Developing a Successful Basketball Program

James H. Brooks

Designed Specifically for Coaches of 6th to 12th Grade Players!

©2003 Coaches Choice. All rights reserved.
Printed in the United States.

No part of this book may be reproduced, stored in a retrieval system, or transmitted, in any form or by any means, electronic, mechanical, photocopying, recording, or otherwise, without prior permission of Coaches Choice.

Throughout this book, the masculine shall be deemed to include the feminine and vice versa.

ISBN: 1-58518-643-0
Library of Congress Control Number: 2002104558

Cover photo: Jonathan Daniel/Allsport
Cover design: Kerry Hartjen
Text design: Jennifer Bokelmann

Coaches Choice
P.O. Box 1828
Monterey, CA 93942
www.coacheschoice.com

DEDICATION

This book is dedicated to my loving wife, Mary, who has been so understanding and supportive. She understood my need to write this book. Without her support, this book would never have been possible.

This book is also dedicated to my children, who have allowed me to share their athletic experiences. Working with them has been one of the joys of my life.

Special thanks has to be given to those special coaches who have been so helpful to the children they coached. Pat Pennick taught her players the true meaning of teamwork. She often took players with limited talent and molded them into excellent teams. Lynn Poole exhibited great communicative skills that helped eliminate the doubt and confusion that often occur during these years, thereby making her players' athletic experiences even more enjoyable.

Table Of Contents

Dedication.. iii
Introduction... xiii
    What is Different About This Book on Basketball
    Who Should Use This Reference Manual?
    Questions for Coaches

SECTION I: COACHING

Chapter 1: Coaching Basketball 3
    Who coaches our children?
    What is success in coaching?
    The coach as a leader
    What is the current player-coach-parent paradigm?
    What are the basic problems coaches face today?
    Why do so many new coaches give up on coaching so soon?

Chapter 2: Traits of a Successful Coach 11
    Characteristics of successful coaches
    Utilizing auxiliaries
    Fifteen suggestions for being a good coach

Chapter 3: Coaching at the Junior High School Level 18
    Aggressive vs. passive children
    What do the parents expect from the coach?
    How to decide which players will make the team
    How does the style of play affect player development?
    Problems junior high coaches may have
    Substitutions

Chapter 4: Communication 35
    The coach should be the leader in communication
    Non-verbal and verbal communication
    Three basic types of communication in basketball

Chapter 5: Internal Problems Can Destroy a Team 53
    Examples of internal problems
    Preventing internal problems on the team

Chapter 6: Player Evaluation........................... 57
    Team selection
    Team skills
    Determining the starters
    Individual evaluation

Chapter 6: Player Evaluation (continued)
Statistics
Team evaluation
Outside evaluation

Chapter 7: Player Development 68
A player's development is determined by five factors
Rules for developing confidence in players
Motivating players
Situations that may affect player development
Summer is the time to develop new skills
The player's responsibility for his development
Team development
Summary of tips for player development

Chapter 8: Noticing the Little Things 89
A great coach pays attention to the little things
Praising the little things
Suggestions for correcting player mistakes

Chapter 9: Teaching New Concepts 92
The KISS principle
Videotape as an aid
Teaching an offense
Teaching defense
Designing a defense

Chapter 10: Utilizing Auxiliaries 99
Training the managers as assistants

Chapter 11: Practice 104
Planning practices
Be organized
Practice suggestions
Correcting bad habits and developing good habits
Matching players in drills and scrimmages
One-on-one situations
Teach quickness during practice
Make scrimmages game-realistic
Variety in practices
Practicing special game situations
Unusual practice segments
Practice expectations

Chapter 12: Drills 116
    Pairing players up for drills
    Types of drills
    Great seldom-used drills
    Drills that players can do on their own

Chapter 13: Game Demeanor 124
    The coach as a role model
    Communicating with the player who made a mistake
    Handling the shooter who is having an off night
    Do not overreact to players during a game
    Putting pressure on the players
    Coaching no-no's
    Tips for game demeanor

Chapter 14: Game Management 130
    Game plan and objectives
    Managing difficult game situations
    Substitutions and playing time
    Types of substitutions
    Coach's talks with the team

Chapter 15: Players 143
    Questions players may ask

Chapter 16: Players with College Potential 153
    Expectations of the players and parents
    What responsibilities does a coach have to players with college potential?
    Getting discovered isn't easy
    What type of player impresses coaches?
    Scholarships and grants-in-aid
    When a player gets a college scholarship

Chapter 17: Dealing with Parents 163
    Classification of parents
    When a parent is a coach's boss

SECTION II: FUNDAMENTALS OF BASKETBALL

Chapter 18: The Team 173
    The roles of the players
    The five positions on the basketball team
    So you are a substitute?

Chapter 19: Basketball Attitude 184
How does a player demonstrate a basketball attitude?
Proving yourself
Develop a basketball attitude, not just an attitude

Chapter 20: Ambidextrous Players 187

Chapter 21: Basketball is a Game of Quickness 189
Exercise and weight programs
Other ways a player can appear quicker
Anticipation vs. reaction

Chapter 22: Getting the Edge 194
Know your opponent
Deny your opponent's strengths
Scout yourself
Be a well-rounded player
Use your body
Anticipation vs. reaction
Court awareness
Team defense
Other seldom-taught skills

Chapter 23: Defense 209
Who can play sound defense?
Defense and offense are equally important
Defensive skills are learned faster than offensive skills
Defense is played with your head, heart, and feet
Finish the defensive effort
The defensive position
When your man doesn't have the ball
When your man has the ball
Intercepting the reverse pass to the backside (offside)
Man-to-man defense
Zone defense
Special defenses
Defensive considerations for coaches
Defensive tips

Chapter 24: Getting Open 236
Helping teammates get open
How to get players open for a three-point shot
Getting open on a fast break
Getting open against a man-to-man defense
Getting open against a zone defense

Chapter 25: Screens 247
    How to set a screen
    Rubbing off the screen
    Passing to a cutter coming around a screen
    Resetting a screen
    Practicing screens
    Defending screens (picks)

Chapter 26: Passing 257
    Why do so few great passers exist?
    Timing of the pass
    What to do after passing the ball
    Types of passes
    The post as a passer
    Entry passes to the post
    The guard-post two-man game
    Outlet passes
    Inbound passes
    Teaching passing
    The no-dribble scrimmage

Chapter 27: Catching the Ball Skills 268
    Passing is a two-man game
    Developing "hands"
    Why players bobble passes
    Catching and pivoting

Chapter 28: Rebounding 273
    Essential traits of a successful rebounder
    What should a player do when he gets a rebound?

Chapter 29: Dribbling 279
    Types of dribbles
    Suggestions for dribbling properly
    Hesitation dribble
    Picking up the dribble
    Being trapped at midcourt
    Learn to dribble with either hand
    Dribble penetration breaking down the defense
    Dribbling in special situations
    Dribbling on a fast break
    Cardinal no-no's of dribbling

Chapter 30: Fakes 289
    Types of fakes

Chapter 31: Moves **293**
    Beating your man
    Know your man and test him early
    Moves are learned
    The simplest moves
    Initiating a move to the basket
    Practicing moves
    Moves for a guard
    Moves for a forward
    Moves for a post

Chapter 32: Two-man Games. **309**
    The give-and-go
    The pick-and-roll
    The pass-and-screen
    The backdoor cut
    The inside-outside game
    The inside-outside-inside game

Chapter 33: Offense **313**
    Creating Lanes
    Spacing
    Timing
    Offense is a series of two- and three-man games
    Types of offenses
    Half-court offenses
    Man-to-man offenses
    Zone offenses
    Last-second plays or shots
    Teaching an offense
    Drills for developing an offense

Chapter 34: Shooting **336**
    Shooting is a learned skill
    The basic process of developing shots and moves
    Shooting tips
    Common mistakes in shooting
    How does a scorer find ways to score?
    Shot selection
    Getting "the feel" for the shot
    Shooting areas
    Practice shooting sessions
    Types of shots

Chapter 35: Free Throws. 351
    The proper technique for shooting free throws
    Who shoots free throws?
    Making the important free throw
    Free-throw shooting drills
    Teaching young players to shoot free throws

Chapter 36: Fouls and Referees. 358
    Players must adjust to how the game is being called
    Players must learn how to play with fouls
    The silly foul
    Referees seldom determine who wins
    Coaches must set good examples

About the Author 362

INTRODUCTION

Coaching young athletes and seeing the joy in their faces and the self-confidence they have developed from their athletic experiences have provided me with some of my fondest memories. It isn't the star athlete I remember most vividly, but those individuals who developed more than they believed they could—sometimes in spite of physical limitations. These kids discovered the joy of sports in a can-do environment where the only goal is to improve each player as much as possible. They learned that hard work in practice results in a good team, a feeling of pride, and an increase in self-confidence. The wins seem to take care of themselves in this environment.

The hours spent playing ball with my children have provided me special pleasures. Through the years, it has been rewarding to see my kids excel in their activities by giving 100 percent and using their mental and physical abilities to their best ability. There have been some special coaches who were very important in the development of my children. Unfortunately, my children were also unlucky on occasion to have new coaches who were ill-prepared to work with children. The helpless feeling a parent has in trying to assist his child in working through these situations, and the realization that this feeling is, regrettably, not an uncommon one are the two driving forces behind this book. Coaches should be able to read this book and find something helpful for these precious years of our children's lives.

Coaching is a very difficult and sometimes thankless job. The coach's happiness and satisfaction should come from knowing the difference he made in the lives of his players, and not from the numbers of wins. As a former coach told me as we were discussing the writing of this book: "When I started coaching, I knew the x's and o's, but I knew very little else. I knew very little about the things that are important in leading children through these challenging years. No one taught us. It was always, Win! Win! WIN! The other skills that were so important to coaching, I had to learn the hard way." The two following stories demonstrate my reasons for writing this book.

"The small, twelve-year-old boy had moved from a rural Oklahoma town to a much larger city. Odessa, like a lot of Texas towns in those days, was a football town. In seventh grade, his first year in Odessa, the boy played football, although he was one of the smallest players on the team. He was excited when basketball season came around because this was his true love.

As a child he had spent countless hours dribbling on the uneven dirt that served as a court in the plowed field outside his yard. He would shoot at a bare rim supported by a backboard made out of two by fours. Now was the time he had waited for—junior high athletics. He couldn't wait to display his skills when he tried out for the team. After the players turned in their football equipment, the junior high coach lined the football team against the wall and picked the 10 largest and best football players. He looked at the other players and announced that they were the seventh grade basketball team. There would be no tryouts! What a wonderful introduction to competitive junior high athletics! I know this story very well because I was that small boy."

Another true story influenced my desire to see every child be given an opportunity to develop to their fullest and not be prejudged regarding their future potential.

In the 1983 and '84 school years, my children's junior high school played another school four times in football and six times in basketball. The other team had one boy who was almost two years older and was much faster and stronger. He outran, outjumped, and overpowered the younger and smaller players. The other school's teams humiliated ours every game during those two years. At one basketball game, the father of one of our players said, 'Look down at our bench. Have you ever seen 15 smurfs lined up in a row?' Well those 'smurfs' learned their fundamentals. They grew up and never gave up! During their junior and senior years in high school, the smurfs won district championships in football and basketball!

My question to you—the new coach—is: If the students from the two small schools had been attending one large junior high competing against each other for spots on the team and for playing time, how many of those smurfs would have been discouraged and run off or never been given a realistic chance?

After all, isn't winning everything, even in youth leagues and junior high? If major colleges and professional teams can't determine who is going to develop, even after seeing them play at a competitively high level for several years, how can a young, inexperienced coach be expected to predict who the best players will be in four or five years? A new coach can buy numerous videos and books that describe in detail all types of drills, offenses, and defenses. However, where does the coach go to learn about the problems he or she may face in coaching, especially if the inexperienced coach has never had children go through the youth league, junior high, high school, and college experience of competitive basketball?

A coach's preparation and planning are not only for the season, the practices, and the games. A coach must be prepared to handle unexpected situations, not only in games, but also in his relationships with players (and their parents). How often do we look back on situations and wish we had handled them differently? Since we had never before encountered a similar situation, we were caught off guard. Hopefully, this book will present a few ideas that will help better prepare the coach for the moment when a problem arises or better yet, will help prevent the problem.

WHAT IS DIFFERENT ABOUT THIS BOOK ON BASKETBALL?

Developing a Successful Basketball Program is a resource designed for coaches who are entrusted with our most special possession—our children. Every coach wants to do an excellent job, but with limited training and little experience, many coaches are learning "on the job" with our children. Coaching is much more than knowing the x's and o's. In addition to possessing a knowledge of basketball, a coach must develop excellent people, organizational, management, communication, and player-developmental skills. Few college graduates possess these skills when they start their coaching experience, and relatively few school districts have training programs for new coaches. Where can these new coaches turn for assistance?

Many excellent books describe in detail the drills, basic fundamentals, offenses, and defenses of basketball. Some of these books offer a brief discussion of the basic concepts of coaching. However, few (if any) books are currently available that guide the coach in developing essential non-basketball skills, discuss problems the coach and the players may encounter, or discuss player and parental expectations and concerns.

The fundamentals of coaching, including non-basketball skills, are covered in the first section of this book. Ideas are presented that hopefully will prevent many of the commonly encountered problems. Most problems are not caused by the coaches' lack of knowledge of the game of basketball, but by the fact that many coaches are inadequately prepared for the task at hand. New coaches, in particular, need a basic reference source that will assist them in deciding what and how they need to coach. A new coach must first decide on the way he wants to coach and the type of coach he wants to be. He must understand that his philosophy of coaching will permeate every aspect of his coaching experience and may ultimately determine his success or his happiness with his profession. If the coach is to be the coach he wants to be, he should make certain his philosophy is totally reflected in the way he coaches and deals with players and parents.

This book addresses many of the problems and questions faced by the players, parents, and coaches during their youth league, junior high and high school athletic experience. Although the concepts stressed are relevant for any grade or age level, one chapter is devoted to the special problems a youth or interscholastic coach may encounter. The coach is expected to be the leader of the player-coach-parent paradigm. How can a coach lead the player and his family through their athletic experience if he is unaware of the problems all three will face? The first section also discusses the skills needed to be a good coach. There are chapters addressing the seldom-taught skills of communication, player evaluation, and player development. The chapters about game demeanor and management review how these aspects affect not only the game, but also the players.

The second section of this manual is the quick-and-easy reference source a coach needs as he prepares for his next practice. No matter how skilled the coach may have been as a player, it is often difficult to explain even the most basic skills simply and concisely to younger players. The basic fundamentals of basketball are described in a manner similar to the way a coach would explain them to his players. Before the next practice, it is nice for a coach to be able to clarify his thoughts by having a reference source from which he can quickly review a topic he plans to explain or emphasize.

This manual does not tell the coach how to run a practice, design and execute an offense, or describe specific shooting or dribbling techniques. Rather, it covers ways to teach fundamental skills simply and more effectively, while stressing team concepts.

Teaching the fundamentals of basketball involves more than teaching players how to dribble, shoot, and rebound. It concerns teaching the little things that will make these skills even more effective. Seldom-discussed concepts, such as how to teach a particular offense, how to teach a player to play quicker, or various ways to initiate a half-court offense, are a few of the subjects reviewed. Coaches also must teach players to accept the responsibility for their own improvement, including how to practice smartly on their own.

Developing a Successful Basketball Program emphasizes teaching players how to "get the edge" by emphasizing seldom taught skills and teaching the players ways they can play smarter. As players learn the fundamental basketball skills and the fundamentals of team play, they must learn the keys that will assist them in knowing when and how to execute those skills within the team concept. Once the players get to a certain skill level it is important that these game-situation decisions become as natural as the skills themselves.

A coach should first read this manual to get a feel for the way he wants to coach and to understand some of the problems he may encounter. It can also serve as a basic reference source for basic basketball fundamentals and how to teach them. At this point, the coach is ready to get into the details of planning practices and drills as well as studying the intricacies of offenses and defenses that will be used. *Developing a Successful Basketball Program* is one of several reference sources a well-prepared coach should have available, along with books or videos that address skill techniques, drills, offenses and defenses. The coach will then have the necessary information to make his and the players' basketball experience even more successful and enjoyable.

WHO SHOULD USE THIS REFERENCE MANUAL?

Any professional who wants to improve his or her skills should be receptive to looking at the profession from different perspectives. This factor is especially true for the inexperienced coach who has never had children go through the athletic experience. As the saying goes, "There is no substitute for experience." Knowledge should be able to be passed on without coaches having to repeat the same mistakes.

This manual can be helpful for both the varsity coach, as well as the young, inexperienced youth, junior high or sub-varsity coach. The book is written with a two-fold emphasis, since each level of competition has its own unique problems and rewards:

- The inexperienced coach starting his career at the junior high level should have a reference source. The problems he will encounter will be vastly different from those on the varsity level. The third chapter is devoted entirely to the youth or junior high coaching experience.

- The varsity coach should be able to find suggestions or considerations that might be helpful. New problems arise at the high school level as the classes are merged and as players struggle with basketball and their teenage years. Coaching players with college potential is a special treat, but this also presents new situations that require consideration. This manual is appropriate for all grade levels up to and inclusive of the junior varsity and varsity teams.

Great coaches are individuals who pay attention to details that others overlook. Their teams are fundamentally sound, have great individual and team skills, understand team concepts, and are always prepared. Their players have learned and accepted the responsibility of learning how to practice outside of school, how to practice and play smarter, and how to gain the "winning edge."

Many great athletes have flopped as coaches, while less athletic players have become excellent coaches. The less-athletic players had to learn every trick and technique to make up for their athletic deficiencies. As a result, they learned the intricacies of individual and team skills that allowed them to compete successfully against more athletic players. One of the purposes of this book is to encourage coaches and players to strive to do the little things that are necessary for success.

QUESTIONS FOR COACHES

Please answer the following questions on a sheet of paper now. Save the answers. After you have read the book, answer the questions again and compare to see if any of your answers are different.

1. Are parents a problem for you as a coach? How? Why? Please describe the problems you encounter and how you handle them. How much involvement from parents would you like?

2. How would you feel if you were a biology teacher and the principal yelled and chewed you out in front of your fellow teachers because your class did not do as well as expected? Do you feel this is the best way to improve your teaching abilities? If this occurred periodically, would you continue to work in such an environment?

3. Did you ever have a coach who screamed and humiliated you in front of your teammates and fans? Did you feel this was the best way to get your attention and to motivate you to do better? If not, what would you have preferred?

4. Do you adapt your system to your players or do you adapt your players to your system?

5. Who is expected to initiate communications between the player and the coach, the player or the coach? Do you have a plan of communication for the players and their parents?

6. When you practice your offense or defense, how much of the time is spent with the starting five players?

    50%   60%   70%   80%   90%   100%

7. As a coach, what would you consider to be the definition of success?

8. How would you respond if a parent said that his or her child was not being treated fairly? What if the parent felt the child was not given quality practice and game time? The parent may also state that when their child gets in a game, he or she is allowed only one mistake before being benched, while starters are allowed to make several mistakes without being benched.

9. Assume you are a new teacher applying for a ninth grade coaching position. The other finalist is a former player on a nationally-ranked team. The athletic director tells you that he is hiring you both for one year on a trial basis. The other coach will coach the best five players, who will get most of the practice and game time. You will coach the second team. At the end of the season, the athletic director will retain the coach of the group with the best stats. The losing coach will no longer be allowed to pursue his life-long dream of coaching. Would you feel that you were given a fair chance to develop and prove yourself as a coach? How is that different from an inexperienced player who is never really given the same chances to improve in practice or in games as the current best five players are given?

10. You are coaching a youth or an interscholastic team. Eleven players are suited up for the game. Your team is playing your chief rival in a close game. There are four minutes left in the game. As you look down the bench, you realize you have forgotten to play two of the players. Your team is nursing a one-point lead. Do you play the two players or do you go with the best players down the stretch? What was your rationale? How would you handle the situation? What messages are sent by either decision?

11. What do you do if a player isn't improving as much as expected?

12. What do the player and his parents expect of the coach if the player has the potential to play college basketball?

SECTION I
Coaching

"Good coaching may be defined as development of character, personality, and habits of players, plus the teaching of fundamentals and team play."

— Claire Bee

"Knowledge alone is not enough to get desired results. You must have the more elusive ability to teach and to motivate. That defines a leader; if you can't teach and you can't motivate, you can't lead."

— John Wooden

CHAPTER 1

Coaching Basketball

For a young person, coaching basketball can be either one of the most challenging and rewarding times in his life, or one of the most frustrating and disappointing times. If the coach is ill-prepared for the complex task of coaching or he is in coaching for the wrong reasons, he will soon become disillusioned. Why do so many young coaches drop out of coaching within in a year or two? Coaching is so much more than putting five players on the court and telling them what to do. In addition to having a working knowledge of basketball and good teaching skills, a coach must develop excellent people, organizational, and management skills. Few college graduates possess these skills when they start their coaching experience.

Most great coaches are successful because they are teachers of the game, excellent motivators, and exceptional communicators whose desire is to have each player on the team develop and play up to his potential. The joy coaches receive isn't only from the wins, but also the self-satisfaction they feel when players develop and succeed.

The reward is the look in the player's eyes and face immediately after succeeding in doing something he didn't know or believe he could do. These are the moments the coach remembers. Each memory is a coach's win! Through the years, the games will blend into each other except for a few, but the memories of the players will last a lifetime.

When a coach takes over a team, there is always pressure to win. The coach's philosophy is reflected in every aspect of his handling of the team. The coach should be alert to never be so concerned with the short- term emphasis of winning that he doesn't emphasize those things that are important in developing a good program.

A coach is a teacher. Any excellent teacher knows that the only limit to a student's ability to learn is the teacher's ability to teach, inspire, and motivate! Considering the answers to the following questions can help clarify this point.

The joy coaches receive isn't only from the wins, but also the self-satisfaction they feel when players develop and succeed.

- Who was your favorite teacher and/or coach?
- Why was that person special?
- What did they do that made you think so highly of them?

These questions have been asked of hundreds of teachers, coaches, and parents. They all elicited similar answers, such as: my favorite teacher and/or coach made me feel special, cared for me, had confidence in me, and challenged me to be better than I thought I could be.

Who Coaches Our Children?

Young, inexperienced teachers are usually assigned to coach at the lowest rung on the competitive ladder in their school system. One coach may be expected to coach 15 to 30 children with no assistants. Many excellent young coaches do a wonderful job on a daily basis. Without help, even the best coach would find it nearly impossible to adequately develop the players and the team. Parents and fans expect young coaches to make mistakes, especially in game management, but they expect the coach to be a leader in people skills as well as motivational—and player—developmental skills!

What training do new coaches get to adequately prepare them for coaching our children? Besides personal knowledge of basketball, what is their training in organizational, communication, and motivational skills? Do they have the ability to teach simply the fundamentals of basketball? Has the school district thoroughly evaluated these abilities? Due to financial limitations, school districts often require a coach to teach multiple sports. This step often results in teachers being assigned to coach sports they know little about. Has the district implemented a thorough training program for these young coaches to help them be better prepared for the challenge ahead?

What Is Success in Coaching?

Success in coaching is often measured in wins and championships. In such situations, the coach's job and his chances for a better job are determined by his win-loss record. Winning is important, but a coach's belief that a good win-loss record equates to success will often lead to burnout and disappointment.

The true joy of coaching is seeing the excitement and pride on the face of the player as the player finally accomplishes a difficult task, that he thought he could never do. That joy is available to the coach many times everyday in practice. If the coach tries to make every player on the team as fundamentally sound as possible, the wins will take care of

> *The true joy of coaching is seeing the excitement and pride on the face of the player as the player finally accomplishes a difficult task, that he thought he could never do.*

themselves! Years later, the coach will typically remember very little about most of the wins, but he will remember in detail the players who worked hard and played up to their potential.

The Coach as a Leader

The player and the parent expect the coach not only to be a basketball genius but also a warm, caring individual who will help the child develop skills and self-confidence. Along the way, the coach is expected to have an open line of communication with the player and parent, since the player and parent often don't know what to expect or how to deal with problems that will arise during the season. In other words, the coach is expected to lead them through the basketball experience.

Before the season, the coach must lead the players and the parents in developing a common goal and philosophy for the team. If the coach doesn't bring everyone together in accepting a common goal, problems can develop. The coach will generally be forced to walk a fine line between winning while giving both his starters and the substitutes quality game time. At the sub-varsity level, if a win-at-all-cost attitude is developed, the parents of the starters will be upset if they do not play all the time. On the other hand, if the substitutes do not get quality playing time, their parents will be upset. This is a lose-lose situation that can be prevented.

What Is the Current Player-Coach-Parent Paradigm?

All too often, the parent-coach relationship has been a less than ideal—if not adversarial—relationship. Experienced coaches have warned new coaches about interfering parents. The new coach tends to keep the parents completely out of the picture and expects the players to learn to handle their own problems. As a result, the coach often makes the following statement to the players at the beginning of the year: "If you have a problem, you come to me. I don't want to hear from your parents." This is great in theory, but it is not realistic!

As a rule, many players are immature, insecure youngsters who are dealing with their own age-related problems and issues, and the coach is the ultimate authoritative figure who determines the athletes' playing time. The players want to make a good impression. As a result, they will not often risk going to the coach with their problems, concerns or doubts! This approach places the responsibility of initiating and maintaining an open line of communication on the player. This approach doesn't work well because communication is limited. Conflicts result when problems aren't addressed early, and things build up until finally they get so bad that a confrontation develops.

Before the season, the coach must lead the players and the parents in developing a common goal and philosophy for the team.

If the player isn't addressing the problem and the coach isn't aware enough to sense something is wrong, the parent is caught in the middle and feels something should be done. Most parents realize their child's window of opportunity is very small, and they want their child to have every chance of succeeding. Wouldn't you?

The responsibility for initiating communication belongs to the coach—the leader! The coach's challenge is to become confident enough in his coaching, human relations, and communication skills that he is not afraid to establish and maintain an on-going, open relationship with both his players and their parents, based on open communication. If the coach is a good, hard-working coach who functions by the cardinal rules and who communicates well with the players and the parents, the parents will usually be content.

The Cardinal Rules of Coaching

- My goal as a coach is to never prejudge the potential, the desire, and the heart of a player. Instead, I will strive to help every player on my team to improve every day and week.
- I will work as hard in practice to develop the player on the team with the least amount of skill as I do the best player.
- Positive motivation and constructive criticism will be the foundation of my coaching technique.
- Every child on my team will get quality practice and game time.

What Are the Basic Problems Coaches Face Today?

The following fundamental issues create many of the problems in basketball that many coaches currently face:

- Emphasis on winning (not on player development).
- Coaches learn on-the-job (their mistakes impact our children and their dreams).
- Prejudging and limiting the potential of players.
- Poor communication between the coach, player, and parent.

Discussing each of these problems in more detail can help clarify the factors involved.

The Emphasis on Winning

Most kids play basketball because they love the game and they want to have fun! They want to be a part of a school team with their friends. In

> **The coach's challenge is to become confident enough in his coaching, human relations, and communication skills that he is not afraid to establish and maintain an on-going, open relationship with both his players and their parents, based on open communication.**

today's society, winning is very important. Players take the court with the intention of winning each game. However, every game has a loser; few teams win championships, and very few teams win state or national championships. In life, you must learn that you can't always have your way; sometimes you will lose. Winning isn't about which team scored the most points. It is about knowing you gave your best effort in practice and in the game. The problems arise when parents, coaches, fans, and the media stress winning the game at all costs.

Does that mean you don't play to win? No! Every time the team steps on the floor, they should give 110 percent effort. A team with a strong, fundamentally sound and defensive-oriented second team will not only push the starters to improve in practice, these players will be able to compete effectively in games.

If winning is at the expense of player development, then everyone loses—the player, the coach, and the program. Unfortunately, that is often what happens at the sub-varsity level and sometimes at the youth, sub-varsity, and sometimes varsity level. In the seventh through ninth grades, for example, some coaches (particularly new, inexperienced coaches) often feel only three to six players will eventually be able to contribute years later at the varsity level. Therefore, these players are given special attention and most of the playing time so the team has the best chance to win now. Sadly, other players are denied the opportunity to fulfill their potential, which sometimes is greater than those players who get the most attention have.

The irony is that some of the players who are given all the attention will either not be living in the school district, or the players will have lost interest in basketball by the time they reach their junior and senior years in high school. The lack of time spent developing the other players at the lower level is now reflected by a downturn in the talent level of the program. Coaches cannot measure heart, desire, and potential; so why try? Coaches should teach everyone. When they do, everyone wins!

Every time the team steps on the floor, they should give 110 percent effort.

Coaches Learn on the Job

After many years, many professionals look back and realize how little they really knew and how much better they could do the job now. Their mistakes, as they learned on the job, were made at the expense of the children they were coaching.

Few new coaches are old enough to have children who have played competitive sports. Coaches should realize their perceptions often might be quite different from those of the players and the parents. As an older coach once said, "Things look different when your child is on the court and you aren't the coach."

As coaches work with young athletes, they need to remember how difficult it was to grow during their adolescent years. They should remember problems that they or their friends had while growing up. At a child's impressionable age, what the coach says and does may have a dramatic effect on a young athlete's desire and self-esteem. What a coach doesn't do or say can also have a powerful effect, sometimes negatively.

When a new coach gets his first assignment, the very first thing he must realize is how little he may know and how poorly prepared he may be to handle kids during their formative years. The point to keep in mind is that every new coach must have the willingness to work harder than his players if he is going to become an excellent coach.

Prejudging and Limiting the Potential of Players

Colleges and professional teams spend millions of dollars each year evaluating the so-called blue chip players so they can select the "can't miss" prospect. The truth is, more often than not, they are wrong. Small colleges and professional teams are loaded with players who were told they weren't good enough. If large staffs of famous coaches and scouts misjudge talent badly every year, how can a young, inexperienced coach expect to know which youth league or junior high school players have potential?

> Players mature physically and emotionally at different rates. Remember Michael Jordan was cut from his high school basketball team.

In today's fast-paced society, many couples or single parents haven't had time to teach their children basketball. Some parents know nothing about basketball, but their children may have a burning desire to play. These kids may be less skilled when they try out for a team than those children fortunate enough to have had someone spend many hours helping them develop fundamental skills. Coaches need to develop and encourage every player. Each player's heart, desire, and athletic ability will then determine that individual's ultimate potential and success.

Poor Communication Between the Coach, Player, and Parent

Effective communication is one of the most important skills that any individual can learn. A lack of communication can create problems and failure in an individual's personal and professional life. Remember the coach is often a very authoritative figure to the player and the parent, and they will be very hesitant to openly discuss their concerns unless the coach shows a genuine interest and seeks their input. (Communication is so critical that a whole chapter in this book is devoted to it.)

Sometimes coaches are so busy struggling to organize and run practice and to decide how they can best teach basketball that they forget that a coach is the leader of the player-coach-parent paradigm. For a coach to be an effective leader, he must understand the problems, concerns, fears, and expectations of the players and the parents.

The players and parents expect the coach to lead them by clearly communicating what he expects of them, by teaching the players how to handle new situations, and by actively keeping the lines of communication open. Remember, the player and their parents are looking to the coach to help them through their basketball experience! In the coach-player-parent paradigm, when the parties are not aware of the other's expectations or when expectations are not being met, disappointment and conflict are likely to follow!

Success in coaching, like success in other professions, depends upon a person's human relations and organizational skills. Many people know basketball, but only great coaches can teach simply and exhibit the following desirable human relations skills:

- The ability to motivate and encourage.
- The ability to lead an open line of communication with players and parents.
- The ability to bring the team together as one.
- The ability to prevent future problems.

Why Do So Many New Coaches Give Up on Coaching So Soon?

Why do so many young coaches drop out after only a year or two of coaching? Among the possible reasons are:

- ➢ The coach wasn't prepared to coach. The coach was thrown to the wolves without adequate training. Coaching basketball is much more than walking out on the court and telling the players what to do. Without proper training, the coach may feel lost, do a poor job, and/or have conflicts with parents.
- ➢ Coaching wasn't what the coach expected. The coach discovered that he didn't enjoy coaching as much as he thought he would.

For a coach to be an effective leader, he must understand the problems, concerns, fears, and expectations of the players and the parents.

> Coaching and teaching took too much of his personal time. Some coaches are unaware of the amount of time required to teach and coach and the resulting difficulty of raising a family at the same time. For example, coaching basketball in a public or private secondary school can be very challenging since the coach also has a teacher's normal responsibilities such as developing lesson plans, grading daily work, and making and grading tests. The additional duties involved in coaching can put tremendous demands on an individual's time. Time is not only spent during practice and games. A coach spends an inordinate amount of time traveling, evaluating game films, developing practice schedules, and consulting with players and parents when needed.

With all these demands, a coach must learn to be organized, prepared, efficient, and learn to use auxiliaries if he wants to excel. The coach must learn to teach the fundamentals of basketball in a simple manner that is easy to learn and easy to teach.

Summary Points

Basketball can be one of the most wonderful or one of the most discouraging experiences of a player's, parent's or coach's life, depending upon the coach's goals and approaches toward coaching. As a parent, it is truly wonderful to see children develop under the guidance of a terrific coach who understands them.

Each player may be at a different level of skill, maturity, experience, and confidence. A coach's challenge is to find ways of developing their players' skills and confidence, while giving every player a chance to participate meaningfully and be an integral part of the team. If you accept this premise as your primary goal and you do your best in preparing your team to play, you will cherish the growth and development of your players. In the process, you will always be a winner in the eyes of your players and their families.

CHAPTER 2

Traits of a Successful Coach

The basic fundamentals involved in coaching are the same, whether an individual coaches youth leagues, junior high, junior varsity, high school varsity or college. While each level has its own unique problems and rewards, certain skills and traits exist that are common among successful coaches. At least three general basic skills are necessary to be an excellent coach. As such, coaches who have the following skills are usually quite successful:

- Knowledge of basketball and teaching skills
- People skills (communication and motivation skills)
- Organizational and management skills

Characteristics of Successful Coaches

Successful coaches tend to possess and exhibit the following traits:

- Is knowledgeable about the game of basketball.
- Possesses a desire to improve every player on the team.
- Is organized, prepared, and disciplined.
- Emphasizes fundamentals.
- Exhibits sound basic teaching skills.
- Pays attention to details.
- Communicates well with players (and parents).
- Adjusts style of play to the strength of players.
- Teaches players how to "get the edge."
- Desires to improve as a coach.
- Offers constructive, not destructive, criticism.
- Develops an offense that allows every player the chance to score.
- Encourages teamwork and unselfishness.

Reviewing each of these traits can enable coaches to better understand how and why each of these factors are essential to effective coaching.

Is Knowledgeable About the Game of Basketball

Being a good coach does not require that you were a great basketball player in your younger days, but it does require that you develop a thorough knowledge of the game and that on an on-going basis you keep building on your understanding of the game. In basketball, as in other sports, the best coaches may well be the ones who have studied the game of basketball in such detail that they are able to "get the edge" and make up for their lesser natural athletic ability. A thorough knowledge of the game is essential if the coach is to properly teach every player the individual fundamentals and skills essential to prepare the team to perform in a cohesive, coordinated manner.

Possesses a Desire to Improve Each Player

The desire to fully develop each player on the team is the fire that motivates successful coaches. Success to a thoughtful coach is seeing a player accomplish feats the player never dreamed possible. The memory of the excitement and pride on the face of the player who has performed well is the fuel that kindles an individual's desire to continue coaching and is proof of a job well done.

Is Organized, Prepared, and Disciplined

As the leader of the team, the coach must set the standard that he expects the players to maintain. If the coach has thoroughly prepared and organized each practice and is disciplined enough to follow through with the plan, he is demonstrating to the players that he is working hard to help them improve and is setting an example of the kind of effort needed to be successful.

If practices are to be as productive as possible, the players must be ready to start practice on time. No time should be wasted during the practice. The practice schedule should be modified to meet the needs of the individual players and for the team based on the results of the previous day's practice or game. An assistant coach or auxiliaries can be used extensively to observe the small group drills and to re-emphasize to the players when they perform the required exercises incorrectly and to praise them when the drills are done right. One assistant should be responsible for ensuring that the time allowed for each section of practice is followed. All factors considered, the teams that utilize practices to the maximum are better prepared to win. Winning teams, like winning coaches, are prepared and disciplined.

Emphasizes Fundamentals

Fundamentals must be stressed every day, starting the first day of practice until the last game of the year. The best designed offense or defense will not work properly if the players aren't skilled in the fundamentals and aren't confident of their abilities to perform the essential techniques and skills.

A skill is best developed through hard work, proper instruction (paying attention to detail and technique), and repetition until the skill becomes instinctive! Unfortunately, some coaches are so busy scrimmaging or working on the offense and defense that they devote relatively little time to fundamentals each day. Scrimmaging, while very important, is not an efficient way to quickly teach skills and develop the players' confidence.

As a rule, all basic individual fundamentals can be taught more quickly and effectively in small group drills. Drills provide players the opportunity to work in small groups on basic individual skills, such as dribbling, shooting, passing, rebounding, and defense, as well as other techniques such as faking, spacing, timing, executing screens properly, and defending the screen. Other skills such as posting-up, entry passes, and help-defense can also be taught using small-group drills, as well as concepts such as quick-ball movement and the inside-outside game. Drills enable mistakes to be corrected immediately and proper techniques to be practiced and reinforced until they become natural. Any team—at the youth, interscholastic, collegiate, and professional levels—must emphasize fundamentals if they are to improve. Teams that do not will never develop to their fullest potential!

Drills can also be employed to teach the basic team concepts of offense and defense. For example, certain drills can be designed so they simulate various aspects of the offense. To teach the offense, the coach simply adds various drills together, modifies them as necessary, and teaches concepts such as floor spacing and timing, keys to running the offense, and keeping the weakside defenders busy. During these drills, teammates can also be taught proper defensive technique and how to help each other defensively through communication and proper defensive position.

The best designed offense or defense will not work properly if the players aren't skilled in the fundamentals and aren't confident of their abilities to perform the essential techniques and skills.

Sound Basic Teaching Skills

The basic tenets of teaching hold true for coaching. Teach simply. Establish a good foundation and build upon it, while developing the confidence of the student.

Pays Attention to Details

The ability to pay attention to small details is an attribute that many great coaches possess. The successful coach emphasizes and works on small details that other coaches often never consider. As a result, his teams always seem to have the advantage and are prepared for any circumstance.

Communicates Well With Players (and Parents)

An individual can have all of the other skills necessary to be a great coach, but if the coach cannot effectively communicate, he will have innumerable problems. (Communication is discussed in detail in Chapter Four.)

Adjusts Style of Play to the Strength of the Players

Coaches have a style of play they prefer. Most coaches understand that the natural talent and athletic ability of their team varies from year to year. There are years when the players do not have the skills or athletic ability to execute the coach's preferred style of offense or defense effectively. In those instances, the coach must be flexible enough to adjust the team's style of play to what the players can do best. The coach must be able to accurately evaluate the abilities of his team. For example, the primary objective of defense is to prevent or make it difficult for the other team to score; it doesn't matter how it is done. If a coach prefers a full-court, pressing defense, but he has one or two players who aren't very quick and are often out of position, his preferred defense will be ineffective, resulting in easy lay-ups for the opponents. In that situation, his players might play better in a conventional half-court defense starting just outside of the three-point line.

> **The coach must be flexible enough to adjust the team's style of play to what the players can do best.**

During the course of a game, the coach may want to consider utilizing the offensive and defensive schemes that best fit the athletic ability, skills, and confidence levels of the five players who are on the court. The team may play differently when one or two substitutes are in the game. The coach's flexibility will allow the players the best chance of playing up to their potential while developing confidence. Isn't that success?

Teaches Players to "Get the Edge"

"Getting the edge" means learning the little things that are necessary to gain an advantage over another player. Basketball is not a game played only by the fastest and highest leaping players. There are opportunities for players who are less athletic, but who possess sound basketball fundamentals and are willing to work and to do whatever it takes to get the edge. Such a combination of factors can allow a less athletic player to compete with and beat a more athletic opponent.

"Getting the edge" also means learning complementary skills, such as faking, as well as other seldom taught skills, such as anticipation, setting up an opponent, and being unpredictable. The players need to learn how to evaluate and scout the opposing team and individual players before and during the game. If a player knows the strengths, weaknesses, tendencies, favorite moves and shots of an opponent, the player can adjust his game accordingly. Players need to learn to think during the game. A player who has "the edge" plays closer to his or her potential. A team of players who play to their potential are often called champions.

Desires to Improve as a Coach

A strong desire to improve is one of the most motivating factors for a successful coach, as well as players who excel. Great coaches have the willingness to work extra, doing the little things that other people are not usually willing to do. Do you have that desire?

Offers Constructive, Not Destructive, Criticism

Criticism must be constructive not destructive! The manner in which the criticism is delivered may be as important as what is said. Always criticize the action, never the individual. Every player must hear several positives everyday; positives should outnumber negatives by at least five to one. Early in the year, it may be difficult to attain that goal since the players are learning what is expected of them each day along with the fundamentals. However, no player should ever leave practice without hearing something positive from the coach that day.

Develops an Offense That Allows Every Player the Chance to Score

Every player expects to have a chance to score when the offense is run to completion. If a particular offense doesn't offer that opportunity, the coach should make sure another offense the team runs will allow the player to have the chance to score. Everyone wants his name in the box score.

Encourages Teamwork and Unselfishness

The coach should encourage teamwork everyday in everything the team does, whether in games, drills, or scrimmages. The coach teaches teamwork by:

A player who has "the edge" plays closer to his or her potential. A team of players who play to their potential are often called champions.

- Developing offenses and defenses that utilize the strengths of every player.
- Reminding players to help their teammates on defense.
- Showing players every time they miss an opportunity to pass to an open teammate in a better scoring position.
- Teaching the team to acknowledge their teammates when they give extra effort, make a good play, set a good screen, make a good pass or help the team in other ways. Players should also be encouraged to acknowledge teammates who finally succeed when they have been struggling. Peer encouragement (a form of positive peer pressure) is a very powerful motivational tool that helps develop a sense of team spirit.

Utilizing Auxiliaries

One of the major drawbacks a coach faces is that he can only watch one match-up at a time, whether running drills, teaching offense and defense, scrimmaging, or during a game. As such, coaches should make maximum use of everyone who might help them fulfill their developmental responsibilities.

Since practice time is relatively limited and most youth and interscholastic programs have very few, if any, assistant coaches, it is important for the coach to effectively use every resource available. For example, coach's aides (managers) can be of tremendous help in the development of players. Coaches who only assign menial responsibilities to their managers must rethink their position on the issue. In fact, most team managers have a strong love of the game and can do much more for a team if given the chance.

Fifteen Suggestions for Being a Good Coach

An effective coach needs to:

- Know the game of basketball.
- Truly care for each player.
- Teach simply.
- Communicate clearly and often with all the players.
- Design drills that simulate game situations and game speed.
- Be organized.
- Pay attention to details.
- Teach fundamentals every day.
- Find something a player does well and build on it.
- Encourage, don't discourage.

> **Players should also be encouraged to acknowledge teammates who finally succeed when they have been struggling.**

- Teach players seldom taught skills and how to get the edge.
- Clearly define each player's role on the team before the first game and periodically throughout the season. Explain your expectations for the players, but let them know their role can change if they improve their skills.
- Mix up practice and make it as much fun as possible.
- Be firm, but flexible.
- Emphasize the team concept and positive peer pressure.

Chapter Summary

No individual coach naturally has all of the aforementioned traits of a successful coach. What is required is an inner desire by the coach to be as good as he can be and a willingness to work harder than he would ask of any player.

CHAPTER 3

Coaching at the Junior High School Level

If you are reading this section, you are probably are a new teacher whose first coaching assignment is or will be at the junior high level. New or inexperienced coaches often start at this level. Hopefully, basketball is your first love. In some schools, football or track coaches have been asked to teach basketball. That can be a difficult situation for the coach as well as the players. If you find yourself in this position, you can still be a great coach. The varsity coach should be more than happy to offer suggestions. Typically, the junior high programs are where fundamentals are first learned!

Many books are available that describe various offenses and defenses as well as drills to help develop fundamental skills. One of the purposes of this book is to help the new coach with some of the other facets that are very important, yet are often learned the hard way years later.

A coach should know the policies and expectations of the administration.

A new coach may feel lost because he isn't sure where to start, and how to teach kids who have so much to learn. Hopefully, your school district has a training program to assist new coaches. A coach should know the policies and expectations of the administration. Were you given any training or were you just told you were the basketball coach when the season started? Coaching at this level often forces an individual to deal with too many "too's":

- too many kids.
- too little time.
- too little help.
- too much to do.

For that reason, you may have to learn more than you ever dreamed. However, this situation could be the most challenging and rewarding time of your career. The first coaching assignment is quite a thrill, and yet quite scary. If you looked back 20 years later, would you say, "I could do it much better now?"

The dilemma for the coach is that the future of your children is now! They need your best now, as a coach, a motivator, and a developer of talent. Teenage years are exciting, yet emotional times. The importance of everything is exaggerated. These children have only a year or two to develop enough skills to continue playing at the high school level when grades are merged on the junior varsity or varsity.

In junior high, inexperienced coaches often assume that the best players at the beginning of the year will later be the nucleus of the varsity. They assume their job is to get these players ready for the varsity. These players are quickly designated as the starters. Since many young coaches assume that all children have had an equal background, these must be the players with the most potential.

The reality for players is that if you are one of the best five or six players on the team at the beginning of the season, you will get most of the quality practice and game time. The other players usually share what little time and attention is left. The result is that the starters get a lot better, and the subs improve, but not nearly as much. The coach then appears to have been a good judge of talent. No one will ever know what potential went undeveloped, except the child who really wanted to play, but was never given an equal opportunity.

No coach intentionally hurts the development of a child. Everyone wants to do a good job, but inexperience sometimes blinds one to the truth. The coach may be correct, and the starters may truly end up being the best players. However, occasions will exist when players will surprise you if they are given the opportunity to develop. These will be the kids you remember throughout your life.

Players with previous athletic experiences will have a distinct advantage. The best players have had someone spend a lot of time teaching them basic skills either in various youth sports or on the playground courts. These players will be more advanced than those children who haven't been as fortunate. Children who have played other sports, such as soccer, will have been exposed to concepts that carry over into basketball, such as aggressiveness, anticipation, no fear of making mistakes, attacking the goal, beating their man, as well as team offensive and defensive concepts.

In a great many ways, society has changed in recent years, and many children may not have had the privilege of anyone helping them until they start junior high athletics. As such, the following factors may apply:

The dilemma for the coach is that the future of your children is now! They need your best now, as a coach, a motivator, and a developer of talent.

- Many single parent families exist in today's society who are struggling to get by day-by-day and have little time for playing with their children. In other families, parents are working two jobs to keep everything going.
- In some families, the parents may simply not be interested in sports.
- The most depressing situations are when the parents are not involved in the lives of their children at all. Unfortunately, some children are forced to raise themselves. The parents never show up for games and are often not home until late in the night.
- Passive children who want to play will take longer to develop. The "perfectionist" children are tentative and afraid of making mistakes.

As a coach, the aforementioned are but a few examples of the many children you may encounter. Keep in mind that they all deserve the chance to develop to their potential.

Aggressive vs. Passive Children

In junior high, the performance and rate of development of some players are modified by factors other than skill levels. For example, coaches at the junior high level frequently have players with varying degrees of aggressiveness. All factors considered, basketball is best played with an aggressive attitude. In this regard, the very aggressive or passive nature of some players will strongly influence their play and development. As a rule, girls will be more passive than boys, but most young players are passive about certain parts of their game.

Coaches must realize that some players will be late developers.

The more aggressive player will usually do better at the start of the season, and is more likely to get the attention of the coach. Players who have a more passive nature or who are lacking in self-confidence may not do as well initially. Remember, first impressions are hard to overcome. Coaches must realize that some players will be late developers. As such, the coach must be patient and encouraging.

Why are some players more passive or tentative? No easy answer to this question exists; many factors can come into play, including:

- Each person has his own natural level of aggressiveness and passiveness.
- The child's environment influences the child's level of aggressiveness, for example:
    - Interactions with siblings and play partners influence children

as they develop. A child may assume a more passive role if a sibling is very aggressive.
- Parents in some homes discourage aggressive behavior at an early age. In other homes, aggressive behavior is normal.
- How the parents play with the child may influence how aggressive the child becomes.

➤ No previous participation in sports will often result in the player being less aggressive than those children who have played in basketball or other sports. As a child plays in his first sport, he learns many things that will carry over to other sports. In soccer, for example, the young athletes learn the concepts of offense and defense, as well as other more fundamental concepts such as competing and trying to beat an opponent one-on-one. They also learn about attacking the goal and being aggressive. Skills such as foot movement, passing the ball, and helping teammates on defense are also learned. These experiences are carried over to the basketball court when these young athletes start to play competitively for the first time. These players will have a definite advantage over those players who have not yet played a competitive sport.

➤ Intimidation can make a player more passive and can slow down player development. For example, a passive player or a player lacking in confidence can be intimidated if he believes all the other players are more skilled and experienced. Even when a good player moves up to the next level or joins a new team, the player may be intimidated if he is lacking in self-confidence. If the best players can occasionally be intimidated, how must the less skilled players feel? Young players may also be intimidated by a coach who is loud, emotional, and/or stern, especially if the players have never been around someone with that demeanor.

➤ If a player is afraid to make mistakes, he will be tentative and reserved. These players need to learn not to be afraid to take a chance and that it is okay if they make a mistake. These players are so afraid of making a mistake that they never make anything happen. If a coach gets on these players too hard before they start to develop confidence and before they realize the coach is there to help them get better, the player will probably pull back and be even more passive. They may even decide to quit.

Can Passive or Tentative Children Become Good Ball Players?

Yes. A tentative player may take longer to develop than the players who have more experience or natural aggressiveness. How the coach handles these children can have a tremendous effect on who develops. First, the coach must know his players. Who has played basketball before and for how many years? Do they play with older siblings or kids? Have they played other sports and for how long? This information will be a beginning step in understanding each player.

Taking a risk and trying something new is a big step for the passive player. The coach must understand that passive players are afraid of looking bad by losing the dribble, missing a shot or having it blocked, or getting beat after going for a steal. These players are so afraid of making a mistake that they are afraid to try! The coach must assure the players that mistakes are a part of the game and that they will make mistakes as they learn to play. Notice and comment to the players when they are more aggressive and try what you have been encouraging them to do. Let the players know they did the right thing at the right time. Once the players begin to develop confidence initially, their defense will improve and then their offensive skills. These players must learn that it is okay to make a mistake, and you, the coach, won't be mad at them. Praise the effort.

A passive child will seldom get called for a foul since they think a foul is bad. These players need to learn that if they are being aggressive and making something happen, they will occasionally be called for a foul. The player needs to hear from the coach that fouls are part of the game, and they are okay. If a coach is encouraging players to be more intense, he shouldn't get upset if the child fouls, unless it was a senseless foul. Stress aggressiveness during drills and scrimmages. Compliment the player on being more intense; then tell them what they need to do differently. If this situation is handled properly, the players will be more likely to try again. The power of encouragement from the teammates cannot be underestimated. It is up to the coach to inform the team from day one that the players are expected to encourage one another. The joy of watching these players develop may be as rewarding as helping a good player become a great player.

The power of encouragement from the teammates cannot be underestimated.

This point can be illustrated with a story from another sport. It is one of my fondest memories of working with children. The ten-year-old girl standing near second base was new to the team, as were all the girls. Joy saw the rolling ball come ever so slowly toward her. Rather than step toward the ball to pick it up, she screamed and moved out of the way so the ball could roll past her. When the ball stopped, she picked it up and aimed to throw the ball back to home plate. After she released the ball, it went almost straight up in the air and toward first base. I looked in disbelief and asked myself "How could a girl play softball for two years and not learn anything?" It soon became apparent Joy was afraid of the ball, had no basic skills, and had no confidence.

Joy had been on different teams each of the last two years. The coaches had put her in right field and ignored her. They must have thought they would waste their limited time trying to help her. It is amazing that Joy still wanted to play since she was so far behind all the other kids.

During the season, the team worked on fundamentals every day in practice. I told the players that I would be at the field 45 minutes early to work with my daughter and that I would be happy to work with any other player who wanted help. It was not mandatory, and it wouldn't influence any player's status if they didn't come. Every day, Joy and her mother were sitting in the hot Texas sun waiting for my van to drive up. By season's end, Joy could catch most ground balls and pop-ups, as well as throw the ball very accurately to home plate. Each day now, a smile decorated Joy's face as if it were permanently painted on. The season ended, and I didn't know if I would ever see Joy again.

The next year, I had a new team again. As we got ready to start the first game of the season, I realized Joy was the shortstop on the other team. In the first inning, the bases were loaded with two outs when our batter hit a screaming line drive to the left of the shortstop. Joy lunged to her left and dove for the ball. As she hit the ground, the ball was still nestled in her glove. As she got up and dusted the dirt off her uniform, she looked at me and grinned.

My heart smiled back. What greater "joy" could a coach have? That moment will always live in my heart. Did we do anything special for Joy? No, we treated her exactly the same as every other player on the team.

Basketball players are no different. They respond when coaches care enough to help them get better by giving their time, instructions, and encouragement.

What Do the Parents Expect From the Coach?

Most parents realize a junior high coach will often be new and inexperienced. They expect the coach will have to learn how to be a good game coach. However, they expect the coach to know how to run effective practices and how to teach their children. They expect the coach to have good interpersonal and motivational skills. At this level, parents expect their children to get an equal chance to develop and to get quality playing time if they are on the team.

Basketball players respond when coaches care enough to help them get better by giving their time, instructions, and encouragement.

How to Decide Which Players Will Make the Team

At this age level, a coach's primary goal should be to develop the skill levels of every child on the team. Winning should be important, but not if it comes at the expense of children with potential being denied the opportunity to improve. Ask yourself the following questions. Keep in mind that no one has any way of knowing the answers to these questions when the players are twelve or thirteen years old:

- Which players will be the tallest or fastest in five or six years?
- Which player will have moved from the school district during this time?
- Which player has the heart and desire to work extra on their own to improve?
- Which player will develop when given encouragement, good coaching, and a chance to play?

If the junior high program is geared to developing only the best five or six players each year, what happens to your program if several of the players are not in the program when they are junior or seniors in high school? Players leave basketball for many reasons including the fact that society is currently much more mobile than it was years ago. The following story illustrates the problems that can arise when a coach's attention and efforts are concentrated on only a few players.

An eighth-grade coach played six players 75 percent of each game, and the other 14 players split the remaining time. This team had far too many players, but if it had only twelve players, a problem would still have existed. The coach assumed that the varsity would eventually depend on these six players in several years. The problem was that by the next year, three of the six players had moved to other school districts. This is not unusual in today's mobile society. The next year, the ninth grade coach could not understand why the remaining players weren't better prepared. The program suffered greatly because the potential development of these players was hindered by the well-meaning eighth-grade coach.

Winning should be important, but not if it comes at the expense of children with potential being denied the opportunity to improve.

Selecting a Team at the Sub-Varsity Level

Selection of a team at the sub-varsity level implies to the players and their parents that each player will be given quality practice and game time. Teams usually will have at least 13 to 15 players. This number of players ensures the coach will have at least 10 players at practice even if there is illness, thereby allowing the team to practice and scrimmage with complete teams. The problem in having this many or more players on a team is that it is more difficult for the coach to ensure that each player is given quality game time. Fortunately, it can be done! A written schedule of substitutions is helpful. For example, a student assistant can be assigned the responsibility of reminding the coach when it is time to make a substitution.

If a coach wants problems every year with parents, one of the best ways to guarantee such problems is to be concerned only with winning and to play only seven or eight kids for most of every game. In doing so, you will run the rest of the kids into the game for a minute or so to fulfill the requirement that they play. If the coach takes this approach, he may win a few more games, but, as a rule, coaching won't be as much fun because of those darn meddling parents!

The parents have an obligation to ensure that their child is given an equal opportunity to improve. They don't expect exactly equal playing time, but they do expect it to be fairly close. At this level of play, if a coach picks players for a team and asks them to work hard at practice, then he has an obligation to play them since there is no substitute for game experience. Parents are likely to assume that their child is getting little attention in practice if they get very little game time. Parental dissatisfaction and/or conflict are sure to follow.

The large number of kids wanting to play often creates a logistical problem. Many schools now have two or three teams per grade level, so most players with a realistic chance of improving are given the opportunity. This concept lets the truly interested children have time to develop if they have the desire. The challenge is to provide each team with excellent coaching.

How Does the Style of Play Affect Player Development?

One of the most important issues a coach must be aware of is how the style of play of the games at the junior high level affects player development. Usually at the junior high level, the game turns into a racehorse type of game in which the players steal the ball or get a rebound and go as fast as they can to the other end of the court. This is all there is to the play of some teams, and some of these teams win a lot of games. As a result, these teams do not learn the basic skills necessary to be successful at the high school level. When these players reach the next level, they need to have already become fundamentally sound in all aspects of the game, since the defense and skills of the opposing players will be much improved. The following true story will help demonstrate what can happen if they haven't.

If a coach wants problems every year with parents, one of the best ways to guarantee such problems is to be concerned only with winning and to play only seven or eight kids for most of every game.

"Ninth grade players comprised the very successful high school junior varsity team. The players, parents, and junior high coaches thought these kids would have a great team in high school. Many parents were even quietly mentioning the possibility of going to the state tournament in the future. After all, this group had blown away every team except one in the last two years. The problem was most of these games were racehorse-style games, and most of the players never learned the skills and concepts of a half-court game. By the time their senior year had ended, only three of the players made the varsity, and only one player was ever a starter."

Players Need to Learn the Basics of Basketball

If all the players do is shoot layups and short shots, they may win the game now, but they may be losing the future. Players need to learn how to shoot outside, post up, make entry passes, and how to execute a half-court offense. It is the coach's responsibility to ensure that their players master these skills, even if it means losing a few games at the junior high level.

Coaches should control the style of play in every game to ensure the players develop the basic skills and confidence in those skills before they reach high school. If a game is turned into a track meet, the teams should only play this style of play for a portion of the game. In turn, the coach should take control of the situation and instruct the team to walk the ball up the court and set up the half-court offense.

This philosophy should be communicated to the players and to the parents at the beginning of the season to avoid any concerns later, since some parents are focused on winning now. They will not understand the importance of developing the players' "other" skills.

Problems Junior High Coaches May Have

Coaching at the junior high level often means dealing with numerous unexpected problems. The young coach can easily be frustrated as he deals with these problems. The talent levels in each grade may vary greatly from year to year, thereby creating new problems. A list of a few of the more common problems that junior high coaches may face includes the following:

> ➤ Players must learn how to practice. A junior high coach will have to teach the players what is expected of them during practice since many of them may never have experienced a well-organ-

ized, hard practice. Practice is hard work, and sometimes it can be boring. However, games are won in practices. Players need to learn that they have to work hard if they want to be good athletes. Coaches should make practice fun if possible.

Players need to understand the importance of practicing well since that is the way the coach evaluates the player. The coach should clearly communicate to the players what is expected of them during practices. This may include attitude, hustle and effort, and knowledge of both the offense and defense. The coach should also explain those things he will be looking for as he evaluates the players and identifies their role on the team.

> Learning to compete. Young players have to become comfortable competing for a spot on the team and for playing time. Most children have never had this experience and will look to the coach for guidance. If these children played in recreational sports leagues, they were usually guaranteed a spot on the team and a minimum amount of playing time. The competition becomes more serious when players reach junior high. Young players have to learn how to be good teammates. Teammates don't have to be the best of friends, but they do need to be good teammates. They have to learn to be encouraging and supportive of one another.

> Jealousy. Individual or class jealousy can destroy a team. It should be addressed the first day of practice.

Jealousy can exhibit itself on and off the court. Class jealousy sneaks into the picture when grades start being merged together at the junior varsity or varsity level. High school students are very class oriented. They often expect younger players to wait their turn. If younger players excel, the older players sometimes resent it because they feel threatened. Jealousy manifests itself off the court by talking bad about someone. Some players have been known not to talk to a younger teammate who had a good game the previous day. On the court, the jealous player may avoid passing the ball to the younger teammate or may run the offense away from that player. The coach should be alert to look for signs of jealousy and stop it immediately!

The coach should clearly communicate to the players what is expected of them during practices.

> The more passive child can learn to be more aggressive and competitive on the basketball court, but it will take longer and will require encouragement by the parent, as well as the coach. The coach should keep in mind that, as a rule, such a child will not make a good first impression.

> Players taking instructions literally. Most players take things literally when they are first learning the game of basketball. On occasion, even older players can take things too literally when they are under stress in an important game. It is important for the coach to be aware of times when the player may have misunderstood what was meant and has taken things literally. For example, the comment "guard your man all over the court" seems like a simple statement. In the sixth or seventh grade, some players will take it literally when they should know better.

The following story illustrates the potential problems with a player taking instructions too literally. A young player who had played basketball in youth leagues for three or four years was now competing for a starting guard position on the seventh grade team. Everyone was surprised to see the player shadowing the opposing guard out near mid-court, while the other eight players were under the opponent's basket.

After the game, when asked why the player was guarding the inexperienced opponent so far out of position instead of sagging down and helping teammates, the player stated the coach had made it perfectly clear that they were to stay with their man no matter what. The coach should have corrected this obvious problem during the game. Instead, the coach never told the player what to do in this situation.

The more passive child can learn to be more aggressive and competitive on the basketball court, but it will take longer and will require encouragement by the parent, as well as the coach.

The player refused to deviate from the coach's original instructions, even though the player had previously been a smart and good defensive player. The player's response was that if she was not doing what the coach wanted the coach would have told her. That should have been true! However, the problem persisted for several games. During this time, the player's playing time started to dwindle. The first-year coach never explained why. Common sense would make an individual think that if the coach looked out on the court and always saw a defender so totally out of a good-help defensive position, then she probably thought the player must not understand the concepts of basketball, and will never be a good player. Kids often take things literally, and they expect the coach to inform them if it isn't correct. Coaches should never believe that children know exactly what is expected. Communicate!

> Unrealistic expectations. Recently a young coach with several years of experience was relating how frustrating this year's seventh grade team was. The previous year's team was better skilled and understood what the coach wanted and could do it. Last year, the coach could tell the team what to run, and they could to it. This year's team did not seem to be able to do anything.

Further discussion revealed that last year's team had four different presses, as well as several offenses and defenses.

The coach was expecting too much from these players at their level of development. Most varsities do not have as many offenses and defenses as those seventh graders. This was too much to try to teach at one time. Why try to teach too much, too fast to players who are struggling? Would a math teacher try to teach addition, subtraction, multiplication, and division simultaneously? No, it should be learned individually over time, building on the principles learned previously.

If your team is not very skilled and confident, you should:

- Stress fundamentals! Do not worry about teaching offenses and defenses in the off-season or very early preseason. Minimize scrimmaging! Scrimmaging is fun for the kids, but they learn fundamentals very slowly when they scrimmage. Scrimmaging should be a situation when the players put to use and develop confidence in the skills they learned while working on drills.

Skills are learned much faster in drills, and drills should take up most of the practice time early in the season. Skills are best learned through executing a skill over and over correctly until it is second nature. During this time, confidence is developed in the skill. The two go together! Drills allow such a learning opportunity. Although scrimmages do not offer this opportunity, some coaches have their players scrimmaging most of the practice day after day. All other factors considered, these teams seldom beat those teams that stress working on fundamentals.

- Simplify and reduce! It is better to teach a few things well, than many things poorly! Select one offense and one defense initially, usually a man half-court offense and defense. The skills attendant to this particular offense and defense should be developed first. Other offenses and defenses can be built upon these basic skills. Weeks later, a simple transition offense, a zone offense, and a zone defense can gradually be added. One press defense and offense and one or two out-of-bounds plays should be added gradually. Keep in mind that teaching too much too fast will overwhelm even the best players; it will destroy the less-skilled or less-confident players.

- Find things players do well, and build on it! Confidence is usually developed slowly—one small step at a time! Defense is a good place to start because the techniques and skills involved in

Skills are best learned through executing a skill over and over correctly until it is second nature.

sound defensive play can be learned quickly if the player commits to giving his best. The first skill to learn on defense is to move your feet. It should be the focus of the first drill taught, and it should be emphasized every day. Defense wins games, and defense develops confidence quickly. As the players' confidence gradually grows, their attitude will also change in a positive manner.

Discipline involves complying with the coach's expectations.

Developing confidence and a basketball attitude is necessary if the player is to develop good offensive skills. As a rule, offensive skills often take longer to develop. The players need to know that the coach understands it will take time. The coach should also explain to the players that he expects them to be able to execute both the non-dribbling and non-shooting skills. Players should also understand that they are expected to give 100 percent on defense, move without the ball, set and use screens, rebound and block out, and shoot free throws well.

- Discipline. The young coach mentioned in the previous story also said the players keep missing passes even when they are told how important it is. Or, they will keep shooting with two hands when they have been instructed to shoot with only one hand. A legitimate question to this particular coach is what happens if they keep missing the passes or keep shooting with two hands?

Discipline involves complying with the coach's expectations. The players need to know they are expected to comply. In these situations, telling the players may not be enough. The coach should demonstrate proper technique, have the player do it, verify that the player understands, and then tell the player he is expected to do it from now on. Drills should be modified for the individual that day or at the next practice to emphasize what he has been told. Extra drills should be assigned to the player that he can do outside of practice to improve. The coach should expect and demand proper execution by his players. If it is not important to the coach, it will not be important to the players!

Be consistent!

If the players keep making the same mistakes, what are the consequences? Find something the players do not like to do, and use that as an incentive to do better. Running is one of the things players typically despise. For example, if a player repeatedly misses an easy pass in practice, the coach should immediately have the player take a couple of laps as play continues. This step immediately stresses to the player and the rest of the team that proper execution is important. Be consistent! If another player misses a pass, send them also. Running after missed free throws is another way to get the team understanding that it is important to make every free throw. When they execute well, praise them as quickly.

If expectations haven't been met, the player's role on the team or the amount of his playing time can be reduced. This is especially useful when the player has an attitude problem, exhibits a lack of effort, or is continually making the same mental mistakes. The player should be warned ahead of time of the possible consequence if the problems aren't corrected. If he improves, give him the chance to earn back his previous status.

> Positive and negative motivation in practice. There are appropriate times for both positive and negative motivation. However, negative motivation is okay only if it is focused on the result, not the person. Try to have at least five positives to every negative for players every day. This may not always be possible, especially the first few days of practice when the players are trying to learn what is expected of them.

Positives aren't always the verbal praising of someone. A positive can be a pat on the back or demonstrating encouragement or confidence in a player. A list of examples of positive and negative motivation can include the following factors:

Positive motivation can be gained from:

- Praise and/or encouragement from the coach.
- Positive peer pressure.
- Allowing the players to play something that they consider fun at the end of practice, if they had a great practice.
- Rewarding the team by not doing something they usually hate or by shortening practice a couple of minutes that day if the team has done well.

Negative motivation can be applied by:

- Running laps.
- Engaging in extra drills or practice.
- If players are always dragging down the team by inattention or lack of effort, the coach may want to generate peer pressure from their teammates to conform. If the team is given extra work because of a few players, there will be peer pressure to comply.

Note: It is important that coaches are always consistent in applying any punishment to players.

Try to have at least five positives to every negative for players every day.

Substitutions

Substitution schedules and the determination of the amount of game time each player gets involve a difficult choice for coaches. Collectively, this is also an extremely important decision for the child and his parents. It not only determines the success or failure of the team in that game, it also affects the development of every player on the team!

The logistics of coaching 11 or more players with no assistant coaches can be very difficult. During practice and games, even the simple task of substitution is not as simple as an individual may think. It seems obvious that the best five players play, then eventually the substitutes keep coming in until everyone has played. This is probably a good scenario for the best seven or eight players on the team.

How Does Player Substitution Affect Player Development?

Players get better when they play with better players. The starters in basketball routinely play only with the best players on the team. As a result, they are able to develop more quickly than the second- and third-team players. The challenge that coaches face is how to improve the other players as quickly, while giving all the substitutes quality practice and game time. Will the team on the floor execute better if one or two good players are playing with the substitutes, rather than putting the worst five players on the floor together? Yes.

If you have five of the weakest players on the court, someone will usually be out of position, forget what to do, or turn over the ball. Even if a player is capable of playing well, he may not get the opportunity if a pass is not made or if a teammate has clogged a lane to the basket because he did not run the offense correctly. These are lost opportunities to improve, develop confidence, and gain the attention of the coach in order to get more playing time. Such is the life of the fourth, fifth, or sixth subs off the bench.

If the subs get to play with the better players periodically in practice and games, they will be more likely to make good plays which, in turn, will help them build up their confidence. Remember, confidence comes from repeated success! How can you help your players develop confidence? Among the steps you can take are the following:

> ➢ Each substitute should know his status and role on the team, as well as what the coach expects from the player during a game. If the player hasn't yet developed good scoring abilities, the

The challenge that coaches face is how to improve the other players as quickly, while giving all the substitutes quality practice and game time.

coach may need to tell the player he expects him to play good defense and rebound well. The player needs to hear from the coach that offensive skills will take longer to develop. The player needs encouragement and should know what skills he needs to improve. The coach needs to look for ways to encourage players as they work to improve.

➤ Players should seldom be pulled from a game for making a single mistake. Players can't play if they are afraid to make mistakes. Even the professionals make mistakes. If a player is pulled from the game after making a mistake, the coach should not be angry. The coach should ask the player if he knows what he did wrong. If he does, ask him if he can do better next time. Encourage him. If you pull a player for making a mistake, it is important to demonstrate to the player your confidence in him by putting him back in the game fairly soon.

If the Coach Doesn't Play the Substitutes, What Are the Consequences?

Among the consequences of a coach not playing the substitutes are the following:

➤ Players with potential will be prevented from developing.
➤ Unhappy substitutes won't work as hard in practice, therefore denying the starters quality practice.
➤ Dissension may be created on the team.
➤ Angry parents may be grumbling in the stands, and may later confront the coach, athletic director, or school administrators.

Summary Points

Since it is difficult to predict potential or to know who will be in the school district in four or five years, the coach's goal should be to develop each junior high player to his maximum potential. Your challenge as a coach will be to find ways to teach individual fundamentals to every player each day, as well as team fundamentals. You should give positive encouragement to every child every day, but expect and demand team spirit and 100 percent effort in practice and in games. Learn to be the best possible coach. It will take preparation and hard work on your part, but the rewards are great.

Each substitute should know his status and role on the team, as well as what the coach expects from the player during a game.

All other factors being equal, all children will be happy playing on a team where:

- The coach helps each player every day to strengthen his skills.
- The coach has designed the offense and defense so every player can contribute.
- The coach communicates to the player what the player needs to do better, how to do it, and encourages the player.
- The coach establishes an open line of communication with the players and their parents.
- The coach has no favorites who get preferential treatment.
- The team has fun while they work hard.

Although the junior high coach should have less pressure to win than the varsity coach does, but in many other ways a junior high or middle school coach has a much more difficult job. Programs that have been successful for many years often have junior high coaches who have been teaching and motivating children for years. Those coaches are very special to the players and the program.

The point to keep in mind is that a coach creates a well-organized environment in which hard work, discipline, teamwork, and fundamentals are stressed, and if players are rewarded daily with positive encouragement as well as challenges to be better, players will want to participate.

Programs that have been successful for many years often have junior high coaches who have been teaching and motivating children for years.

CHAPTER 4

Communication

A coach's ability to communicate should be one of his greatest assets. Unfortunately, many coaches do not possess good communication skills. Over the years, too many coaches have communicated effectively only when a crisis has arisen. Communication involves much more than that.

The Coach Should Be the Leader in Communication

The coach should lead the players and the parents through their basketball experience. The coach must understand that he is expected to lead and help both the players and their parents understand what to expect, all-the-while maintaining an open line of communication. Such communication can involve numerous channels and forms, including team meetings, parent meetings, daily practice comments and instructions, as well as face-to-face consultations with the players. A coach can eliminate doubt and confusion among the players by:

- Defining his expectations and rules for the team.
- Defining each player's role on the team as well as expectations for the player.
- Discussing the player's strengths and weaknesses and areas in which the player needs to work.
- Keeping each player updated periodically on his progress.

The coach should lead the players and the parents through their basketball experience.

Some coaches have trouble communicating, and they put the responsibility of initiating communication on the player or the parent. As a result, they are increasing the likelihood of conflict because the coach is the ultimate authoritative figure; neither the player nor the parent is likely to approach the coach unless emotions are about to explode.

A leader should create an environment in which people feel comfortable and are relatively at ease. If players are accustomed to communicating with the coach on a periodic basis over everyday matters, it will be much easier for a player to approach the coach with his concerns or problems.

Communication

> It's not just what you say—it's how you say it.
> It's not what you say—it's what you do.
> It's your body language.
> Communication isn't just what you say or do,
> It's what the other person hears or perceives!

Coaches should remember that perception is reality for their players. Communication is what we say and what we do—both consciously and unconsciously. Many questions that players struggle with each season occur because there is inadequate communication or the verbal communication is not supported by the non-verbal actions of the coach!

Non-Verbal and Verbal Communication

Non-Verbal Communication

Everything an individual says or does as a teacher or coach says something to someone. Much of what is said is through non-verbal communication, whether it was intentional or not. A person's actions, tone of voice, and attentiveness all send signals. Ask yourself: do your everyday actions validate what you have told the team? Some examples of non-verbal communication that coaches may not have considered include:

> *Everything an individual says or does as a teacher or coach says something to someone.*

- Time spent with each player in practice. Do some players always get most of the instruction?
- Giving all players quality practice and game time.
- Are suggestions and encouragement given to all the players during games or just the starters?
- Criticizing and praising favorite players while basically ignoring the players against whom they are paired.
- The excitement a coach shows when a player finally accomplishes a difficult task with which he has difficulty.
- Substitution patterns. If a player finally gets to play more in a game, does well, and is excited about working harder, what signal is sent if the player doesn't get to play in the next game? What would this do to any individual's confidence, much less an insecure teenager's?

Several instances of verbal communication not being supported by the non-verbal actions of the coach are subtle. For example, a coach tells the team that every player is equally important. On the other hand, if the coach subconsciously believes that only a handful of players will ever be able to develop in four or five years, the coach may spend disproportionately more time trying to help those few players at the expense of the others on the team. In this instance, the coach's actions will send signals to the other players that the coach does not believe they will ever develop. While these actions may be subtle and unintentional, the message that is delivered to the other players is powerful!

The amount of quality practice and game time given to the lesser skilled players sends a message. Coaches send signals to the players when they spend considerably more time during drills trying to improve the skills of the better players. Does the second team exist only so the starters will have someone to practice against? Or, is the practice structured to try to improve everyone equally on the team? Do all the players get quality game time? Is the substitution pattern such that the eighth-through-the-tenth players on the team each get an opportunity to play with several of the starters, or do they only play with second- or third-team players? All factors being equal, a player improves much more quickly when playing with better players.

How many times have you seen a coach talk with the starters when they come out of the game, giving them suggestions to use when they go back in the game? Too often, well-meaning coaches never bother to make similar suggestions to the other players when they come out of the game. They are told to have a seat! Such non-verbal actions send a subtle message that the coach does not have faith in these players.

Non-verbal communication is powerful. Non-verbal communication will sometimes express our inner feelings of which we are unaware. Coaches must be alert to always send positive signals to all players. All coaches who deal with athletes should realize that both their words and their actions send messages to their players. As a coach, what message do you want to send?

Non-verbal communication is powerful.

Verbal Communication

Any player, whether the star or the last player off the bench, will have questions and self-doubt during the course of the season. This is true at the junior high, high school, college, and even the professional levels. Often this self-doubt is because the player is trying to figure out his role on the team, what he needs to do to get more playing time, or how the coach feels about his performance. This doubt can be even more exaggerated if the player is struggling with his game.

It may be helpful before the season begins for the coach to develop a schedule of times to communicate with players and, occasionally, with parents. By doing so, the coach is initiating and maintaining an open line of communication. Many college coaches have planned periodic conferences with players. However, it is seldom done at the youth or interscholastic level. Why?

Three Basic Types of Communication in Basketball

- Player-coach communication
- Player-player communication
- Coach-parent (and player) communication

Player-Coach Communication

A coach has several possible methods of communicating with his players, including:
- Team meetings
- Daily communication during practice and games
- Player-coach conferences
- Special situation conferences:
    - Team captains
    - Players who are struggling (individual conference)
    - Player promotion to the varsity (individual and team meetings)

• *Team meetings.* The first meetings of the year should define what is expected of the players trying out for the team and later of the players who have made the team. A coach can use the following suggestions as a guide and as a means to help develop an organized system of communication that fits his personality.

1) Meeting for players trying out for the team. At this first meeting of the year, the coach should inform the players of his expectations for them as individuals and collectively as a team. It is important to clearly define what is expected during practice. Some players may never have experienced well-organized, efficient practices. The coach should inform the players that he realizes practices are sometimes hard, tedious, and may get old, but this team will not waste any practice time. If the team wants to win, the players' primary goal should be to work harder than any of their opponents to improve.

2) Meeting with the players making the team. After the team is selected, the coach should meet with the players to go over team rules, the coach's expectations for the team, the practice schedule, and any questions the players may have. The coach

> **The coach should inform the players that he realizes practices are sometimes hard, tedious, and may get old, but this team will not waste any practice time.**

may want to have a conference with each player individually at this time. The coach should inform the players that player-coach conferences will be held periodically throughout the year.

• *Daily communication with players.* Most coaches do a much better job of communicating daily than they do in player-coach conferences. A coach's daily communication is when players will see if the coach's promises come true. What messages are you sending? A coach communicates that he cares about a player by:

- ❏ Working with a player on technique.
- ❏ Praising a player in public.
- ❏ Encouraging a player who is struggling by telling him he knows he can play better.
- ❏ Reviewing with the player something he did well in the last game or scrimmage.
- ❏ Challenging a player to work harder or do better.

Much of the daily communication that a coach has with his players occurs in practice. As such, for a coach to have time to give individualized attention to each player during practice, he must have qualified assistants who will allow the coach to better establish a one-one-one relationship with each player. A minimum of five positives to every negative are often mentioned as the ideal ratio of criticism if practices are to be positive in nature. There will be bad days when a player feels negative because he can't seem to do anything right. This player needs encouragement from the coach before he leaves for the day; a few positive words may mean a lot to a player.

An excellent coach once said after an exasperating defeat, "We need to get back in practice and build up the players' confidence. When they are down we have to build them up, and when they are up, we need to challenge them to do better than they have."

Coaches should not assume their players know anything until proven otherwise.

In any profession, people forget how much they have learned a little bit at a time over the years. Coaches, like parents, sometimes expect young people to know things they have not yet learned or have never even considered. Coaches should not assume their players know anything until proven otherwise. For example, coaches tell players on the bench to "keep their heads in the game". So, the kids watch the game. The coach actually meant the players should analyze the other team's offensive and defensive play, and the players should scout the players they are likely to play against when they get in the game. That is not what the teenager heard!

Coaches should keep in mind that one of the most effective communication tools at their disposal is film. Verbal communication is limited by the speaker's ability to effectively verbalize what was meant as well as the listener's preconceived perceptions. Film captures an individual as everyone else sees him, not as he sees himself. The saying "A picture is worth a thousand words," has never been more accurate. Videotape can be a great communicative tool.

In team meetings, game film can be used to stress the things the team needs to do. Film also offers the opportunity to find positives that can be reinforced. In individual player-coach conferences, game film can be invaluable in demonstrating to the player what needs to be improved. Often, players either don't realize what they are doing or think they are doing it correctly.

Communication during the game is also important. A mature coach realizes his job is to have the players prepared and fundamentally sound enough before the game so that he can calmly tell the players what they need to do during the game. The preparation needed for winning is made during practices. The coach is the role model for the team, and the players look to the coach for leadership. A coach must learn to suppress expressions of disappointment, frustration or anger.

❑ What signals do you send to your players during the game? What you say, how you say it, and your body language express your feelings. Ask a friend to videotape you as you work with the kids during the official scrimmages and the first few games. Objectively critique your actions. Are you the role model that you want the team to reflect? How do you talk to your players when things aren't going well? If a player has made some dumb mistakes, what is your response? What was said to the player? What body language did you have as the player was coming to the bench? Was it encouragement, anger, indifference, or was the player ignored? The coach should never get so caught up in the emotions of the game that it affects the way he communicates with the players. A coach who is "ranting and raving" will not be focusing on proper coaching decisions. If the coach is always calm, confident, and well-prepared, the team will be more likely to respond to what he suggests.

❑ The player who is hard on himself. A player sometimes is so mad at himself that he is seething. Such a player may appear to have a bad attitude, and a coach may have a hard time knowing how to deal with this player. If the coach prefers to visit with players as they come out of the game, this player will create a challenge to the coach. The player is so mad at himself that he wants to go to the end of the bench. When a player is this upset, he will not be in the mindset to listen well. The coach doesn't want the player to have an attitude problem, or the team to think that the player gets special treatment by being allowed to act in this manner. These are usually intense players, and these actions have been developed over the years. The player can change, but it will take time. In these situations, it is important to address the problem as early as possible in practice. At the beginning of the season, the coach must explain to the player that:

- He will play better if he isn't so hard on himself.
- His actions may give the appearance of having a bad attitude, and bad attitudes aren't acceptable.
- If they work together, the problem can be avoided.

The player may act in this particular way for many reasons a coach may never learn. On the other hand, once the player learns that the coach is there to help him get better and not to get on his case, his attitude will usually improve.

• Player-coach conferences. Player-coach conferences can play a very important role in eliminating doubt and confusion in the mind of the player. Even though the coach communicates with the players daily in many ways, it is not the same as sitting down and exploring the feelings and thought processes of one another. When self-doubt and misperceptions exist, a player's imagination can create an emotional roller coaster. Once the player clearly understands where he stands, what is expected of him, and that the coach truly wants the player to succeed, the player should develop and perform at a higher level.

❑ The player-coach conference. The coach may want to find out if the player has any questions. The coach should ask the player what he feels his strengths and weaknesses are and what he feels he needs to improve. The player should be asked what he thinks his role on the team is.

After gaining an insight into the player's perception of his status, the coach should tell the player what he thinks the player's strengths and weaknesses are and what the player should try to improve. This is an ideal time to review the coach's opinion of the player's role on the team. The player should also be informed that if he works hard to improve his skills, his role on the team might change during the season. The player should be asked if there are any questions or concerns he might have.

Player-coach conferences can play a very important role in eliminating doubt and confusion in the mind of the player.

If the player wants to work to improve his skills at home or after school, the coach can provide a list of things the player should work on, as well as drills that will help the player become more fundamentally sound. The player should be informed that there will be future conferences as the season progresses so that the player will always understand where he stands on the team and what is expected of him. The player should be told that there will be times when he is struggling and he may have doubts about his status. Such times are perfectly normal, but the player should feel free to come visit with the coach anytime he has questions or concerns.

The coach should plan on player-coach conferences throughout the year (e.g., after the team is selected, periodically during the season, after the season, and before the summer recess begins, as well as when special situations arise). Many problems develop in the minds of the players as the competitive season progresses. Outside forces and problems can easily be carried into the gym and have an effect on players and the team. The earlier the problems are dealt with, the better everything will be.

> **The coach should plan on player-coach conferences throughout the year.**

- ❏ The end-of-season player-coach conference. The end-of-season player-coach conference is an opportunity for the coach to thank each player for working hard during the year. In this session, the coach should be positive and encourage his players:

  - ➤ <u>For the seniors.</u> It is a great time to say thank you to the seniors for their years of sacrifice and hard work. They will soon be busy with other activities and preparing for the end of school. You may not have the opportunity to express how much you have appreciated the chance of sharing their lives. This may also be a good time to discover if the seniors have suggestions that might be helpful in the future or if there were problems of which you were unaware. It is a great time to express your feelings and desire to be helpful in their future. No matter how the season went, this moment of caring may last a lifetime.

  - ➤ <u>For the returning players.</u> The end-of-year player-coach conference is an opportunity to once again discover each player's sense of where he stands and what he needs to work on during the summer. It is important for the coach to let the player know where he envisions the player will be the following season. The coach should review the player's strengths and weaknesses and how he will fit in next season's plan. If the coach isn't sure if the player will be on the junior varsity or varsity, he should let the player know. The player should be asked if he would prefer being on the varsity and sitting on the bench quite a bit, or playing more on the junior varsity. The coach should encourage and inform the player of drills, as well as other ways, to improve himself during the summer. The player should be reassured that you will reevaluate each player again once try-outs begin the following season, since you realize some players may sometimes improve drastically in a few months.

- ❑ The new school year player-coach conference. The new school year player-coach conference is an opportunity to find out what the player did during the summer. If the players are in an off-season practice program, it might be advisable to give them a couple of weeks to show what they have learned. The coach can usually tell who really worked during the summer. The player should be asked what he has worked on during the summer, and what he did to improve. The coach should ask the player what he feels his strengths and weaknesses are and what he feels he needs to improve.

After gaining an insight into the player's perception of his status, the coach should tell the player what he thinks the player's strengths and weaknesses are. At this time, the coach can make suggestions on things the player should work on until the formal practice time begins. This will allow time for the player to make significant improvements in fundamentals before the season begins. If the player wants to work extra at home or after school, the coach can provide a list of things on which he should work, as well as drills that will help the player become more fundamentally sound.

Finally, the player should be asked if he has any questions. The player should then be informed there will be further conferences as the season progresses. The player should be encouraged to feel free to visit with the coach anytime he has questions or concerns.

- • Situations that may require additional communication: During the course of the year, situations will often develop that require special effort to communicate by the coach. Handling the following situations properly will result in far fewer problems.

- ❑ After the team is selected. It is very important to meet with each of the players who are being cut from the team. It can be a very difficult and trying time for these young athletes. Remember you cannot measure heart, desire, and potential! So never destroy their belief in their dreams. Be realistic about their chances but try not to prejudge desire and potential.

If a player has a strong desire to play, the coach should try to find out if there are alternative leagues the player can participate in to gain experience. The coach should tell the player what he needs to improve and provide him with a list of drills to work on at home. The player should be informed of off-season leagues that are available, as well as camps that might be helpful. The player should be told that there is no guarantee he will make the team next season, but he will be given a fair chance if he works hard to improve and if he wants to try again.

- ❑ A player who is struggling. A player who is struggling with his confidence needs encouragement. The coach should find something a player does well and build upon it. The player's hustle and effort should be acknowledged. An emphasis should be placed on doing the little things that determine success. The coach should also acknowledge that the player made the correct decisions, even if the results weren't successful. The player should be encouraged to continue to give a 100 percent effort and reassured that you have confidence in him and that everything will soon turn around if he hangs in and keeps working hard. Remember, confidence develops slowly but is destroyed easily and rapidly, especially if the coach demonstrates anger and frustration with his words, actions, and body language.

All players will struggle with confidence problems. During these times, the players will worry about what the coach is thinking. Is everything okay? Will their status on the team change? Communication and positive encouragement are especially critical when players are struggling with their confidence.

The coach should find something a player does well and build upon it.

- ❑ A player promoted to varsity (or junior varsity) during the season. If the coach promotes a player during the season, it is important to remember that several potential problems need to be addressed before they occur. First, the player may be tentative and hesitant to shoot (which may be the reason the player was promoted in the first place). The player may be afraid to come out shooting because he wants to be accepted by the upper-level players and doesn't want to appear as a "hot dog" or a "ball hog." Second, class jealousy often exists in high school and players are subjected to it unless the coach prevents it from ever starting.

The coach should explain privately to the player:

- Why he is being promoted.
- What the coach expects the player to do.
- Asked if he has any questions or problems with performing his role. What is expected of him and
- The coach should tell the player that the team will be informed that same day.

Furthermore, it is important for the coach to explain to the team:

- Why the player is being promoted.
- What is expected of the player.
- That they are expected to make the new player feel comfortable and an integral part of the team.

The coach should be alert the next few practices and games to watch for subtle signs of class jealousy. It is during this time that the coach should encourage the player if he is hesitant, and the coach should emphasize that the offense should be run as it is designed.

- ❑ Defining the role of team captains. The role of team captains should be clearly defined. Many players who are designated as the team captain have no idea what is expected of them, and few players can easily define leadership. What is leadership? Each coach has different expectations. The coach should define the duties and expectations of the team captain. Leadership qualities will vary greatly from one year to another depending on the individuals. However, the captains will more likely fulfill their roles in the desired manner if their roles have been fully explained to them. The following two examples demonstrate how leadership can vary.

The role of team captains should be clearly defined.

The seniors called the freshman and invited her to come to the gym each day during the summer. The seniors wanted other players to work hard during the summer because they knew they had a chance to have a good team the next year. Since the player was too young to drive, the seniors said they would take care of the transportation. The two star players were caring and unselfish on and off the court. They worked harder than anyone else and always tried to make everyone else better. The next year was a dream season for the team. In a subsequent year, the senior captains were vastly different. There was insecurity and jealousy among the captains, and they did very few of the things that made the team in the previous example so special. Jealousy of the younger players by the senior leadership was one of the team's problems. Although the team played well, the players never came close to realizing their potential or their dream.

- ❏ Getting a player's attention. Does the coach have to yell at or intimidate a player to get his attention? The military coaching style of the past, in which the players were intimidated and humiliated, is no longer acceptable. The coach should have enough people skills to know how to communicate with and motivate his players. Does that mean a coach can't raise his voice? No, of course not. Raising one's voice is one way to emphasize a point and get the player's attention. A coach should keep in mind that raising his voice is most effective when it is seldom used. If the coach raises his voice, he must remain calm, cool, and instructive.

Player development is a complex issue. The coach walks a fine line between being coach, motivator, and taskmaster. On one hand, the coach needs to be positive and encouraging. At other times, he must be challenging and demanding. He must discover ways to stimulate the players to be better than they ever thought they could be.

A coach's greatest motivating tool is the young athletes desire to play! The truth is the coach controls the playing time. He shouldn't threaten players with it. The players are already quite aware of who controls their destiny. The coach should simply and calmly explain to the players what he wants and what they need to do. If the players don't do what the coach wants, they should have their amount of playing time reduced or their starting status changed until they are ready to do so.

A coach should keep in mind that raising his voice is most effective when it is seldom used.

Player-to-Player Communication

Coaches must teach and encourage players to communicate with each other. Players should learn to help each other by communicating on and off the floor. Coaches understand this, but young athletes often don't. Teams will have players with drastic differences in skill levels, as well as maturity levels. Players are learning to communicate and interact in a competitive environment. For some players this can be a challenge, and a coach's guiding hand can be very helpful in this regard.

- • Create a supportive environment. The coach should teach the team to be supportive, encouraging and open to helping each other. This attitude can only be taught in practice. A supportive relationship brings the team closer together and makes it much easier to discuss problems or make suggestions.

During the first practice of the year, the coach should set the tone for the team by being very positive toward those players who hustle and try hard, as well as players who make an outstanding play, whether it be a pass, shot, move, screen, block, or denial defense. The coach should also inform the team that he expects the players to acknowledge the effort and hustle of their teammates, as well as those instances when a player finally has success at something at which he has had difficulty in the past.

Positive peer pressure is a powerful motivating force.

The best players should learn to lead by encouraging and praising teammates. Positive peer pressure is a powerful motivating force. We all love people who help us and make us feel better about ourselves. All other factors being equal, we are more likely to listen to anything they say in the future.

On the court, players need to communicate to make the offense or defense more effective. Players need to be able to discuss what is happening on the court so they can make the appropriate adjustments. The following examples illustrate the point:

- Communication is critical on screens. A player should warn a teammate when he is about to be screened on the blind side.
- If an opponent switches defenses, someone must take charge in notifying his teammates of the new defense. The point guard is usually the offensive quarterback that takes charge of the team.
- In transition defense, communication is critical to ensure that all players are defended and no player is left unguarded.

Coach-Parent Communication

If a player is on your team, you have a relationship with the parent! How a coach treats the player and how the coach leads the player and the parents in their basketball experience will determine whether the parent-coach relationship is co-operative, tolerant, or adversarial. Communication with the parents is critical if a good relationship is to be maintained. Parents need to know that they can visit with the coach, if necessary, and they need to know that the coach has their child's best interest at heart. It is the coach's responsibility, not the parent's, to initiate and maintain an open line of communication. This communication is initiated with a pre-season meeting with the team and the parents.

If a player is on his team, the coach has a relationship with the child's parents.

Preseason meeting with the team and parents. The preseason meeting is the perfect opportunity for the parents to be brought into the basketball experience. The coach has already explained to the players at the initial team meeting most of what he is going to say. He should reinforce his points as he explains how the team will be run, what his philosophy is, and what his expectations are. He should solidify parental support by involving them in the process. Some points a coach might want to cover during his preseason meeting with the parents include:

"Our style of play each year is based on the talent level of the team, utilizing the players' strengths while trying to cover up their weaknesses. Several factors remain constant. You cannot coach height and speed! We play with what we have; we just need to get as good as we can be! A coach's job is to get the best out of our teams while developing the players to their fullest potential."

The coach could also expand on the following factors:

What his philosophy is regarding the team:

- Defense allows us to win games. We play DEFENSE.
- Everyone contributes in our team offense.
- Turnovers and missed free throws lose ball games. We will avoid them!
- Transition offense allows scoring opportunities and discourages pressing defenses.
- Practices will be hard and efficient, and we will learn in practice. Practices are work so games can be fun!
- Teams win! No one loses if they give their best every day!

What he expects from the team:

- Our team should be in the best physical condition. We will be in better shape!
- Defense and rebounding will allow our offense the opportunity to win games.
- We will attack on offense any chance we have. A good transition offense will allow our team to get better scoring opportunities after a made basket or a change of possession.
- Team play is mandatory! There will be no petty jealousies or squabbles!
- The team should learn to be as prepared as possible and to use their brains by figuring out ways to get any advantage they can over the opponent.
- Free throw shooting will be a strong point!
- We will give 110 percent in practice. Our practices will be hard work, and the reward will be the fun we have as we play and do

It is the coach's responsibility, not the parent's, to initiate and maintain an open line of communication.

well because we are prepared and have improved.
- The substitutes should quickly learn to play defense as well as the starters; offensive skills will take longer. If we are to win, our players off the bench must play well.
- Players will be assigned roles on the team based on their skills. If the players work hard and improve their skills enough, their role on the team can change during the year. Every team must have role players!

Every team must have role players!

What each player should expect from him:

- Our team will be as prepared as possible.
- Our offense and defense will be designed to utilize the strengths of all our players.
- Each player will be treated as equally as his teammates.
- I will have favorites, but I will not play favorites.
- I will work as hard to improve the player with the least skill on the team as the best player. It will then be up to the player as to how much he progresses.
- Players will be given quality practice and game time.
- I will correct players immediately when they make a mistake in practice, and I will praise them immediately when they are able to do it correctly.
- I will lead the team and the parents in an open line of communication. My goal is to help you to enjoy your basketball experience. Each player will know his role on the team, his strengths and weaknesses, and what he must do if he wants his role to change.

What will get a player in trouble?

- Lack of effort.
- Arguing.
- Talking back.
- Not following the team rules.
- Not following instructions.
- Not knowing the offense or defense after we have worked on it.

Each player will know his role on the team, his strengths and weaknesses, and what he must do if he wants his role to change.

What the team rules are:

- Be the teammate you would want.
- Be supportive and encouraging of your teammates.
- Pass all your courses.

- Be on time.
- No excuses.
- Be attentive even when I am talking to someone else. You might learn.
- No smoking, drinking, or drugs. No exceptions.

What approach regarding team discipline he will take:

The coach should clearly discuss what issues will demand immediate suspension from the team, for example:

- Violating team rules.
- An attitude detrimental to the team.
- Not attending classes and/or failing a class.
- Being caught with alcohol, drugs, or tobacco. This means on campus or off.
- Being in trouble with the law or any school official.

What he expects from the parents:

- Let the coach do the coaching.
- Be supportive of the players and the coach.
- Be a positive fan. Do not yell directions or negative comments.
- Be ready to help your child at home, if they ask for it.

What the parents can expect from him:

- I will give a 100 percent effort to help your children get better.
- The players will work on fundamentals every day! This is how they can improve quickly.
- I will try to teach the players how to get every advantage we can.
- I will be demanding, but caring and positive.
- Our goal is to win every game. But we will not win at the expense of developing players.

What do parents want of the coach?

- A caring coach who is knowledgeable about basketball.
- A coach works hard to make the players as good as they can be.
- A coach who gives their children a fair and equal chance to be successful or to fail.
- A coach who practices the cardinal rules of coaching and leads the players and parents in an open line of communication.

- ❑ Getting a formal commitment of support from the parents. At the preseason coach-player-parent meeting, it is wise to get the parents to agree with and make a formal commitment to support the way the program will be run so there will be fewer problems during the course of the season. A strong unity among the parents is needed before the season starts because if the team or a few players are struggling, problems sometimes arise. It is important for the parents to verbalize their support. Ask the parents if they have questions or concerns about what has been discussed previously. Does it seem fair and reasonable? Is there anyone who has a problem with what has been outlined? The pressure is now on the coach to follow through with what he has promised.

- ❑ At the subvarsity level. The coach should ask the parents if they want a win-at-all-cost philosophy where only the best five or six players get most of the playing time at the expense of the other players. The parents should be required to raise their hands if this is what they want. In reality, few parents will want this philosophy since they aren't sure of their child's playing status. The coach may then ask, "Are we in agreement? I will not coach this team to win only by playing the best players most of every game. It would deny the other players the opportunity to develop. But we will play every game expecting to win."

The coach should then restate his fundamental rule concerning playing time: "If a player is on the team and works hard in practice, he will get quality playing time unless he is being disciplined. I may put the best players back in toward the end of the game if all the players have had quality playing time." At this point in the meeting, the coach should ask the parents: "Is this agreeable with everyone?"

- ❑ At the varsity level. The attitude at the varsity level is to win games. There is no guarantee of playing times at this level. Coaches routinely use at least the top seven or eight players on the team. However, if the other players develop good fundamentals, work hard in practice, and play great defense, they often can contribute. On the other hand, there will be no guarantees that they will get in a particular game.

The team will be better if the substitutes are able to develop to the fullest possible extent during the course of the season.

The team will be better if the substitutes are able to develop to the fullest possible extent during the course of the season. The better they are, the more they can challenge the starters during drills and scrimmages. Ideally, the second team will challenge the starters so much in practice that games will seem easy to the players. Strong competition makes players and teams better!

Parents like to be involved. The coach should find ways for them to be involved. He should ask for their help in the future. When a coach involves the parents (rather than isolates them), the parents will become allies, not people to fear. Most parents like to do for the kids and the team. The coach should encourage the parents to be involved within interscholastic guidelines.

At this meeting of the players, parents, and the coaching staff, it is appropriate to discuss with the parents what communication with the coach is acceptable. The coach should invite the parents to feel free to visit with him anytime. His door should always be open for the players or the parents. The coach should clearly define to all parents what topics will and will not be open for discussion!

What subjects are open for discussion with the coach? What can be discussed:

- The strengths and weaknesses of the player.
- What the player can do outside of practice to improve.
- If the player is having personal, school, or basketball problems.
- Other pertinent general information.

What subjects should not be open to discussion with the coach?

- The selection of the team.
- The starters on the team.
- How much playing time a player is getting.

Other player, coach, and parent meetings can be scheduled, if needed, during the year.

Summary Points

People play mind games on themselves when they do not know what to expect or where they stand. Being human, most people usually assume the worst. An open line of communication can help reduce or eliminate such worries and help free the player to improve his ability to play the game he loves.

CHAPTER 5

Internal Problems Can Destroy a Team

Internal problems can destroy a team, and the coach may not have a clue of what the problem is! As a rule, the players will not come to the coach with the problem; however, they may confide in their parents.

Examples of Internal Problems

A. Personal Problems of the Player

A coach at a very good program recently stated that he used to think that the X's and O's were the most important aspect of coaching. Now he believes that dealing with the day-to-day problems and keeping the player confident and focused is just as important, if not more important. The challenge is to continually address these problems in a helpful and caring manner. Some of the common problems that players have include:

- The player is losing confidence.
- The player is uncertain of his role on the team or how he is doing.
- The player may not know what he needs to improve to get more playing time.
- Players on the team may not be friends and they may be having problems off the court.
- Boyfriend-girlfriend problems.
- Family or academic problems.
- Teammates may have a drinking or drug problem, but the players may not know what to do or say.

B. Jealousy

Class jealousy is a serious problem in high school. Seniors often look down on the younger students, especially freshmen and sophomores. Seniors do not think of them as equals in anything. Seniors who have

> Internal problems can destroy a team, and the coach may not have a clue of what the problem is!

waited for their turn to start on the varsity tend to resent anyone younger who excels and threatens their status on the team. Individual Jealousy can also be a problem. Individual jealousy can involve any player, regardless of grade level. These individuals are immature and are lacking in confidence.

Jealousy may be manifested by in many ways. The most obvious is when the player shuns or ignores a teammate off the court. The jealous individual may talk negatively about the other player behind the player's back. On the court, the jealous player may do things that will insure the other player isn't successful. For example, the jealous player may look to pass to the open teammate then realize who it is, and quickly decide to pass to another teammate even if he isn't as open. The coach may think the player didn't realize where the open player was. It was, in fact, a conscious decision on the part of the player to not pass there. Jealous actions start in practice, and they must be corrected early before they are carried over to games.

The parents are in a dilemma because they know what the problem is, but they may not be able to do anything about it because the child has asked the parent to not say anything to anyone. The parents do not feel comfortable bringing up these kinds of problems to the coach, and they feel or wish the coach were aware enough to know there is a problem. The following story demonstrates this situation perfectly: In preseason scrimmages, the team looked unbelievably good. In the first regular season game against a much larger school, the smaller school destroyed its opponent in the first half. The first sign of jealousy surfaced at halftime when the two senior starters on the team snubbed the sophomore, who had scored fourteen points in the first half. They refused to talk to the sophomore during halftime. During the second half, the sophomore passed up many easy, short shots and instead passed to older players who were guarded closely. The coach could be heard yelling for the sophomore to shoot, but the young player did not shoot the entire second half.

Jealous actions start in practice, and they must be corrected early before they are carried over to games.

The sophomore later confided that the cold shoulder was a common occurrence after a good practice or game. The coach never asked her why the sophomore didn't shoot the second half, even though the coach had yelled instructions to do so. The younger player was not about to complain to the coach because she felt she would be an outcast for sure. The problem persisted throughout the year, and the team gradually got worse. The team made it to the playoffs, but was quickly eliminated and only a shell of the team that started the season.

For some reason, some high school seniors think that they automatically should be the stars of the team because they have waited their turn. These players are selfish and put their interests above that of the team. The coach must make certain that the older players accept the younger players as equals. The coach must pay attention in practice for any signs of trouble. Resentment and jealousy make poor teammates.

How Does the Coach Know There is a Problem?

The players or the parents will generally not be comfortable coming to the coach and bringing up the subject. Therefore, the coach must assume that periodic problems will occur that he must prevent. The coach must pay attention to the little things on and off the court. Little details may give the coach an idea if there is something wrong on the team.

Not passing to an open teammate or not including the teammate in the offense is a common way of punishing a teammate. Is the pass made to the correct person? Did the passer not see the open teammate? Did he even look, or did he not want to pass to the open teammate?

How do players get along on and off the court? Players do not have to be best friends or hang out with each other off the court. However, the coach can get some ideas if there are internal problems by discreetly being aware of the players' attitudes on the court, before and after practice, and out of the gym. In high school, coaches often hear rumors about students.

How is the team playing? Is the team playing up to its potential? Is the team getting better, staying the same, or getting worse? If there are problems it will show up in the performance of the team.

How is a player developing? Is the player developing as expected? Is the player playing worse lately? A player's performance often will be influenced by his personal or jealousy problems, insecurity or a lack of confidence exaggerated by doubt about his role or status on the team as well as meeting the coach's expectations. A coach must clearly communicate to every player on the team on a regular basis if he wants the players and team to develop.

The coach should also be aware that other factors also affect performance. Poor coaching and poor interpersonal skills by the coach also cause problems. If the coach is truly evaluating the performance of the team, he should be ready for answers he may not want to find.

If the coach is truly evaluating the performance of the team, he should be ready for answers he may not want to find.

Preventing Internal Problems on the Team

The best way to handle problems is to prevent them. The coach can do this by doing the following:

- Coach by the cardinal rules.
- Help the team to bond together. Great teams must bond together. The players on the team don't have to be great friends, but they should respect and want each person to succeed. Teams will have players from different grade-levels and players with different friends and interests. The coach must set the tone of teamwork in practice. He should work with the team captains to encourage group extra-curricular activities to help with the bonding of the players.
- Communicate. Clearly define the team rules. Define the roles of the players on the team and your expectations for each of them. Discuss your expectations and theirs.
- Expect jealousy or problems when:
  - A younger player is better than older players.
  - A player is promoted to the varsity.
  - A substitute is promoted to a starting position.
- The coach should look for signs of problems. If problems occur, deal with them immediately and fairly.

Summary Points

One of the most important responsibilities of a coach is to create a team environment where internal problems don't exist, and if they do, they are recognized and dealt with in a systematic, positive manner. To the extent possible, the coach should do whatever possible to prevent such problems. When and if internal problems arise, the coach should have a clearly defined, well-thought out plan for addressing them.

Great teams must bond together.

CHAPTER 6

Player Evaluation

People think of player evaluation being done when the team is being selected and when the starters are being determined. Player evaluation is much more. The ability to develop the players and the team is greatly dependent upon the coach's ability to accurately notice and evaluate the little things that are so important. The coach must keep an open mind and continually reevaluate and reassess the players and the team's play on a regular basis!

Player Evaluation is Something Coaches Assumably Do Well

College and professional coaches recruit or draft players whom they think will develop into potential stars. Are they very accurate in their evaluations? The answer is no! With their large staffs and huge budgets, these organizations are quite often wrong. The college and professional levels are full of players who were underestimated and consensus blue chip recruits who never developed. It isn't unusual that many of the blue chip prospects never develop. In fact, a fourth of these "can't miss" players often do not complete their college careers.

If large universities and professional teams cannot evaluate and predict who will develop into a fine player, how can an overworked and understaffed junior high or high school coach expect to do better? In fact, he shouldn't. The coach must realize the first step in having a good program is to understand he can't determine potential! Instead the coach should fine tune his player evaluation skills and develop every player on the team to their maximum potential!

An evaluation is an impression. Many decisions early in the year are based on past reputation and first impressions made during tryouts, the preseason, or early in the season. Since first impressions are so very difficult to overcome, the challenge is to keep an open mind thereafter.

The coach must realize the first step in having a good program is to understand he can't determine potential!

Player evaluation should be a year-long process with the coach updating the evaluation everyday. During the season, a coach will need to do the following types of player evaluations:

- Team selection.
- Team skills.
- Determining the starters.
- Individual evaluation.
- Team evaluation.
- Outside evaluation.

Team Selection

Team selection is one of the most difficult decisions a coach has to make. Usually a few players will be far superior than the rest. The difficulty comes in deciding who makes the team when the rest of the players are very close in skills. A coach must be aware of the probability that a player he has cut may have had more potential than he showed and the coach first realized.

> ❑ The players being cut. Remember, the decision to cut a player impacts a player's dreams. Few young athletes will risk the embarrassment of trying out and being cut a second time. Their willingness to continue to pursue their dreams will be greatly decided by how the coach handles the situation! The coach needs to imagine how he would feel if he had an intense desire to play and was cut. How would he like to be treated? The coach owes it to the kids to meet with the players being cut. Be honest with the player being cut about his strengths and weaknesses and his likelihood of improving enough to make the team the following season if he works hard. Ask the player if he would like a recommendation regarding things on which he should work. If there are alternative leagues or teams, interested players should be encouraged to participate and try out again the next year. Remember, Michael Jordan was cut from his high school team his sophomore year.

> ❑ The players making the team. Once the team is selected, most teams usually will have one to three players who stand out as being more skilled. The coach, as well the other players, will know who they are. The coach's dilemma is to make certain that the remaining players on the squad who are very close to being equal in talent are evaluated continuously and are given an equal chance to perform and be successful. The factors on which the

A coach must be aware of the probability that a player he has cut may have had more potential than he showed and the coach first realized.

players will be evaluated should be explained. The coach should inform the players that during the season their role on the team may change if they work hard and improve significantly.

Team Skills

Once the team has been selected, the coach begins the task of finalizing the evaluation of the strengths of the players so he can decide on the style of play that best fits the team. At the varsity level, great coaches adjust their game to the strengths and weaknesses of the players. They do not always try to make the players fit their style of play!

Don't limit potential by typecasting players by the first impression! As a coach, do you see the tallest player and assume this player should develop only low post skills? The tallest player in the seventh grade may not be the tallest by the age of seventeen or eighteen! If player development is the primary concern, the coach should try to develop every player into as well rounded a player as possible. Posts or power forwards are more effective if they can play further from the basket. Likewise, a small guard with good post-up skills may be very effective in an offense in which the guard is occasionally in the post position. The program will be much stronger in the long run if the objective is to have every player well-rounded and fundamentally sound in all aspects of the game. How many times in the seventh or eighth grade are the tallest players told they will be a post player? What would have happened if Magic Johnson had been told that he was too tall to be a guard? Would he even have become Magic?

Determining the Starters

If the coach is having trouble deciding which player to start, he should make certain each player is given the chance to play with players of similar talent. Sometimes in the team selection phase, the coach should have a written player rotation schedule for drills, practicing offense and defense, and scrimmages. This ensures that everyone is compared under similar situations. For example, if Player A always plays with three or four of the best players and Player B always plays with lesser skilled players on the team, the coach will not get an accurate evaluation of the their abilities. Remember, you look better in a team game when you play with better players!

> **The coach should have a written player rotation schedule for drills, practicing offense and defense, and scrimmages.**

Individual Evaluation

Players are compared to each other when the team is being selected and when the starters are being decided. From that time, it is critical for player development that on a daily basis players are evaluated and compared only to themselves! By doing so, the coach becomes more attuned to noticing the little things the player needs to work on and more aware of the subtle improvements the player makes. *The coach's acknowledgement of these improvements is one key to player improvement and motivation.*

Player evaluation on a daily basis means the coach has to be organized and spend a little more time reviewing the day's practice or game while it is fresh in his mind. Notes made during the practice or a game by the coach or an aide will make the daily evaluation easier. These ideas allow the coach to slightly modify the next day's drills to the needs of each individual, as well as that of the team. Each day the coach should find something positive on which to compliment each player. The coach should make some suggestions to the player with situations with which he recently has had difficulty. These brief moments of working with each player are an effective form of communication. Players not only want positive encouragement and to know their status on the team; they also want to know the coach cares enough to spend time to help each player improve. *A coach's ability to evaluate players objectively every day is closely associated with the coach's ability to develop players and the team!*

> ❑ Statistics as part of the evaluation process. Statistics can be very inaccurate in high school sports since the people keeping them are seldom well-trained and quite often not paying close attention during the game. These statistics should be considered accurate only after they are compared and corrected using the game film.

Player evaluation on a daily basis means the coach has to be organized and spend a little more time reviewing the day's practice or game while it is fresh in his mind.

Evaluate more than the normal stats. Good players do many things that don't go in the box score, but are necessary if the team is to do well. On defense, a great block will get the attention of the fans. However, fans seldom notice the players who deny desirable offensive position or the ball. The player who denies the offensive player his favorite move and causes him to pass is often overlooked, as is the player who hassles the offensive player so much that he makes a poor pass. These are only a few examples of the little things players do which should be noted. The great coaches notice the little things players do to help the team. Championships are often won by the players on the team who get very little recognition.

A very good high school girls team was about to play two of the most important games in the school's history. This state-ranked class 3-A team was to play the top-ranked team in the 2-A division one day, and the top-ranked class 1-A team the following day. The class 3-A team was relatively unknown and the other two teams had won multiple state championships. The class 3-A team had three players who were to later play in college. The team was very unselfish and Gina was a perfect example of a role player who does the little things that help win championships.

During the two games, Gina, a short post player who couldn't jump very high, quietly went about her business of playing excellent defense and rebounding against taller post players, as well as passing and occasionally scoring a basket. During the fourth quarter of the first game, the lead changed every time down the court. In the last two minutes, Gina caused three turnovers that helped preserve the one-point lead.

The following day's game was every bit as exciting as the lead see-sawed back and forth. Once again during the last two minutes, Gina made the difference. She played great defense with her footwork and was in constant motion. Gina sensed the opposing wing was going to pass to the teams all-state post player. As the wing glanced down to grab the ball, Gina quickly moved to the side of the post and deflected the pass to a teammate. The next time down the court, Gina quickly popped in front of the post player just as the wing had stepped forward to pass. The result was a traveling violation call. The final time down the court, the opposing team decided to attack another area of the zone. Gina anticipated the pass, left the player in the low post area, and intercepted a pass at the free-throw line. The write-up in the newspaper discussed the game and who led the scoring, but nothing was ever mentioned about the great defense Gina had played.

During the next few weeks Gina continued to contribute to the team in many ways. Against the second-ranked team in the district, Gina had 22 rebounds as she had blocked out the opposing players better than any player I had ever seen. The team went on to win the state championship. Everyone talks about the great players on that team, and there were several. However, Gina was the epitome of athletics. She played up to her potential and did the little things that often go unnoticed by the fans, but are so important if the team is to be successful. Her basketball days ended the day the team won the state championship, but the memory of her play will last a lifetime.

Good players do many things that don't go in the box score, but are necessary if the team is to do well.

- ❏ Evaluate each player throughout the course of the season. The coach must evaluate each player on the team during the course of the season. Is the player performing as expected? Is the player developing as expected? If a player has done everything the coach has asked, it is critical to his confidence and development that he be rewarded. Players expect that reward to be an acknowledgement of improvement and the reward of playing time. Effort without reward will result in the loss of desire.

- ❏ Is a player losing confidence and being tentative? Talk to the player and ask if there are any problems. Ask the player what he thinks about his play. Inform the player of your impressions. Help the player work through any problems they may have. The problem could be loss of confidence, of being unsure of what his assignment is (but being afraid to tell the coach), technique problems, personal or family problems, or problems on the team.

If the player is struggling with his shooting, help him on technique and rhythm as well as showing confidence in him. Let the player know that everyone struggles with their shot from time to time—even the professionals. Stress the importance of working extra to correct the problem and stress the other things the player can do well.

Team Evaluation

As a coach evaluates the individual players, he does so within the team concept. For example, poor spacing or timing by just one player will clog up lanes and destroy the effectiveness of an offense. Similarly, one player being slightly out of position or slow to help a teammate will cause the defense to fail. Basketball is truly a team game, and the little things often determine a team's success or failure.

Effort without reward will result in the loss of desire.

A coach must be very objective and analytical during this process. The coach must truly see the entire picture. The coach must be able to evaluate each player's performance while they are on the floor. Obviously, the head coach can watch only one area at a time. The coach will have to depend on the evaluation skills of his assistant coaches as well as the game film to get a true appraisal. Sometimes evaluation shows that the coach's first impression of what was occurring was incorrect. For that reason, the coach should not be too critical of individual players after a game until he has had an opportunity to study the film. Unjustified criticism of a player can be damaging to a players' confidence, as well as the coach's credibility.

As the players are being evaluated, the coach must determine what offenses and defenses the players will be able to execute successfully.

Coaches often have a preferred style of play. The problem in high school is that some classes may not have the skills or athletic ability to be successful in this style of play. A good coach is able to evaluate his players and determine if these players will be able to improve enough during the season to play his preferred style of play. If he does not think they will, he changes his style of play to what fits the talents of his players. This evaluation skill is very important.

- When a team is not playing up to expectations. The coach may be severely challenged to discover the problem. Many times the players and parents know what the problem is, but do not feel comfortable bringing up the subject to the coach! They feel as if doing so would cause problems for an individual player or for the overall team chemistry if the coach were to find out.

Sometimes the problem is the self-confidence of the players, a lack of discipline or inconsistently applied discipline, personal problems of the players, jealousy among the players, or players not understanding the concept that competition is okay among friends as well as those they will meet on the court. Obviously, there are no easy answers to these dilemmas. The coach can prevent many of the problems by having an open line of communication and by paying attention to the little details that sometimes give subtle hints that there may be problems on the team.

Outside Evaluation

An outside evaluation can be a very a great asset if the coach is self-confident enough to ask for assistance from a knowledgeable third party, whether it be another coach, a retired coach, or a friend. An objective third party can open a coach's eyes and mind to other possibilities. This person should evaluate the players, the team's strengths and weaknesses, the style of play, and the way practice is conducted. A coach's pre-judgments may prevent him from seeing the potential that is obvious to others.

The evaluator must be free to make suggestions on anything the person feels might be helpful. The evaluator should analyze the practice schedule and techniques, the players and their utilization, as well as how their strengths and weaknesses fit into the overall scheme. Are there other players on the team who aren't being used to their fullest potential? Coaches are human and sometimes "can't see the forest for the trees." Until the coach has a realistic view of what is happening, he will not be able to improve the team.

A good coach is able to evaluate his players and determine if these players will be able to improve enough during the season to play his preferred style of play.

The outside evaluator should also scout the team during games as he would if he were an opposing coach. He should review the scouting report with the coach to see if trends, habits or weaknesses are obvious. Are the strengths of the team being fully utilized? This scouting report may alert the coach of the necessity to make changes, which should result in a much more successful team. Do you have the strength to seek an outside evaluation?

Volumes of books could be filled with stories demonstrating how important it is for coaches to be able to evaluate the players and the team accurately and objectively. The following two stories are true and emphasize the importance of learning this skill and how it impacts the players and the team.

"Beth first caught my attention while playing summer league ball prior to her sophomore year in high school. Beth, at 5'11", had improved as much in one year as anyone I had ever seen. You could see her confidence grow with every game. She started scoring 20 to 30 points in the last few games of the summer season. She scored in a variety of ways and often with a defender in her face.

Beth had been a third-team post player in the seventh grade, and a second-teamer as an eighth-grader and a freshman. Beth had never started a game, but you could tell she loved to play and that she had a lot of potential. Beth's desire to play and her potential could not have been expected since her family had never emphasized sports. Driven by her inner desire to play, she seemed destined to explode onto the basketball scene.

> **An objective third party can open a coach's eyes and mind to other possibilities.**

During her sophomore year, Beth appeared to be the dominant player on the team, even though she never got to start. She led the team in scoring, blocks, and rebounds per minutes played. If Beth entered the game when the team was playing poorly, she completely changed the complexion of the game and the team suddenly played better.

Toward the end of Beth's sophomore year, I asked the junior varsity coach what she thought of Beth playing on the AAU basketball team that I was to be coaching in a few months. The coach was puzzled as to why Beth was being asked. Beth was the only player on the AAU team who hadn't started on her high school varsity for at least one year. Against teams filled with players who had already signed college scholarship agreements, Beth was one of only two players on our team who could more than hold their own. Beth showed great promise, and I knew she would excel on the varsity the following season.

Amazingly, Beth's junior year found her still on the junior varsity and still not starting, even though she still dominated the games. Beth was growing discouraged. Her parents tried to encourage her, but they didn't know what to say or do. By the start of her senior year, she finally decided to give up basketball. This was one of the sad days in sports as a girl with tremendous potential and love for the game finally gave up her dream. Imagine playing all those years and never being rewarded or encouraged by coaches no matter how much you had improved. A sad day indeed! How many more "Beths" are out there?"

The next true story demonstrates how a potentially great team can be destroyed when the coach fails to evaluate the team and deal with team problems.

"A college team, favored to win the conference crown, returned the starting line-up as well as eight of the top 10 players including two All-American players. The team had everything it takes to win a national championship. The team was not playing well as the season progressed, but the coach appeared to be the only person who couldn't see the problems. The coach got on the players about playing better, but the problems still existed. She never realized what was happening on the floor. Some of her practice methods actually made the problems worse.

Let's look at what was happening. The All-American forward was an impressive athlete. Unfortunately, she had never considered it important to play defense well or to block out consistently. Although very fast and tall, the player was often out of position. She never made a commitment to move her feet and hustle on defense. After three years, an all-conference guard who was four inches shorter was moved to the power forward position and the All-American took the three-guard position."

Why didn't the coach consult with the forward and say, "You can be a great player. However, you have to greatly improve your defense. If it doesn't improve, I will sit you on the bench until you decide you are ready to play defense and block out. I know you can do it! If you have questions or concerns, feel free to talk to me about them, okay?" Initially, the player would have been upset, but she would have come around. The player was emotional with a tendency to pout, but she wanted to eventually be a good player. She needed extra counseling, encouragement, as well as self-discipline. This should have been addressed during her freshman year. The problem was the coach's inexperience in dealing with players. Two years before these players were recruited, the coach had been offered the college coaching position after only two years of junior high experience. By ignoring the problem, the coach hurt the player and the team.

The All-American post transferred in after her sophomore year; it was obvious immediately that she could help the team because she was a very good scorer in the paint. However, the post quickly got the reputation among her teammates as being a "black hole player" who shot every time she got the ball in practice or in the games. If she was double or triple-teamed, she was going to force up the shot even though teammates were free. This team was quite capable of shooting well from anywhere on the floor with almost any combination of players. During the two years prior to the post transferring in, nine of the other players on the team had scored 20 or more points in one game or another.

When the post's selfishness was never corrected in practice, it carried over into the games. Opponents quickly realized that if they sagged down on defense when the post got the ball, she would force up a bad shot. The offensive abilities of the other players were never utilized to their maximum, and the players gradually lost confidence. There was no excuse for the coach not correcting "the black hole" syndrome and demanding a total team concept!

The coach wanted to run the offense through the post as much as possible because of this player's offensive abilities. Did the coach evaluate whether the offense was ever run to completion during practice? The answer is no! It was not unusual for the team to go the entire 45 minutes devoted to offense and never have the offense run to completion. The offense would have to be run to completion when the team played against nationally-ranked opponents that played good defense. The players, who seldom got to shoot in practice, were not as confident with their shots as they had been the previous two seasons.

In teaching and practicing an offense, the coach's first responsibility is to teach the team concept, then to ensure that every aspect of the offense is practiced so that every player is prepared and confident! The offense should be run to completion, including all the options. Often, this means instructing offensive players to not take certain shots and instead run a different part of the offense until all the options have been well-executed.

What other signs of selfishness did this player demonstrate that the coach either didn't see or didn't want to address? The post player wanted to be the hero, and she put that ahead of the good of the team. The team held a slight lead in the last few minutes of several very close games. In the team's press-breaker offense, the post would receive a pass in the backcourt and pass to a guard who was breaking open. The post would look at one or both of the cutting guards but would not pass to either of them, even if one or both were open. Instead, she waited to get fouled or she would try to dribble upcourt which often resulted in a defensive foul or a turnover. The All-American post player was a 65 percent free-throw shooter, while the guards shot 80 percent at the free throw line. The team managed to win most of these games during her junior year, but not during her senior year. The first time this happened the coach should have called a time out and told the player that the next time she failed to pass to the open guards she would be sitting on the bench. The problem could have been solved. Instead it persisted, and selfishness gradually destroyed the team.

An outside evaluator would have been of immense help to this team. It is difficult for anyone to objectively critique his own performance, whether it is a player or a coach. In this particular case, the lack of coaching experience before taking a college head coaching job caused the coach to be unprepared not only for player evaluation and player developmental skills, but also player-management skills.

Summary Points

Player evaluation is a seldom-discussed coaching skill that is critical to player and team development! Communication, motivation, and teaching skills are needed to effectively use the information gathered in the player-evaluation process.

The initial evaluation of a player's ability and talent is in no way an accurate predictor of how good he can or will be. To achieve player development, self-confidence and motivation, the coach must carefully evaluate each player on a regular basis, not comparing players to each other but instead evaluating each player's progress. With the information from these evaluations, the coach should be able to make suggestions for improvement, acknowledge the player's strengths and weaknesses, and notice improvement in skills, effort, hustle and knowledge of the offense or defense. Find something positive to say to every player every day. A player who is trying hard to improve is inspired and encouraged when their effort is acknowledged privately and in front of their peers. Player evaluation is a critical part of player and team development!

It is difficult for anyone to objectively critique his own performance, whether it is a player or a coach.

CHAPTER 7

Player Development

It's primarily the responsibility of the player to have the heart and desire to improve. Heart and desire are not enough; the player must be rewarded with acknowledgement of effort, praise, and opportunity.

Aside from his parents, the coach will have more influence on the player than any other individual. For that reason, it is critical that the coach understands player development. A coach not only teaches basketball to the team, a coach's every action, decision, or discussion will have an influence on someone on the team! The following two true stories can help demonstrate how coaches can affect player development.

"During the annual year-end player-coach conference, the varsity high school coach looks across her desk at the skinny, shy sophomore. The coach tells the girl what she perceives the girl's strengths and deficiencies are, as well as what the girl needs to work on during the summer. She explains what she thinks the player's role on the team will be during her junior year. She asks the girl if she would rather be on the varsity and not play much, or receive substantial playing time on the junior varsity. Without hesitating, the player responds she would rather be on the court. With positive encouragement and good coaching the tall, slow guard with an unorthodox shot slowly evolves into a very dependable player during her junior year. Even with all five varsity starters returning from a playoff team, the girl becomes the team leader as a senior and the team's leading scorer. The coach has done a wonderful job in developing a player reach her potential!"

In contrast, the following scenario illustrates vastly different results: "A first year junior varsity coach quickly earns the reputation as "the coach from hell." During the season, the players lose confidence and their love for the game due to poor coaching and the atrocious interpersonal skills of the coach. The team gets worse as the season progresses. By season's end, the parents are sick of seeing their children crushed—not by opponents, but by their coach. Seeing their children crying after games,

> A coach not only teaches basketball to the team, a coach's every action, decision, or discussion will have an influence on someone on the team!

whether a win or a loss, incenses the parents and creates a confrontational attitude. The coach survived one more season. The tragedy was the lost dreams and emotional trauma endured by the players during this two-year period."

Both examples demonstrate how coaches play such a critical role in the development of players. Opportunity, encouragement, and experience play pivotal roles in the development of a young athlete. Deny any one of the three, and the player may not fully develop! How can lost potential be measured? It is measured only by the heartbreak of a child who was denied one of these crucial elements!

A Player's Development is Determined by Five Factors

- Physical status of the player
- Desire to improve or excel
- Basketball skills and knowledge of the game
- Opportunity
- Self-confidence

Physical Status of the Player

The physical status of a player is something over which the player has very little control. A taller or quicker player, or one who can jump higher, will always have an advantage over other players. Coaches will look to give these players every opportunity to develop and be successful because the coach realizes that a great athlete with terrific basketball skills can be a great player. However, being good at basketball requires much more than natural athletic ability. Less athletic players will often have to wait their turn to prove themselves before the more athletic player has played himself out of the starting position! One of the great things about athletics is there is always a place for an athlete who works to improve his physical abilities, who has a burning desire to play and to improve, and who works extra hard to improve his skills and knowledge of the game.

> ❑ Players develop physically at different ages. Since players develop physically at different rates, it is impossible to know if the tallest player in the seventh grade will still be the tallest three or four years later. Generally, girls develop younger than boys do. As a rule, girls have finished growing by age fifteen. Girls tend to grow early and fast; boys tend to grow slower over a longer period of time. Most boys are through growing by the age of seventeen, but it is not unusual for boys to continue to grow after they

Opportunity, encouragement, and experience play pivotal roles in the development of a young athlete. Deny any one of the three, and the player may not fully develop!

reach adulthood. Many young men have grown several inches while in college, with a few growing as much as seven to nine inches.

A player may improve his strength, jumping ability, and quickness. A player has the responsibility to be in basketball shape by the time practice starts each season! An excellent weight program can be developed to add strength, while increasing explosiveness and jumping ability. A player's natural quickness can only be improved so much. However, the player can learn to play a quicker game. A player can react more quickly if he anticipates where his teammates and opponents are and what they are likely to do in a particular situation. The ability to get the edge by knowing the opponent's tendencies, habits, strengths and weaknesses, allows the player to properly position himself to successfully compete against a better athlete.

Desire to Improve and Excel

The desire to improve and excel is the force that motivates the player to work harder and longer than other players. Players who want to practice only in an organized setting will never be as good as they could be. Players who play near their potential are the players who want to work extra every day improving their techniques, moves or shots, even if no one else is practicing. They enjoy spending their time trying to improve. The coach should explain to the players that if they want to get better they will have to work outside of practice. He often has to teach them how and what to practice.

Self-confidence will not develop without success and praise.

The motivation to work hard and develop to his potential is the self-satisfaction a player feels when there is recognition and praise from the people he respects the most. Self-confidence will not develop without success and praise. The coach plays a pivotal role in this process.

Player's Basketball Skills and Knowledge of the Game

The player should work to become well-rounded and proficient at complementary skills. A player cannot be concerned only with his position; he must learn about all the positions. Once the player learns his team's offenses and defenses as well as why and what they are attempting to do, it will be much easier to learn and anticipate what opponents are trying to do. Court awareness is developed through attentiveness, hard work and experience. If a player does not know what he would do in a situation, how can he ever be able to anticipate what others are likely to do?

Opportunity

A player's athletic ability, heart and desire, and skills and knowledge of the game are worthless unless the player is given an opportunity to play. Every player needs quality practice time and game time!

Self-Confidence

The single most important element in any athletic endeavor is confidence! Without self-confidence, a player may never develop, even if the player is a terrific athlete with good skills. Confidence is very hard to develop and very easy to lose!

Confidence is very hard to develop and very easy to lose!

Each player will have his confidence challenged as he begins to learn the game and as he reaches the next level of competition, whether it is junior high, high school or college. This is especially true for adolescents and teenagers, who are not only learning basketball, but also struggling to develop their own identity during their difficult teenage years.

- ❑ How is confidence developed? Confidence is the knowledge and belief that a person can successfully perform the task attempted. Confidence is accomplished only through working to learn a skill and having subsequent success when attempting the skill or task. The coach must challenge the player to be better than he thinks he can be without putting him in a situation in which the player will fail and lose his confidence. Success breeds confidence; confidence breeds success.

One of the greatest attributes of a successful coach is the ability to develop the players' confidence in their own skills, as well as confidence in their ability to execute the offense and defense. Only a small part of a player's confidence is developed in games. Confidence should be developed every day in practice with realistic game-situation drills and scrimmages. A prepared player will then become confident enough to try and successfully execute a new move, skill, or shot.

Success breeds confidence; confidence breeds success.

- ❑ Confidence levels of young athletes vary. Every person is different. Each will have different personalities, family environments, support systems and past experiences. Each child has different desires as well as varied rates of physical and emotional development. Inexperienced coaches must realize they should not rush judgment on the future potential of an individual player. The players are diamonds in the rough waiting for the coach to discover, polish and show them off to the world.

- All players will have self-doubt. How the player, as well as the coach, handles a situation involving self-doubt will determine the player's future development! The natural tendency is for players to have doubts about their abilities or of their status with the team or the coach. This is true for every player on the team, whether the star or the last player off the bench! As players move up to the next level of competition, they must prove again that they can be successful, thereby revalidating their self-confidence.

Players need to be informed of their status! They need reinforcement that everything is okay and that the coach has confidence in them. Developing a player's confidence and maintaining their confidence level may be as important as the basketball skills the player develops. The coaching techniques and communication skills of the coach are critical in preventing self-doubt and in developing and maintaining player confidence.

- Define expectations to the player. Since self-doubt is natural, especially when a player is learning new skills, the coach should clearly define to the player his role on the team and the expectations of him. Players equate improvement with scoring. Coaches realize that scoring is only one part of a player's game, and that offensive skills will be the slowest to develop. The coach should also explain that every team needs players who play good defense, deny good post position, rebound or pass well. The player should then clearly understand what the coach considers a successful effort.

- Each small success builds a delicate foundation of confidence. Confidence builds slowly over time, but is quickly and easily destroyed. Players need to hear more positives than negatives if they are to develop confidence. What can a coach do daily to help build player confidence and prevent losing that confidence?

Rules for Developing Confidence in Players

The following five guidelines can help coaches enhance the self-confidence levels of their players:

- Find something a person does well and build on it.
- Do not prejudge a player's heart or potential.
- Compare a player only to himself.
- Work as hard to improve the player with the least potential on the team as you do the best player.
- Encourage, not discourage.

Find Something a Player Does Well and Build on It

This basic principle is true in sports, teaching, and parenting. Skills and self-confidence develop one small step at a time. Confidence is developed when a parent or coach finds something a player can do (no matter how small or insignificant it may seem), helps him learn to do it better, and praises him for doing a good job. The fire is then lit! The story of a shy, eight-year-old girl, who was playing on the second team in a coed league, can help clarify this point.

> **Skills and self-confidence develop one small step at a time.**

"The league rules necessitated the best five players be on the first team. The team gaining possession of the ball was to be given the opportunity to cross mid-court. At that time, the opposing defenders usually swarmed whoever had the ball. Since only one boy on the second team had any dribbling ability and since the other players had yet to develop many skills, the boy usually lost the ball.

During a time-out, the girl looked to her dad on the sideline and asked: 'What can I do?' Since the girl had watched her older sisters play, the father asked her if she knew how to set a screen. The next time down the court, the boy dribbled to the right as usual, except this time, he was suddenly free of the defenders, and he went in for a score. The girl's face filled with pride and excitement as she discovered something she could do to help the team. The scene was repeated the next two times down the court. From that time on, the two of them were planning where and how to set screens. Without finding something she could do to help, I am not certain she would have played the next season since she was hesitant to play already. Through the next few years her skills and confidence slowly grew, and she fulfilled a desire that the shy, eight year-old girl would not have dreamed possible—being a starting guard on a good high school varsity playoff team."

Since players may be discouraged by how slowly offensive skills develop, it is important there is something the player can feel is improving rapidly. Non-ball skills can be learned much faster than ball-handling skills. Examples of non-ball skills include:

> **Non-ball skills can be learned much faster than ball-handling skills.**

- Defense.
- Blocking out.
- Rebounding.
- Setting, using and defending screens.
- Moving without the ball.
- Seldom taught skills, such as scouting opponents, anticipation, aggressiveness, and executing fakes.

Success for a coach is dependent upon whether his emphasis is on winning or player development. If the emphasis is on winning, the coach is primarily interested in the result: a score, a rebound or a stolen pass.

A coach whose desire is to improve every player is concerned about the result, but he is also excited that a player finally attempted a new move, made a good pass at the correct time, or finally anticipated and deflected a pass. In other words, the player has finally done what the coach has been trying to get the player to do in the manner the coach wanted the player to do it. Success for this coach involves helping the player improve and the seeing player's heightened self-confidence. The coach knows:

- The first step is to attempt something.
- The second step is to work on technique, timing, and other skills.
- The player will eventually perform the task correctly and become comfortable and confident in his execution.

Success for a player may mean not just scoring points or being the star but having the following occur.

- Finally achieving or doing something that the individual has worked hard to accomplish.
- Being rewarded with the opportunity to play more or having a chance to do well.
- Hearing his coach say, "Good job!"

The coach shows he believes in a player and his actions every day by:

- Treating every player on the team as equals, even though they aren't equally skilled.
- Allowing every player to have quality practice and playing time.
- Not prejudging a player's abilities or typecasting players early in their career in a certain position, thereby limiting their all-around skill development.
- Placing a player in a difficult situation, but one in which the player has a good chance of success.
- Spending a few minutes per day showing the player how to get better and that he believes and has confidence in that player. Examples are:
  - Acknowledging the small improvements by saying something positive every day to each player.

- Challenging and encouraging the player to levels beyond his own expectations.
- Communicating well with the players.
- Teaching players how to "get the edge."
- Recognizing hustle and effort.

Do Not Prejudge a Player's Heart and Potential

Major university programs and professional sports teams hire large staffs of coaches for scouting and studying game films, while spending hundreds of thousands of dollars trying to find the "can't miss" prospect. In spite of all their expertise, time and money, few of the blue chip prospects ever turn out to be great players, while the smaller colleges and the professional leagues are filled with players who were told they weren't good enough as seniors in high school. This inability to predict who will develop holds true for all sports and all ages. So why should a young, inexperienced junior high or high school coach with few, if any, assistants and lots of players think he can predict who will be good in two to five years?

- Can you predict at age twelve or thirteen how tall a person will be? The answer is no! People develop physically at different rates, with some young athletes growing four to six inches after they start college.
- Do you know with any degree of certainty that a player's family will still be living in the school district in three or four years? No, society today is very mobile, and it is not uncommon for families to move every few years.
- Can a coach tell who will still have the desire to play in several years? No, he can't. Too many variables exist to predict future desire with any accuracy.
- Can a coach know which players will have severe injuries or medical problems in the future? Of course he can't.

No one can accurately predict any of these factors. Therefore, it is essential to develop every player on the team to his fullest because you never will know who can and will be able to help the team in the future!

It is essential to develop every player on the team to his fullest because you never will know who can and will be able to help the team in the future!

Compare a Player to Himself

Relatively speaking, each player on the team is at a different maturity level with different physical abilities and skills, as well as being at different physical and developmental stages. If confidence is to be instilled, the coach should not fall into the trap of only comparing players to each other. The coach must compare each player to the progress of that individual.

Obviously, the coach must compare the players to each other in order to decide who the starters should be and the type of offense and defense that best fits the team. However, in order to develop players to their fullest potential, the coach must compare each player to himself. By being acutely aware of each player's status, the coach will tend to notice the little things a player needs to improve. He will also notice the subtle improvements and will be more likely to compliment the player.

If a coach's primary focus is on winning and developing only the best players, it is very easy for a coach to fall into the trap of letting his own preconceived ideas of who will be good influence the way he treats the players on a daily basis. These subtle actions send powerful messages. Remember that we all develop one small step at a time, but it only takes one negative comment or action to potentially destroy several small steps.

Work as Hard to Improve the Player on the Team with the Least Potential as You Do the Best Player

If the coach works as hard to improve the player on the team with the least potential as he does the best player, he sends a powerful message to the rest of the team. It says the coach cares, and he will work hard to help everyone develop if they will give a 100 percent effort. The coach's actions tell the players that basketball is a team game, and everyone is important!

Encourage, Not Discourage

We all need encouragement. When a coach is working hard to teach proper effort and techniques, he is sometimes so busy telling players what they did wrong and what they need to do differently that he forgets to praise the players when they finally do it correctly. This praise is even more important if it is given in front of the team. The coach should also emphasize positive peer pressure. The coach should teach the team he expects them to encourage and praise each other when extra hustle is given or when a teammate finally accomplishes something they had been struggling with. Positive peer pressure is a great motivator as well as a builder of team chemistry.

The Power of Praise

The following story illustrates how a coach restored a team's lost confidence. "Three sophomore starters on the high school varsity were so discouraged that they were about to quit the team. The team was not playing up to it's potential, and had lost several games to weaker opponents.

However, the main problem was that they felt they could never satisfy the new coach, and that everything was negative. They were afraid to make mistakes. Basketball had lost its fun.

The players were encouraged to hang in there a little longer. In the meantime, I visited with the new varsity coach. The coach was never told about the players' visit and their growing discontent. Instead, I asked the coach if she had noticed how my daughter's game had gone downhill the past few weeks. The coach stated she was concerned about it and intended to visit with her to find out if anything was bothering her. After reassuring the coach that everything was fine at home and school and that there were no boyfriend problems, I asked her if I could tell her a little about my child. I informed her that my daughter was an over-achiever who wanted very badly to please. My daughter needed positive encouragement every day, no matter how small. We also discussed that my daughter seemed worried about whether or not she was doing what the coach wanted. From our seats on the opposite side of the court, it was obvious that my daughter was constantly glancing toward the coach instead of focusing intently upon her opponent.

A few days later, my daughter came home and stated, "You won't believe what happened today. We were scrimmaging. The coach stopped play, sent someone in for me, and she asked me to come over by her. I thought to myself 'What did I do this time?' To my surprise the coach said she just wanted to tell me what a good job I had been doing and that she appreciated the hard effort I had given. Dad, I was so shocked that I am sure my jaw fell to the floor. She has never said anything like that to me!

The coach made similar statements to other players in the next couple of days. There were no more discussions of being unhappy or wanting to quit the team. The team suddenly caught fire. They went undefeated the next 14 games before a loss several games into the playoffs. During the next two years, it was especially rewarding to see the coach obviously loosening up and enjoying coaching on the sidelines. For the first time, we could see her smiling and enjoying the kids. The players loved basketball again."

What the coach says can light the fire of desire!

The *"power of praise"* can never be underestimated. What the coach says can light the fire of desire! The player's knowledge that the coach believes in him and the systematic acknowledgement of improvement by coach and teammates are two sure-fire ways to motivate a player. Praise is an important motivational tool. A detailed discussion of motivation follows.

Motivating Players

For maximum improvement, players must not only develop skills and self-confidence, they must be motivated to give the extra effort needed to be good. A coach must be a great motivator.

A player's level of motivation can be the result of many factors, including:

- Self-motivation to be as good as he can be.
- Coaches caring enough to spend time helping the player improve.
- Recognition of effort and/or success by the coach in front of the team, parents or media.
- Acknowledgement of improvement and success by friends, family and teammates.
- Rewarding a player with more quality practice time and game time after he has worked hard to do what was asked or suggested.
- Friendly competition.

A coach sends a powerful message when he:

- Reviews with the player a small detail from the previous scrimmage or game. For example, a player sets an excellent screen to free up a teammate for a key basket. The fact that the coach remembers one small part of the game and cares enough to share it with the player the next day is a powerful motivating tool. It says the coach cares for the player, and is excited about what he does.
- Acknowledges effort and improvement by the individual in front of his teammates. This is important for all players. It is even more critical for those players with low self-esteem, players with little family support, for any player who has to work harder to learn a skill, or for any player who has the coach on his case!
- Teaches the team to be supportive of each other during practice and in games! The coach must teach the team to encourage any teammate who is struggling and to take pride and acknowledge when a teammate finally achieves his goal or accomplishes a difficult task with which he has had trouble. This positive peer encouragement and acknowledgement can be a powerful motivating and unifying force for the team.

> **The fact that the coach remembers one small part of the game and cares enough to share it with the player the next day is a powerful motivating tool.**

Yelling at players

Yelling at players is not a good motivational tool. Basketball is game played with intensity and desire. Coaches are usually intense, and they often ride an emotional roller coaster. A coach can be upset with a player, but he can express it in different ways rather than yelling. Raising one's voice is an effective way to make a point and is usually more effective when used infrequently.

A former player was talking about his highly successful—but sometimes controversial—coach. A fan asked the man what it was like to play for such a demanding person, especially someone who yelled and screamed at the players. The former player responded that the players didn't like the yelling, but they liked the coach because they knew he cared for them and wanted to make them better. The reason they could stand that attitude was the fact that, just as quickly, the coach would have his arm around the kid complimenting him on his hustle or a good play.

Challenging a player

In the past, many coaches have challenged athletes by getting mad, yelling and intimidating the players. In actuality, "challenging players" meant a coach embarrassing a player in front of teammates by questioning the player's inner desire. Some young athletes, most often boys, will get mad and work harder to prove this type of coach wrong (which is usually what the coach expects). Other players don't respond that way, they take it personally and believe the coach doesn't like or care for them. As a result, these players typically don't improve—they regress.

Every individual responds differently to similar situations. The way we are raised affects how we respond to out-of-character situations. In many families, the family members are never "challenged" by intimidation and fear. They are encouraged by a supportive family who sets high standards. A child from this family will have a hard time enjoying playing on a team on which they are "challenged" by the coach.

Does this mean a coach can't be upset? Certainly not. Criticize the action, the effort, but not the player—encourage the player! Does this mean a coach should never yell? Of course not. Does this mean a coach should never challenge a player? No, but the coach should be very selective when he does, and carefully follow the player's development to see if that was the correct thing to do.

Every individual responds differently to similar situations.

- ❑ Challenge players in a constructive manner. Human nature seems to cause people to look for the easy way out. For that reason, coaches must challenge players to reach down and give an effort they did not believe they could. This is true in teaching, parenting and coaching. Among the steps that coaches can take to challenge their players in a constructive manner are the following:

  - ➢ Tell the players what you expect.
  - ➢ Demonstrate to the players what is desirable and what is unacceptable.
  - ➢ Acknowledge improvement and encourage the child to work a little harder to reach the next goal. The coach must let the player know that he believes the player can succeed.
  - ➢ If the player isn't giving the effort, let the player know there are no excuses and either there will be improvement or the player's status will change. Do not humiliate or embarrass the player in front of fans or teammates. Talk privately.
  - ➢ If improvement doesn't result, consult with the player and follow through with a reduction in his playing time.
  - ➢ Criticize the actions, but never the player.
  - ➢ Once the player improves, acknowledge it and reward the player with more playing time.

Demoting a Player in an Attempt to Motivate

Demoting a player is a form of public humiliation with the intent that the player will get mad and work that much harder. In some cases, this will work when other attempts to motivate the player have not. However, it can also backfire. Demoting a player is serious and should be done only if the player has not done what was asked of him or if the player has been beaten out. The player must be informed of the reason for the demotion and what he needs to do if he is to regain his spot. Be honest and sincere.

Demoting a player is serious and should be done only if the player has not done what was asked of him or if the player has been beaten out.

The Balance Between Being Demanding and Encouraging

Does emphasizing positives to players and encouraging the development of every player on the team mean that the coach doesn't challenge players or play to win? No! In fact, the coach should expect to win every game, and the team should give every effort in practice to insure they are prepared to win. A coach should demand effort, execution, and excellence, but the coach must also give encouragement.

The coach must have realistic expectations for individuals and the team based upon their skill levels. The coach and players must set realistic and attainable goals. These goals should be readjusted as they are approached. A coach can be both demanding and caring.

Situations That May Affect Player Development

Many situations arise that may affect a player's confidence and/or development. How a coach handles these situations will greatly impact the success of the individuals and the team. A few examples follow.

Moving a Player Up to the Varsity in Midseason

The coach should communicate clearly to the player why he is being promoted and what the coach truly expects from him. Players moving up to the varsity may be intimidated or may not feel they fit in. (Handling this situation is discussed in Chapter 4.)

Players Who Are Intimidated with a New Situation

Players have different levels of self-confidence. Some players never doubt their abilities, while others do. When players with low self-esteem are in a new environment, they are sometimes intimidated by the other players. As a result, they will be tentative and will not perform as well as they could. These players will not make good first impressions. They need time to prove to themselves that they fit in and that they will do well. Once confidence is developed, these players should do well.

The following scenario is commonly seen on all-star and "select" teams. A player is not playing as well in practice as he did for his original team. He is tentative and not relaxed. If the player understands the offense and defense, the problem may be that he is intimidated by the entire situation. With time, the player rapidly starts improving and playing to his potential. For a player with an established reputation, he will be given time to re-establish his self-confidence. For a player trying to make a team, he may never have the same opportunity.

A coach should demand effort, execution, and excellence, but the coach must also give encouragement.

A Player Who Is Down on Himself

The coach will not have to be hard on this player because the player is already too hard on himself. The coach's job is to encourage and motivate the player. The coach can also help the player work on technique or fundamentals to help him recover his touch and his confidence. During this time, try to avoid putting the player in situations where they will not have a chance for success.

When a Player is Doing Well

Players will respond better to new challenges when their confidence is high! The coach should encourage the player while challenging him to do better or try new moves or techniques. The coach should also match him against better players, increase the level of intensity of defense on him, and look for the little things to make the player even more successful.

Playing Scared

Playing scared will impede player development. In fact, the player may regress the longer he plays scared. The player is afraid to make a mistake if he believes he will immediately be yanked from the game and that he might not get back in. If a player is unsure of his status on the team or unsure of the coach's expectations, the player may also be tentative and play scared.

How does a coach prevent a player from playing scared? Playing scared is the player's problem, but it is made worse by the coach's actions that amplify a player's uncertainty and lack of confidence. The coach should clearly communicate with all the players so there is no uncertainty about their role on the team or the coach's expectations!

Players should be told that the coach understands that mistakes will happen during games, and that usually a player will not be pulled from the game for making a mistake, unless the mistake has been repeated. Players need to understand that mistakes lose games and that lack of hustle is forgivable, but that repeatedly making the same mistake is inexcusable.

The coach should review with the team other things that will cause a player to be pulled immediately from a game, including:

- Disobeying a coach's instruction.
- Not knowing the offense or defense or being out of position.
- Lack of hustle.
- Not attempting to help out a teammate who has been beaten.
- Not moving your feet on defense.
- Not knowing the game situation.
- Silly game-situation mistakes, like forcing a shot at the end of a close game when your team has the lead instead of eating up the clock.

Players need to know that the coach will communicate whether or not their status or role on the team is in jeopardy of changing while time still remains to work on it. Every player on every team, whether the best player or the last player off the bench, will have a time when they are worried about whether they are doing okay! Eliminate the players' self-doubt with good communication.

Playing at the Next Level

Will players be prepared for the position they will have to play at the next level? School coaches are forced to use players at positions that is better for the team, but may not be best for the long-term development of the player. This is true going from junior high to high school, and from high school to college.

For example, junior high coaches often put the tallest two players at post positions. Since players develop at different rates and ages, it is impossible to tell how much the player will develop physically over the next four to five years. Some players who were the tallest players in junior high may turn out to be only average height by the time they are juniors or seniors in high school. Other players grow much later, with some boys growing several inches after high school.

If players don't learn all-around skills early, they may not have the skills to be successful when their growth is finished. If a player only learned post skills while in junior high, and now he is too short to be a post in high school, he will have a difficult time catching up the other guards and wings. What would have happened if Magic Johnson had been told in junior high and high school that he could not be a guard because he was so tall? Would he have developed the ball-handling, passing, and shooting skills that made him a special player? Possibly not.

High school players often have to play different positions in college because the other players are taller, faster, and more skilled. A wing with good ball-handling and shooting skills may have to be a point guard in college, while an average sized high school post may have to be a forward or wing. The coach will probably have to encourage the player that he should work on additional skills in case his role should change in the future. It is the player's responsibility to take charge and work on the skills that will prepare him for the future. The off-season and summer are when great players are made!

If players don't learn all-around skills early, they may not have the skills to be successful when their growth is finished.

Summer Is the Time to Develop New Skills

Summer is the time a player should work hard to improve his current skills and learn new ones. Players should attend quality camps and play on a competitive team, such as BCI or AAU teams. Many summer teams have quality coaches who will help the player hone his skills. The coach should inform each player what he needs to work on during the summer. Specific drills are helpful. The summer is the time to work on becoming an all-around player.

If the player is a post player, he should work on developing his facing-the-basket skills. Posts should work on shooting at least 15 feet from the basket. They should also work on passing, dribbling, faking, and making quick moves to the basket. The post should also learn new low-post moves.

Guards should work on any weak areas of their game. If the player is a spot-up shooter, he should work on driving to the basket and learning to be a scorer. If the player is good at driving, he should work on improving his outside shots. Guards should also learn quick post moves and ways to score when they are under the basket. All players should develop better passing skills.

The Player's Responsibility for His Development

The player must assume the major responsibility for his development. It is the player's life, and he must learn life is what he makes of it. Not every coach will help the player in the ways the player would like. In fact, some coaches may be more of a discouragement than an encouragement. In all situations, but especially these situations, the player must have the heart and desire to be a basketball player. The player must take the challenge to work that much harder to prove the coach wrong. The player must not allow anyone to discourage him from his dream.

To achieve this dream, the player will have to give more of himself than any other player on the team. The player must become a student of the game, learning how to get the edge as well as being a fundamentally sound, well-rounded player. He should ask the coach what needs to be worked on to improve and how to practice this on his own. He should read books and watch instructional videos. But most importantly, the player should open his eyes. He should watch college and professional games on television. Then, he should go out and practice the moves, shots, or techniques on the driveway goal, the park court, or at the local gym.

> **Summer is the time a player should work hard to improve his current skills and learn new ones.**

In today's society, many children only practice during organized league or school practices. They devote very little time to practicing outside of school or during the off-season. After all there are so many other things to occupy one's time, from television, video and video games, to skateboards and cars. Many kids are willing to go outside and work a little on their skills, if accompanied by friends with whom they can play a game. Playing two-on-two or three-on-three is extremely beneficial. However, the players who come close to developing to their full potential are the players who learn to enjoy working on shots, moves, and other techniques when they are by themselves. The coach may have to engrain in his players the truth that no one becomes good at anything without working hard at it! He may have to teach a player how to practice smartly on his own.

Team Development

Players develop their skills and confidence in drills, scrimmages, summer play, and with success in games. If the team isn't prepared, is in the wrong offense or defense for the players, or if other players don't execute properly, neither the team nor the individuals will develop fully.

Coaches should develop multi-dimensional teams. A team should develop into a multi-dimensional unit, even if one aspect of the team is totally dominant. A good team can shut down a one-dimensional team. For example, if a team's inside game dominates every opponent, it is important during the course of the season to improve the team's outside game so their inside-outside ability will be difficult to stop. If players have skills they have not fully utilized in games because they weren't need to win, make certain the player is comfortable and confident with those skills before they are needed in an important game. In practice, emphasize to the player the need to play up to his potential for the good of the team.

When the Team or the Players Are Struggling

When the team or players are struggling, the player's level of confidence will be down. In this scenario, the coach should:

- Build up player confidence.
- Teach players how to "get the edge."
- Make sure the offense and defense is best for the players on the court.

If the team is improving, but still losing, encourage them! Tell the players what they are doing well while working on what they need to improve. When the team is winning and players' confidence is high, challenge the players to work harder and play better than they think they can.

Evaluate the Team Throughout the Year

The coach should evaluate both the team and the players throughout the year. If possible, an outside evaluator should be used. The evaluation should include the following issues:

- Identify the strengths and weaknesses of the team.
- Make sure the offenses and defenses are designed to cover team weaknesses as well as utilize to the maximum the strengths of the players.
- Identify what is or isn't working on offense and defense and why or why not.
- Consider whether the players are doing better than expected. Have you complimented them for their efforts?
- Identify which players are struggling. How can they be helped?

Summary of Tips for Player Development

- ❏ Be encouraging and positive!

- ❏ Pay attention to details. The skill of paying attention to the smallest details is often the difference between an average coach and an excellent coach. Noticing and acting on the little things that other coaches ignore is what allows a coach to develop his players to their fullest potential. It means paying attention to details pertaining to each individual player as well as the team as a whole.

  - The coach should pay attention to the strengths and weaknesses of every player, not just during the team selection phase but every day of the season! What is improving? What needs to be worked on more?
  - When working on basic skills, the coach should emphasize the little things that make the skills more successful.
  - Notice improvement and compliment it.

- ❏ Accurately evaluate each player's skills. Carefully and objectively evaluate each player.

The skill of paying attention to the smallest details is often the difference between an average coach and an excellent coach.

❏ Communicate the following factors to each player:

➢ Your evaluation of the player.
➢ The player's role on the team.
➢ Your realistic goals for the player.
➢ What he needs to work on inside and outside of practice.
➢ Encouragement and confidence in him.

❏ Utilize. Basic skills can be developed most quickly in well-designed drills that emphasize fundamentals and simulate game situations. Teach the players how to practice at home.

❏ Teach the players how to "get the edge." Never assume the players know what you expect them to do. The information a coach has learned is gained one small piece at a time over the years. "Getting the edge" allows the player to come closer to his potential and to compete effectively against more skilled or athletic players.

❏ Assign appropriate match-ups. A player should never be put in a situation where he has little chance of success. The coach can easily control the situations in practice, but sometimes there will be a severe mismatch in games. In this situation, the coach's responsibility is to design the offense and defense so that the team can compensate when these mismatches arise.

The coach should challenge the players but not overmatch them in practices. Everyone improves more when they play against someone who is better. In drills, players may need to be paired so they are competing against someone of similar skills. If a player improves enough so this now becomes a mismatch, the players should be paired differently. As long as players are improving, reward them with new challenges.

How does the team match-up with the other team in actual competition? This evaluation considers the other team's individual players and team concept. The offensive and defensive schemes developed by the coach are designed to cover the team's weaknesses and utilize their strengths. Sometimes, no matter what the coach does, an opposing player may be so tall or athletically gifted that your player will not be able to stop him.

For example, if an opposing post player is much taller, the post may not be able to prevent the player from getting off a high percentage shot or getting a rebound. Your player knows how tall or gifted the other player is. Perhaps the goal of the defense should be to make the post work hard to get the ball in the low-post position, to front him if he gets down low, and to expect back-side help.

How does the substitute match up in games? Does the offensive or defensive scheme need to be changed due to the makeup of the five players on the floor? Often it does. If a guard isn't quick enough, he shouldn't be asked to play full-court man-to-man defense. Quite often, a guard can defend his man in a half-court defense but not in a full-court situation. The object is to prevent the opponent from scoring. The coach should put players in situations in which they are challenged to improve, but also have a chance of success.

Summary Points

The coach should realize his every action and word is likely to influence an impressionable youngster in some way. A coach must also be a teacher and a motivator. The coach is the one person who can easily light the fire of desire or can douse it just as quickly. The player looks to the coach for leadership, not only during practices and games, but also for encouragement, honest advice, and recommendations for what he should do outside of practice. Much of this book is dedicated to teaching what coaches' responsibilities are in player development, especially for new coaches who are just embarking out on the wonderful adventure of coaching.

CHAPTER 8

Noticing the Little Things

It is very easy to praise a player when he makes a great play. The challenge for a coach is to notice the little things that usually go unnoticed, but are so important if the team is to do well. The little things help players develop and realize their potential. A coach notices the little things and commenting to the player about them is a powerful motivating tool. It sends a message to the player that the coach cares enough to pay attention to the small details whether the player is a star or a substitute.

A Great Coach Pays Attention to the Little Things

Great coaches pay attention to the small details while teaching individual or team skills. A great coach not only teaches fundamentals very well, he also emphasizes little things that make these skills even more effective. This book stresses this concept for both players and coaches. The chapter "Getting the Edge" was written especially to emphasize the importance of paying attention to the smallest details, whether:

➢ Small details in individual techniques.
➢ Ways to gain an advantage.
➢ Subtle improvements in skills, effort, and attitude.

Praising the Little Things

When a coach notices and acknowledges a player's effort, attitude, or even slight improvement, the fire is lit for future improvement! Everyone wants praise! For anyone developing new skills, acknowledging of the player's small improvements is essential if the athlete is to ever develop to his full potential.

A coach notices the little things and commenting to the player about them is a powerful motivating tool.

Coaches must learn to look for the small improvements. What is only a small improvement to a coach may be very important to the player. Remember, skills and confidence are developed one small step at a time.

Coaches have to learn to evaluate each player individually, compare the player only to himself, and acknowledge the smallest improvement. A coach who acknowledges an improvement by a player, can send a number of signals to the player, including:

- That the coach cares enough about the player to notice the small improvement.
- That the coach wants him to get better and be successful.
- The player is reassured the coach is happy with his effort.

In the process, these signals help to reinforce the player's desire to improve.

The box score reflects only a small part of the overall play of the team and the individuals. During a game, an aide should make notes on those factors that need to be worked on in the next practice. The aide can also make notes on the little things the coach has noticed that he wants to mention to the players after the game or the next day at practice. While coaches are teaching players how to do things better, they often notice and comment only on the negatives.

In fact, they should also emphasize the positive things that demonstrate effort and improvement. Every practice and every game are full of these opportunities. For example, during a game a player rebounds and makes an excellent outlet pass resulting in a transition basket. It will probably go unnoticed by everyone except the parents. It can mean a lot to the player when the coach later mentions the play. The player will probably be much more responsive when the coach gives the player constructive criticism in the future because he knows the coach cares enough to notice the little things.

Great Coaches Immediately Correct Bad Habits and Reinforce Good Traits in Practice

The individual and team habits developed in practice will be reflected in the team's play during games. Remember, good habits are hard to develop, but bad habits are even harder to break!

If a player has developed a bad habit, the coach must point out what the player needs to do to correct the habit. The coach's responsibility does not end there. The coach must continue to be aware whether the player perpetuates the habit or corrects it. This step can be difficult since one or two coaches cannot watch everything that is happening on the court during drills or scrimmages. Therefore, it is impossible for the coach

The individual and team habits developed in practice will be reflected in the team's play during games.

to pay particular attention to one player throughout the practice. But, assistant coaches or aides can be helpful in reminding the player when he does something incorrectly and praising the player when he does it well.

Suggestions for Correcting Player Mistakes

- Correct mistakes immediately when they occur in practice.
- Be consistent.
- Compliment players when they perform the skill correctly and give a good effort.
- Turnovers are eliminated in practice. When turnovers aren't allowed in practice, they are reduced in games. Pay attention carefully and do not allow walks, double dribbles, lane violations, bad passes, bobbled passes or other preventable mistakes. Teams play like they practice.

Summary Point

It is the little things in basketball, as it is in life, that often provide the unexpected joys or disappointments.

Teams play like they practice.

CHAPTER 9

Teaching New Concepts

Teaching new concepts in basketball is no different than teaching any other subject. The process is the same whether an individual is teaching offense, defense, inbound plays, transition game, or the full-court press. When teaching new concepts, a number of guidelines should apply, including:

- Keep it simple as the basic fundamentals are learned.
- Build on the fundamentals, continually reviewing them until they are second nature to the student.
- Add new concepts. Continue to review and fine tune.

The KISS Principle

The KISS principle—"Keep It Simple Stupid"—is very important in teaching. A skilled teacher is adept at breaking down a complex subject so that it can be taught and learned very simply! The ability to breakdown a basketball offense into its most basic elements so it can be taught gradually, simply, and in detail is a learned skill.

A skilled teacher is adept at breaking down a complex subject so that it can be taught and learned very simply!

Players learn more quickly if everything is simple. They should start out having only a few choices. Once those aspects are learned, other options can be learned. Eventually the players will understand a complex subject, but they learned it one small part at a time.

Videotape as an Aid

Reality is often different from our perceptions when it comes to evaluating ourselves. Videotape will prove whether our perceptions of our basketball skills and effort are accurate. Because you are trying to accomplish a task, it is human nature to think we are doing things correctly even though you aren't. Players need to see themselves as the coach and their opponents see them.

Videotape can be an invaluable tool for coaches. Seeing is believing, even for teenagers. Once a player sees what the coach sees, there is an opportunity for more rapid improvement. Videotape is not used daily as a teaching tool. The coach may use videotape for individual consultations or team demonstrations.

Teaching an Offense

Teaching an offense is probably the most complex subject a coach can teach. He has to incorporate five players using all aspects of their individual offensive skills into a smooth functioning offense in which they instinctively know when and where to go in all situations. Teaching a complex concept such as an offense requires teaching new concepts simply and in a systematic manner.

The Sequence of Teaching an Offense

Any skill, such as teaching an offense, should be taught in stages, building upon what the player has mastered. A detailed description of an appropriate way that an offense can be taught:

- Coaches should always KISS.
- Design fundamental skills drills that are parts of the offense.
- Fundamentals—teach options and keys:
    - Teach ball-side options first.
    - Teach backside players what to do while the other side is exercising their options.
    - Add light defense.
    - Emphasize timing, spacing, and keeping defenders busy so they can't help.
    - Emphasize quick decisions, quick passes, and court awareness before a player catches the pass.
- Review, review, review until everyone can perform the necessary steps naturally.
- Add a variation. Review as previously detailed.
- Review the original and the variations.
  Apply moderate defensive pressure.
- Mix up running the two variations and all their options.
  Work on techniques during this entire process.
  Intensify the defense to game intensity.
- Make certain all options of the offense are run to completion so everyone has had equal opportunities to work on their skills. The players' confidence will be needed against good teams who may

Reality is often different from our perceptions when it comes to evaluating ourselves.

shut down the first part of the offense.
- Do not go any further until everyone executes the offense well. Keep in mind that it is more important to do one thing well than several things poorly. It may take one day or five days, but do not go further until everyone is comfortable with what is being taught. If you add new concepts before the team has totally learned the current ones, confusion will result.
- Continue to practice and review what you have already learned as you add other variations or other offenses. what you have already learned. Mix it up. Add new variations early in the practice while the players' minds are fresh. Then, review the old offenses and alternate running the different offenses and their options. If the options can be run from different sides of the floor, do that routinely.
- Establish game realism by:
  - Intensifying defensive pressure while running the offense.
  - Having the point guard bring the ball upcourt under intense pressure before initiating the offense.
  - Mixing up ways to initiate the offense.

Mix it up.

Players need to learn to mix the offense up so they are not predictable. The team also needs to be used to switching offenses and defenses on command. Teams that practice switching offenses and defenses as they might be required to do in a game will have little difficulty executing them during a game. Don't expect the players to switch offenses and defenses in games if you haven't tried it in practice.

Don't expect the players to switch offenses and defenses in games if you haven't tried it in practice.

Creating Proper Spacing and Lanes

As the coach starts to teach an offense, he will realize the offense must be designed and run so that proper spacing and lanes are created at the correct time. The coach must understand how the opposing defenses are likely to defend this offense. Only then can the coach know how to structure the offense so it will dictate to the defense where their defenders will be. Lanes can then be created for cutters and drives.

Remember, if the offensive players are standing, their defenders are sagging. The coach must be concerned with spacing and movement of all the players, including the players on the backside. Are their defenders kept busy so they can not sag off and help clog the lane? Every player should have something to do at all times. Movement of the posts, as well as setting screens to free up teammates, is necessary to create openings and lanes by vacating areas.

Teaching Defense

Teaching defense will be much easier than teaching offense. However, great defense requires an intensive effort. Players must learn to work harder than they thought was possible. Players seldom realize the amount of effort needed to play terrific defense.

How a coach goes about teaching defense is very important. A defense's primary goal is to prevent the other team from scoring. Young players need to learn how to play great individual defense, as well as terrific team defense. Some coaches stress full-court, man-to-man defense, deny defense, and/or pressing defenses. These are all great defenses, but the team must first learn how to play good, basic help-defense in its transition defense and in its half-court defense.

If you watch some high school teams that apply great defensive pressure, occasionally they are so involved guarding their men that they watch a ballhandler go right past them. Sometimes in a transition defense, a player is sometimes so concerned about finding his man that he forgets to defend the ballhandler who is right behind him. Or a player forced to pick up his dribble is allowed an open shot when the defender leaves him to find his man. In the heat of the game, these players have forgotten that they must help their teammate if he is beaten. These players were so concerned with their individual responsibilities that they forgot the team concept.

The Three Most Important Factors in Defense (in Priority Order)

- *The ball.* The defense must stop the ball from being taken to the basket by any player. Do not allow any player to be uncontested if they are in the lane or near the basket.
- *The defender's position relative to the ball, the basket, and his man.* The defender should be in good defensive help position and have good vision of the floor so he can anticipate and play good help defense.
- *The defender's man.* The defender can properly defend his man with good position and technique.

Why Emphasize the Ball First?

- If the team emphasis is on the ball, the team will have maximum help, thereby allowing less athletic players to compete effectively against more athletic opponents because they know they will always have help.

The team must first learn how to play good, basic help-defense in its transition defense and in its half-court defense.

- If defenders are overly concerned in denying their man the ball even when they are not in the scoring area, they will not be able to give adequate help defense. A denial defense requires terrific athletes. The truth is that even these teams with great athletes still must be comfortable playing help defense.
- Most offenses are built around two- and three-man games. A help defense allows the defense to have a five-on-two or a five-on-three situation at all times.

Defense Is Learned in Three Scenarios:

- Drills allow the defense to work on and quickly improve fundamental skills and techniques. At the beginning of the season, the basic fundamentals of defense should be taught, including:
  - Individual techniques.
  - Team concepts of defense.
- As the offense is being taught to the five players on the court, their defensive counterparts should be working on their defensive skills and techniques. During this time, the players are learning to work as a coordinated unit and developing confidence in knowing their defensive teammates will be in the correct position.
- Scrimmaging allows the players to become used to more game-realistic situations. The players will learn to mentally adjust to changing offensive scenarios quickly.

Teaching Guidelines

The concepts of the help defense and the rotation of players to cover for each other can never be emphasized too much.

Drills should be designed to emphasize the important concepts of the defense being taught. Skills are learned much more quickly when they are taught in supervised drills that immediately correct mistakes and praise good efforts. Individual defensive positions and techniques are taught. Players are taught the correct positions for on-the-ball and off-the-ball defense. Players also need to know their responsibilities and positioning when they are one or two passes away from the ball. If the players are in the correct positions, they will be in position to play individual- and help-defense. Players will also be less likely to foul if they are in the correct position.

Players need to be taught to visualize the play developing so they can anticipate properly instead of reacting too late. Sagging off or stepping out on screens to help must also be emphasized. The concepts of the help defense and the rotation of players to cover for each other can never be emphasized too much.

Once the team has the "ball-first" emphasis totally engrained in them, it becomes second nature. Then, the coach can begin to emphasize situations in which there is less help, such as in full-court man-to-man defenses and presses.

Designing a Defense

Before a coach can teach defense, he must decide upon what basic defense he will employ for a particular team. At the beginning of the season, the coach must decide what his basic defensive philosophy will be. He must design and modify a defense that will allow his players to compete effectively. The skill levels, athletic ability, quickness and height of his players will determine how his team will match up against future opponents. In high school, the athletic skill level of teams can vary greatly from year to year.

Selecting a Defense

What is the objective of the coach's defensive plan? Is it to prevent a score or to steal the ball? When intensive defensive pressure is applied, will it be applied full-court, half-court, or inside the three-point line?

Attacking defenses such as pressing and trapping defenses, require quick, athletic players. If one defender is out of position, an aggressive offense will attack it, resulting in an easy shot. The coach must consider if the team will get enough points off turnovers to make up for the points they give up. This aggressive style of defense is also very tiring and requires a good bench.

Half-court defenses initially fall back to inside the three-point line before they play defense, while attacking defenses revert back to their half-court defense after their press has been beaten.

The team has to be able to defend inside and outside the three-point line. The goal is to prevent a score. Therefore, the defense adjusts to deny the most likely scorers or deny high percentage shots. As the coach develops his individual game plan, he will decide whether the defense should emphasize shutting down the inside game or whether to apply more pressure to the wings. Most high school teams do not have five great scorers, so the defense usually concentrates on applying intensive pressure on two or three players with additional help given by the defenders sagging off of the other players.

Once a defense is decided upon, the coach must study and work to understand the basic concepts, as well as the intricacies, of the defense.

Once a defense is decided upon, the coach must study and work to understand the basic concepts, as well as the intricacies, of the defense.

He must also learn how opposing offenses will attack the defense. What are the defense's weaknesses? How can the defense adjust to cover these weaknesses, if needed? Once the coach understands these factors, he must figure out how to simply and effectively teach these concepts to his players. As a rule, the greatest coaches have mastered the ability to teach complex ideas very simply! This may be one of a coach's greatest challenges.

Summary Points

The coach must be flexible in game planning so that he puts his team in the appropriate defense for the situation at that moment. He should keep things simple as the fundamentals that are being learned. The coach should build on the fundamentals until they are second nature to his players.

CHAPTER 10

Utilizing Auxiliaries

It is amazing how a solitary coach in the junior high, ninth grade, or junior varsity level successfully works with large numbers of kids without assistants. To be successful, the coach must learn how to effectively organize practices so that little time is wasted and every player works vigorously on fundamentals every day.

In reality, a single coach can never teach everything that needs to be taught or reinforced in a practice. Paying attention to the little details is a sign of good coaching. During practice it is impossible for the coach to carefully watch all of the players simultaneously to see if they are performing their tasks as desired. Since assistant coaches are not available at the sub-varsity level, a coach must develop his assistants. Each assistant is assigned the responsibility of critically watching small groups of players to ensure the players consistently execute the offense and defense correctly. Skills and techniques are developed much more quickly if good techniques are immediately and positively reinforced and if bad techniques are corrected as they occur before they become bad habits.

Training the Managers as Assistants

One excellent possible source of assistants for a coach is managers. As such, adequate training should be given to the managers before the first day of practice. It is important that they understand they will walk a fine line between being a manager, a classmate, and a coach's helper. Their attitude should always be genuinely constructive and encouraging, not bossy. Managers should not to be derogatory or negative towards the players, since corrective actions are primarily the responsibility of the coach.

The coach should demonstrate confidence in his managers in front of the players. On the first day of practice, the coach should explain his expectations of the players and the managers. The managers should be told in front of the players that their assistance is needed if all the play-

Skills and techniques are developed much more quickly if good techniques are immediately and positively reinforced and if bad techniques are corrected as they occur before they become bad habits.

ers are going to be helped as much as possible and if this team is going to learn everything needed to be a good team. The players should be asked if they want to be an average team or if they want to improve as much as possible. When they say they want to be good, the coach should state, "We need these managers and we need you to listen to them as you would me, okay? Does anyone have a problem with that?"

The coach then reviews what the manager's jobs will be and how they are to be done with the team and the managers. The managers are instructed, in front of the players, that they will be taught what they need to know and how it needs to be done. The assistant doesn't need to know a lot about basketball. The coach will demonstrate to the manager and the players what the player should do. The coach will tell the manager and the players what the manager should look for to assure it is done correctly.

At this time, the coach should select two players to do a drill and demonstrate to the managers and the players what to watch for and how to correct techniques. Allow the manager to supervise a drill and make positive encouragement if the task is done correctly or to make positive reminders if the task is done incorrectly. The manager is told in front of the players to correct the players if they do not do the drill properly and to compliment the players when they do it right. By introducing the concept in this manner, the team should readily accept the managers as an integral part of the team. The players must see the manager as their helper, as well as the coach's helper.

The Coach Can Move Around the Court Supervising Practice

The players must see the manager as their helper, as well as the coach's helper.

The coach is now free to go from station to station during drills and observe players and make individual suggestions to each player, as appropriate. At that point, the coach can go to the next station knowing that good techniques are consistently and immediately being positively reinforced. The same is true when team offense or defense is being taught or even during scrimmages. When the coach turns his attention to a position, he should ask the manager how things are going and if there are any problems or questions. Further observation by the coach may result in new suggestions or encouragement to keep working on the same things. If the coach handles the situation correctly, both the players and the manager will feel comfortable working together as they learn.

Teaching in the traditional manner, a coach spends most of his time focusing on the person with the ball and his defender. The coach finds it impossible to know exactly what the other players are doing at that moment. If an offense is to be run effectively, every position must be given equal attention to detail! Players away from the ball must learn what they should do when the offense has the ball on the other side of the court. Keeping the backside defender busy, letting the play develop, and maintaining proper spacing and timing are hard concepts for players to learn, yet they are essential if the offense is to be successful.

The managers should be honest and state if there are problems of any kind when the coach comes back and asks how everything is going. Among the feedback a manager can provide to a coach is the following:

- If the player is doing a good job, the manager should report out loud what a great job the player is doing.
- If the player is still having trouble executing a skill or is still reverting back to bad habits, the manager should say, "They are still having some problems."
- If a player isn't listening to the manager or has a problem with a student being a manager, the manager should ask if someone else could help. This is a signal to the coach that the manager is not getting the respect of the player. The coach then states, "The manager will stay here, and you will learn how to do the assigned task correctly. Now let's see what the problem is." Have the player and the manager demonstrate what they were working on exactly as they did it the time before.

Several managers may be working under the coach's guidance simultaneously during the practice. Among the duties managers can be assigned are the following:

- One manager can be in charge of the daily practice schedule and ensuring the players stay on schedule by informing the coach when it is time to go to the next thing on the schedule. This manager should be responsible for managing the coach's written player rotation schedule during games. This schedule will ensure that all players get quality game time. The manager should remind the coach when his substitution schedule calls for a substitution in practice or in games.
- During individual and small group drills, managers can be assigned to each basket to observe and correct techniques if needed. Managers will be asked to work with the players on any basketball skill. The coach will use the managers to reinforce what the coach has told the player. The purpose is to have every person develop good technique and skills, while not developing bad habits. This can only be done by consistent and frequent reinforcement.

The managers should be honest and state if there are problems of any kind when the coach comes back and asks how everything is going.

- During scrimmages or team drills, managers may be positioned on both sides of the court and under the basket so they can be in position to watch the ballside and the offside of the court. They should reinforce what the coach wants to emphasize, such as offside defensive help, anticipation, proper timing of screens and cuts, spacing, and keeping the defender busy.
- A manager can be assigned to make notes for the coach during games and practices. The manager sits beside the coach during a game to take notes of things the coach wants to remember or emphasize during a time-out, at halftime, or the next day at practice. This step makes it easier for the coach to pay attention to the little details that are so important in coaching, while not taking his focus off the game. These reminders could be anything from team concepts, ideas for offense or defense, and things to work on with individuals during the drills. At the appropriate time after the game, the notes should be given to the coach.
- Managers can also be assigned any routine tasks that they might normally perform, such as making certain that everything is ready and in its place before and after each practice and game. Once this system of using managers has been in place for several years, the coach will become spoiled. Managers will feel important and will want to be part of the team. As a result, the team should have experienced managers who can set positive examples the younger ones can follow.

Managers Are an Extension of the Coach

During the first few weeks, the coach should meet privately with the managers every day for a few minutes after the practice to get their input as to how things are going and to counsel them how to handle certain situations that have occurred. Phraseology and a positive experience are very important early during the time the players and managers are learning to work together.

Managers can be wonderful assets to the team if the team understands their importance.

Managers can be wonderful assets to the team if the team understands their importance. Early during the season, the coach will need to keep a close eye on the managers and the players to be certain that no one oversteps their boundaries. Any player or manager found to be acting inappropriately should be reprimanded or the integrity of the relationship will be jeopardized. The first time someone is reprimanded, the team will learn the lesson.

The managers who return the next year will be even more helpful. This technique can be a wonderfully efficient and effective way to teach and reinforce the techniques that are important to a team's success.

Some coaches may find it hard to trust managers with all these responsibilities. One plausible suggestion is to try them first with a few small tasks and see how it works. If it works well, continue with additional responsibilities.

CHAPTER 11

Preparation is the key to winning. A poorly prepared team has little chance of winning. Effective practices allow the coach to teach fundamentals, the basic offensive and defensive schemes and their variations, and to develop the confidence of the players and the team. Two important rules to remember when coaching players are:

> ➢ If something is important to the coach, practice it.
> ➢ Never assume players know what you want or expect.

An effective formula for good practices involves the following steps:

> ➢ Plan.
> ➢ Be organized.
> ➢ Work hard; have fun and laugh.
> ➢ Define your expectations to the players. Expect their best effort.
> ➢ Pay attention to detail.
> ➢ Offer more positives than negatives. Find something positive and build on it.
> ➢ Praise the little things.

Preparation is the key to winning.

Planning Practices

A coach must plan practices properly for the daily and long-term needs of the team to ensure that the team has developed the individual and team skills needed to be successful. There is so much to teach and so little time! Great coaches realize the importance of utilizing every minute of practice. Planning, organization, and efficiency are skills not often taught in college courses.

The Season Plan

It is important to have a general plan for developing the team. The season should be broken down into the following smaller segments:

- Preseason
- Non-league play
- League play
- Playoffs

There is so much to learn that the players would be overwhelmed if the coach tried to teach everything early in the season. As a result, the coach should teach the team in stages. It is more important to learn to do a few things well than do a lot of things poorly.

As the team develops the basics, the coach should have a plan of what he wants accomplished by the end of each portion of the season. A coach who tries to keep the plan in his head will find himself unprepared and disorganized. The plan should be written out and filed. Does every week have to be planned out before the year starts? No, but the objectives and the target dates must be written out before the season. Plans always have to be adjusted. Since unexpected problems often arise, allowances should be made for the team to be a day or so behind by the end of the preseason. Notes should be made as to the team's progress and problems, as well as suggestions for the future. This information will be very helpful when developing future plans in coming years.

Preseason

As practices begin, the coach should have an idea of the strengths and weaknesses of his players. The coach can plan what style of play best fits a particular team. With that in mind, as well as a knowledge of the style of play and strengths of the future opponents, the coach should have an idea of what his team will need to accomplish. The following itemized list illustrates an example of a preseason plan:

By the end of the preseason, the high school team should be comfortable and efficient with the following team concepts:

- Man-to-man defense.
- One zone defense.
- A basic man-to-man offense.
- A zone offense and the principles of attacking a zone.
- Two out-of-bounds plays under the offensive basket.
- Two sideline out-of-bounds plays.

It is more important to learn to do a few things well than do a lot of things poorly.

- A press breaker against full court man-to-man trap defense and a half-court trapping defense.
- Transition offense and defense.
- Set plays for best guard, wing, and post to get off an important shot.
- Three-point plays.

Non-League Play

By the end of non-league play, the team should be proficient with basic team skills and have added the following:

- The team must be comfortable switching quickly between different defenses or offenses. This mental mindset must be learned in game-situation practices, not in games!

- Additional man-to-man and zone offenses can be learned while continuing to perfect the basic offenses.

- The defense should be tightened up during this time. The defense should learn how to adjust to counteract the strengths of an opponent. A team may want to play strong deny-defense all over the court against one opponent, while it may want to deny the low post and/or the best outside shooters in a half-court defense against another team.

- A team should have a second zone defense or know how to adapt its basic zone to deny the other teams' strengths, whether inside or outside.

- A stall or four-corner offense should be learned for use at the end of the games.

- Additional out-of-bounds plays and special game situations should be reviewed regularly.

League Play

By the end of league play, the team should have learned all the basics necessary to have a successful playoff season. The team should have fine-tuned the offense and defense, and the players should be confident and hungry. Practices should be enthusiastic. Errors or sloppiness should not be allowed.

All the planning involving offenses and defenses is worthless if the players are not fundamentally sound. The team must continue to work on fundamental individual skills at every practice. The skill level and confidence level of the players and of the team should increase as the season develops.

Never get so busy teaching team skills that the individual skills are ignored! Sometimes practices get so busy that the players don't spend enough time reinforcing their shooting skills. If so, players may need additional quality shooting time outside of practice. (Refer to the section on practice shooting sessions.)

Weekly Planning

Once an overall plan has been developed, one that details what should be taught and the deadlines for doing so, the coach must decide how many weeks (and daily practices) are available to accomplish the task. After a weekly schedule has been developed, the coach can devise a daily planning schedule.

Evaluation of the Weekly Progress

At the end of each week, the coach should review the master plan and compare to see if all the planned tasks were accomplished. If further work needs to be done in certain areas, the practice plan for the next week should be adjusted.

Daily Planning

Daily planning should be undertaken to ensure that each player develops his individual skills as much as possible and that the team learns all the concepts needed to be fully prepared. Daily plans should be written out with the understanding that each day's plan can be modified as needed prior to practice. The coach should plan the amount of time for each drill. The players should have just enough time to get ready to do the next drill. Time should be allowed for short explanations or discussions by the coach. Players should not have idle practice time.

The team must continue to work on fundamental individual skills at every practice.

Practice Analysis

After each practice, the coach should take a few minutes of quiet time to review the day's practice. The notes that managers have made for the coach should be reviewed. (Managers' notes from a game should be considered before the next practice.) This attention to detail allows the coach to immediately customize the next practice to the specific needs of the team and the individuals.

The time allowed for the players to work on individual fundamentals should never be sacrificed for catching up on team concepts. However, individual and small group drills can and should be designed to simulate parts of the offense and defense being used so the players are working on team concepts as they work on fundamental skills.

Be Organized

Once a coach has a plan developed, he must organize his practice so that everything gets accomplished. If the coach does not have a written daily and weekly plan, he will waste a lot of precious practice time. As the coach works up the daily plan, he decides how much time is allocated for each drill or scrimmage.

A written schedule for the practice, along with the times to start and stop each drill, should be copied. A written schedule can be posted for the players to review when they come into the gym. The other copies should be given to managers. One manager should be assigned the responsibility of keeping track of the time and reminding the coach when it is time to go to the next phase of practice.

Players must be kept busy at all times during practice. If they finish a drill early, the players should work on other skills. There should be no stand-around time.

Practice Suggestions

Day after day of practice can get boring. As a result, the coach needs to structure his practices to be efficient, effective, and fun. All players would rather play than practice. Individual attention and praise are very important to every player. Drill time is an excellent opportunity for the coach to enhance the player-coach relationship by teaching and encouraging! Among the steps that a coach can take to conduct an effective practice are the following:

- Plan and schedule every minute of the practice the day before and stick to it.
- Emphasize defense the first day of practice!
- Keep kids busy. If players finish a drill early, they should know to work on their weaknesses.
- Keep it simple and short—no long lectures or verbal demonstrations.
- Teach every player how to play from every spot on the floor. (Don't typecast players into limited roles.)

109

- Emphasi... ...tion to sm... the playe... ful when...
- Teach ne... ers' min...
- Vary the...
- Use sho... e drill too long or...
- Follow ... drills.
- Stress f...
- Develo...
- Stress ... working on them e...
- End ea...

Basic compon...

- Stretc... tart of practice.
- Warm...
- Indivi...
- Defe...
- Scrim...
- Spe...
- Free...

The first few...

The first pra... ...aching players the drills. S... ...ing basketball skills, it is c... ...ects. A significant part o... ...nt on these or similar drill...

Cor... Habits

Practice d... ...fect! Correcting bad habit... ...requires paying attention ... ...reak bad habits and deve... ...ne he falls back into a ba... ...y. If a player is reminde... ...me and is then

It is easier to break bad habits and develop good habits if a person is reminded each time he falls back into a bad habit and praised when he does it correctly.

allowed to do it incorrectly a number of subsequent times, the bad habit will be very hard to break.

One of the primary problems for a head coach is that he can only watch two or three players critically at one time. A coach cannot spend the entire practice watching these players. He needs help. Unfortunately, many of the high school varsities have only one assistant coach, if that. Even worse is the fact that the junior varsity and junior high school coaches, by whom fundamentals are first taught, often have no assistant coaches. How can these coaches pay enough attention to everyone? It is amazing they do as good a job as they do. These coaches need help reinforcing what each player needs to be doing. In this regard, managers can be of tremendous help to a coach.

Matching Players in Drills and Scrimmages

The starters will have to practice together enough so they become a cohesive unit. The challenge is how the coach mixes and matches the remainder of the team so the players are all given an equal opportunity to learn and improve.

Defense is where the lesser-skilled player can quickly improve enough to compete with the better player. For that reason, defense should be emphasized in practice for several days before offense is ever worked on. Since a large degree of defensive success is determined by heart, desire, and hustle, along with good technique and scouting, it is important for the coach to explain to the players that their most rapid improvement will come in defense if they work hard and smart. Let the lesser-skilled players know you expect them to compete effectively against the best players by playing good, smart, hustling defense.

As his skills improve, the lesser-skilled athlete needs the opportunity to periodically test himself against the better players, both in drills and scrimmages. The coach should be alert to notice the improvement in each player and communicate it to the player with a challenge to continue to improve. As a coach matches up players for drills and scrimmages, he should remember that players should be matched with players of similar ability.

- Try to avoid pairing players against each other if there is a large discrepancy in talent levels. If players are grossly mismatched, the lesser-skilled players will become intimidated and discouraged while the better players are not challenged to improve.
- However, the lesser-skilled players must have quality practice time against better players if they are to improve rapidly.

Remember everyone looks better when they play with better players.

Lesser-skilled players need to know what the coach expects of them when they are matched against the best players. This is a situation where communication is very important. The player needs to know that he is expected to play good defense, block out his man, rebound, and pass to an open teammate if a good shot isn't available. If the shot is there, he should take it. If the player is concerned about his scoring ability, encourage him and tell him that it will come with time and hard work.

One-on-One Situations

In one-on-one situations, both players must learn and develop confidence. This is true in drills, scrimmages, and games. In drills and scrimmages, the coach must make an effort to correct mistakes and teach technique while encouraging and challenging players. This should always be done in a manner positive to both athletes. Most coaches do a good job, but a few inadvertently develop the confidence of one player at the expense of another. This is an unforgivable sin of coaching. An example can help clarify this point:.

"On one team, a freshman substitute told his parent that in his practices, the coach praised the starters and seldom said anything positive to the others. The player stated that if a starter beat the substitute then the starter was praised and the other player was ignored. No suggestions or any type of criticism were given to the substitute. If the sub beat the starter in a one-on-one situation, the starter was chewed out for being lazy or using poor defensive technique and the substitute was never given any praise or recognition. The parent told the child that he was just upset with the coach, and that he was blowing things out of proportion. A few days later, the parent learned that another player had told his parents the same story, and stated that practice had been like that all season long. Not surprisingly, the team got worse as the season unfolded. By year's end, half the players on the team had lost their desire to play. There is no excuse for this type of teaching in athletics—or in the classroom!"

Players often are in the habit of practicing at a slower pace than the speed at which the game is actually played.

Teach Quickness During Practice

Basketball is a game of quickness. Players often are in the habit of practicing at a slower pace than the speed at which the game is actually played. When faced with a much faster pace in the game, these players are not comfortable. Keep in mind that players who rush shots seldom make them. The problem is many players could play quicker if they had worked on improving quickness in practice. When a player is working on techniques in drills, it is important to execute the move or shot at a slower speed until the player is proficient at the skill. As the player starts to develop confidence, he should practice at game-situation speed.

The coach should emphasize the importance of quickness in drills while working on team offense and defense, and in scrimmages by emphasizing quickness in all aspects of the game, including:

- Quick cuts, stops, and fakes.
- Quick change of direction, quick outlet pass, quick passes and ball reversal against a zone.
- Quick jumping, quick shots with a quick release.

A coach can improve his athletes' reaction time by teaching players to anticipate, to be prepared to react quickly, and to execute more quickly. To play quicker, the player needs to have court awareness before he ever touches the ball.

Teaching quickness is like teaching other concepts. The team must be reminded of its importance each day, not only by telling them what you expect, but by reminding them when they don't do it and praising them when they finally get it right. Coaches need to insist on quicker execution, since the players will seldom see the need. Players can often do things more quickly than they are in the habit of doing. Breaking habits requires repetition. If it isn't important enough to remind the players frequently, they forget that it is important.

Make Scrimmages Game-Realistic

Players need to be accustomed to quickly switching offenses or defenses in practice so they can comfortably make a smooth transition in games without costing the team several points. This transition is often more mental than physical! Teams that are not prepared to quickly shift styles of play often allow the other team to score several baskets before adjustments are made.

An offense or defense is usually taught by continually reviewing the same points until the players have learned what to do in a particular situation. That does not mean they are comfortable quickly switching to another style of play. Players may seem to understand what to do when they have been doing the same thing over and over in practice for 15 or 20 minutes, but switching will allow the coach to see how prepared his team really is.

The coach should prepare the team for quick adjustments. Once the players seem to have a good grasp of the offense and defense, the coach should start varying the offense and defense used during scrimmages. Scrimmaging in this manner will assist the players in feeling comfortable, prepared, and confident when the opponent switches strategies during a game.

<u>Free-Throw Shooting</u>

Free-throw shooting is a lot different in a game situation, when the player's legs are tiring and the game is on the line, than it is shooting 20 free throws in practice. The coach should simulate game-situation free throws in practice so the players are comfortable in these situations.

Variety in Practices

Practice can get boring after a couple of weeks, and players' attention spans decrease when they are bored. Make hard work more fun by adding some variety to practice each day. Players get tired of practicing the same drills and going against the same players day after day.

Practicing Special Game Situations

Teams that perform well under pressure often do so because they have practiced special situations. Placing players in unfamiliar situations while under extreme pressure will often result in failure.

The coach should attempt to prepare the team for any situation that is likely to occur. Special game situations should be practiced briefly several times a week. The coach should select the players that are most likely to be on the court at these times. However, never forget to give the other players the opportunity to develop these skills since injuries and fouls sometimes remove the best players from the coach's game plan. The following circumstances illustrate examples of special game situations:

> ➢ Shooting at the end of a quarter or half. Players need to learn to be aware of the clock and comfortable getting the desired shot off. Selected plays at the end of a quarter are for one of the following situations:
> • Little time is left and the team is at the other end of the court.
> • Adequate time is left, but the team wants to take the last shot.
> • Defending these situations.

Teams that perform well under pressure often do so because they have practiced special situations.

- Executing out-of-bounds plays from different locations for the last shot.

- Stalling. Teams must practice spreading the floor, passing quickly, and moving to open areas to eat up the clock and/or get a layup. Quick, precise movement and passing will eat up the clock and prevent turnovers and traps. The goal should be to move the ball so well that the other team cannot get close enough to foul.

- Defending the stall. Defending the stall is contrary to the normal defensive instincts that are engrained in the players. For that reason, this defense must be practiced periodically. While it may be needed only a few times per year, it can be the difference in winning a close game.

    When protecting the lane and the basket, the basic instinct is to immediately step back and play help-defense when your man passes the ball. Against the stall, this is the worst thing to do since it leaves your man open for an easy pass. When defending the stall, each man must play an aggressive, excellent denial defense. Make the dribbler pick up his dribble, pressure the ballhandler, and deny all passes.

- Fouling in the stall. Foul the right man. Deny the good free throw shooter the ball, and foul the bad shooter.

Unusual Practice Segments

The following drills or scrimmages are examples of unusual practice segments that are reserved for times when the coach feels he needs to correct bad habits:

A no-dribble scrimmage is useful when a team knows the offense, but the players and the offense are sluggish.

- The no-dribble scrimmage. A no-dribble scrimmage is useful when a team knows the offense, but the players and the offense are sluggish. Dribbles are not allowed no matter what defense is employed, even a full-court press. If a player dribbles, it is a turnover. After using this scrimmage, the crispness of play is usually better. The no-dribble scrimmage emphasizes:

    • Moving without the ball.
    • Meeting the ball.
    • Teamwork.
    • Quick, crisp passes delivered on time.

- The role reversal scrimmage (or drills). When players don't appreciate the difficulty of playing other positions, it is often helpful to let the players switch positions for a few minutes. Guards and posts often do not understand the problems facing their teammates. When the drill is finished, the players appreciate the difficulty of each other's position and will understand the importance of trying to make it easier for each other.

The guards become posts and vice versa. The defense should be run with the defensive players not switching positions. Later the defensive players should also switch positions. This drill is usually done only once or twice a year and for only a few minutes.

Practice Expectations

Coaches should never expect players to know how to practice and what is expected of them at the start of the season. The coach must teach the players:

- What is expected of the players during practice sessions.
- What it takes to become a special player.
- How to practice intelligently at home or after school.

Teaching players how to practice at home will be a challenge. Kids think that if they go out and shoot a little or play a few games that they will get better. Players need to learn that if they want to improve drastically they will have to practice smart and practice hard. Certain sections of this book stress how to practice certain skills at home. In the shooting section there is a discussion on extra shooting sessions and how they should be practiced.

Teaching players how to practice at home will be a challenge.

Summary Points

A coach is a teacher. The gymnasium is his classroom. Excellent coaches, such as the legendary UCLA coach John Wooden, for example, enjoy planning and conducting practices more than they enjoy the games. During practices, the coach gets to know his players and develop a rapport with them. The coach assists the players in not only developing individual and team skills, but also self-confidence. This outcome is the true reward for a teacher.

CHAPTER 12

Drills offer a player the opportunity to develop skills and confidence rapidly. Learning and perfecting any skill is dependent on learning how to do the task and repeating and improving the task until it is second nature. As a rule, scrimmaging is an inefficient way to develop basketball skills, since players seldom get to repeat the same task. Most fundamental skills are learned much more quickly in individual and small group drills. Drills offer the player the opportunity to develop skills and confidence, while developing an open, communicative relationship with the coach.

Drills offer an opportunity for the coach to develop a relationship with his players. By spending a few minutes each day helping the player improve, the coach demonstrates that he cares enough to give his personal attention. To a degree, an enhanced ease of personal communication develops. Encouragement can easily be given during this time. The feeling that the coach cares for him and wants to help him get better can help motivate the player.

Drills offer the player the opportunity to develop skills and confidence ,while developing an open, communicative relationship with the coach.

The coach should design drills that get maximum efficiency from the team and that simulate game situations. Drills can be designed to teach or stress any skill or concept. The only limitation is the imagination of the coach. Among the factors that drills should address are the following:

- Teach fundamental skills.
- Develop confidence.
- Teach a segment of the offense.
- Teach defensive concepts as other players work on offensive skills.
- Emphasize team concepts:
    - Quick-ball movement, quick-ball reversal, and mixing up the offense
    - Two- or three-man games with and without defenders
    - No-dribble drill or scrimmage to emphasize the importance

of moving without the ball, breaking to open areas, quick-ball movement, and looking for open teammates. Players will find that the team can play better as a group, and that a lot of dribbling isn't necessary.
- Role reversal. Guards and posts sometimes don't appreciate their teammates as much as they should. After a few weeks, a few minutes of role reversal can help teammates realize how difficult a teammate's role is.

Pairing Players up for Drills

Players with similar skills should be paired up when doing two-man drills. Players should be pushed to their maximum ability without being overmatched; a total mismatch of talent hinders, rather than helps, player improvement. However, the coach must also give the players the opportunity to prove themselves against better players. Whenever possible, a player should match-up against a player who is a little more skilled. By doing so, the player will be even more motivated to work harder. A substitute may be able to defend a starter very well. The only difference may be in their offensive skills. While working on one-on-one drills, the coach should consider the following factors:

➢ Pair players according to similarity of their skill level.
➢ As the players work in pairs or small groups, customize each group's drill for its skill level. The coach can go from group to group individualizing the drills for each player.
➢ Return to the first group: if everything is now being done well, intensify the drill and work on new skills.

By working in this manner, all players can work on the factors that will make them better. Over the course of the year, the discrepancy in skill levels between the players should diminish. As their skill levels improve during the course of the year, the coach should acknowledge that improvement by mixing the pairings up more than was possible at the beginning of the year.

The coach must also give the players the opportunity to prove themselves against better players.

Types of Drills

Many books are available describing all types of drills. Serious coaches or players should study these references. The purpose of this section is not to list and describe all these drills. Drills can be designed to develop or reinforce just about anything. The coach's imagination is the only limiting factor. Once he decides something needs to be worked on, it can be accomplished by modifying a current drill or by developing an entirely new drill.

This chapter emphasizes the importance of drills and other aspects that sometimes may be forgotten or overlooked. Drills fall into three basic categories: individual, small group, and team drills.

- Individual-skill drills:
  - One or two people.
  - Quickly develops fundamental skills such as dribbling, shooting, passing, defense, rebounding, or blocking out.
  - One-on-one drills can be customized to the players' skill level.

- Small-group skills drills:
  - Four to six people.
  - Emphasizes offensive and defensive skills simultaneously.
  - Can focus on parts of the offensive or defensive schemes.

- Team drills:
  - Five offensive and five defensive players working on team skills.
  - Reinforces and coordinates offenses and defenses.

When utilizing small-group drills or individual drills, the amount of lateral area the players have to work in should be limited so they do not have the entire court to make a move. Players need to have a narrow alley toward the basket in which to work, so that the drill is more game realistic. In a relatively confined space, the players are forced to mix up their moves and make quick fakes if they are to be successful.

Zone Offense

- Quick-passing drills (no dribble); outside-inside emphasis; ball reversal emphasis; stress being unpredictable in the passing tendencies.
- Quick-passing drill with defense.
- Quick-passing drill with defense and dribble penetration.

Entry Passes to the Post Drills

Making a good entry pass to a post player is not as easy as it looks. The pass is bad if the post has to give up his hard-earned post position to receive it. The scoring opportunity may no longer exist. This drill should be done with two or three offensive players and their defenders. It is good for practicing defensive position and techniques, as well as learning how to recognize the proper entry pass angle and when to rotate the ball for a better entry angle.

Fast Break Drills

These fast-break drills that attack the basket may be conducted on one-on-one, a one-on-two, or a one-on-three basis. A good ballhandler should attack the defense in a fast-break drill. The player should take it to the basket every time the player is in a one-on-one situation. In high school, coaches sometimes tell the players not to attack the basket if it is a one-on-two or one-on-three situation. For most players on the team, this may be a good rule, but not for an excellent ballhandler and scorer. These players should be encouraged to attack the basket and make the defense stop the drive. If the defense is slightly out of position or out of synch, the ballhandler can often find a crease in the defense and either go in for an easy score or draw a foul.

Layup Drills

Inexperienced players sometimes have the habit of shooting "bricks" for layups. This situation often occurs because they have never learned to lay the ball up softly with their fingertips. These players shoot with a forward flick of the wrist, as they would a normal shot. Since they are dribbling at a relatively high rate of speed toward the backboard, some players soften the shot by slowing down before they get to the basket. They start slowing down around the free-throw line, thereby allowing the defender to catch up. This problem is quite common in junior high school and sometimes in high school, since many players cannot yet jump up near the rim to lay the ball up.

Players need to learn to make layups from either side of the basket after dribbling at full speed. Players need to learn to make the layup without being defended. Once players are confident, these drills should be repeated with a defender.

Layup from Half-Court with Defender Drill:

The offensive player gets the ball at half=court and goes in for a layup. The defender starts five or six feet behind and tries to block the shot or cause the player to miss the layup. The offensive player should focus on the square painted on the backboard and not look for the defender. The offensive player goes straight for the basket and shoots the ball correctly with the ball in front of him, using his body as a shield to prevent the defender from having an opportunity to block the shot. The ballhandler should concentrate on the following:

➢ Beating the defender down the court.

Players need to learn to make layups from either side of the basket after dribbling at full speed.

- Focusing on a small part of the square.
- Laying the ball up softly, rather than shooting it.

Great Seldom-Used Drills

Shooting with Contact Drills

This drill can be done as a separate exercise or incorporated without notice to the offensive player during regular drills. In the latter situation, the coach quietly instructs a defender to foul the offensive player when he shoots. The contact can be grabbing the arm or pushing gently as the shot is taken or as a rebound is about to be gathered in. Situations where this drill can be employed include:

- When a wing is driving into the lane.
- When posts and forwards are shooting or faking and shooting with contact.
- During offensive and defensive rebound drills.

The shooting-with-contact drills should be initiated once the players have developed the proper shooting fundamentals. They are often used during the off-season and preseason. However, it is important to reinforce this fundamental skill every week by spending a few minutes on specific drills or by secretly instructing a defender to periodically foul the player during drills or scrimmages.

Clock and Situation Awareness Drills

Clock and awareness drills should be done for a few minutes during the preseason and reviewed once a week for a couple of minutes, while working on plays for the end of the quarter, a half, or the game. The point guard is usually the quarterback on the court, but every player should have outstanding clock-and-situation awareness. It is an attribute that requires thinking, not great physical abilities.

Keep in mind that players never see what they don't look for.

Court Awareness Drills

Court awareness is a skill that is seldom taught, but is expected of every player. Players need to have their heads up and their eyes and minds open. Keep in mind that players never see what they don't look for. As such, players should be taught to be aware of what is happening in other areas of the court and not just where they are standing at the moment.

During dribbling drills, the following points should be emphasized:

- Seeing the trapping defender.
- Recognizing the screening teammate.
- Visualizing the cutter coming off a screen or breaking into an open area.
- Finding the open man on a fast break.

During fast-break drills, the following factors should be stressed:

- Rebounding near the basket and making a quick outlet pass.
- Quickly initiating the break after getting a long defensive rebound near the free-throw line.

Peripheral Vision Drill

As a rule, few athletes ever try to develop their peripheral vision because it is so easy to turn their heads. On the other hand, peripheral vision can be very helpful to a basketball player. For example, better peripheral vision will improve the player's vision of the court, as well as making it more difficult for the opponent to anticipate what or where the player is going to make a move, shot, or pass. This drill is easily done either in the gym during formal practice or on any court informally.

Drills That Players Can Do on Their Own

The coach should teach the players the importance of performing drills on their own. Players seldom know how to practice smartly and effectively on their own. They shoot a few hoops or play a game. However, they do not practice with a purpose, and they seldom simulate game situations as they practice. Drills are typically thought of as being used only in formal team practices. However, players who are serious about improving need to learn how to practice as efficiently as they can—regardless of whether they're in the gym with the coach or on their own.

The coach can prepare a list of drills for the player to work on by himself or with another person. The drills should be worked on every opportunity the player gets (e.g., after school, on weekends, during the off-season and summer). The list of drills that should be performed and instructions on how to do the drills can be presented at a player-coach conference. Existing drills can be modified, or entirely new drills can be developed by the player, once he realizes how to practice and what he needs to work on. Once the basic techniques involved in the drill are fully understood, the player should imagine ways to make the drill as game-realistic as possible.

Players who are serious about improving need to learn how to practice as efficiently as they can—regardless of whether they're in the gym with the coach or on their own.

The following drill illustrates an example of how drills can be modified to continue to challenge the player as he becomes more proficient. Once the basic drill is learned, variations can be added to the drill to improve the players' skill level even more.

The Perimeter Shooting Drill with a Defender

In this two-person drill, the passer defends and rebounds. He has the responsibility of simulating game situations. The purpose of the drill is to develop confidence in catching and shooting without and then with one defender. As the shooter develops his scoring confidence and scoring ability, the defensive pressure is intensified. In this drill, the players should use their imagination to predict where opposing defenders are likely to be. The drill involves the following steps:

- The rebounder passes to the shooter, who practices three-point shots from the right wing area. The shooter continues to work on technique and a quick release. Occasionally, the rebounder should make a less-than-ideal pass.

- Once the player is confident and is making a good percentage of his shots, the rebounder should charge straight toward the shooter and try to block the shot. The rebounder will have to adjust the speed of the pass and how quickly he charges, so the shooter has a reasonable chance to make the shot while being seriously challenged. The charging defender will have to increase his intensity as the shooter develops his confidence with game-speed shots.

- The rebounder then passes to the shooter and charges from a different angle, the right side of the shooter.

- Once the shooter is confident, the defender should increase his attack so the shooter cannot get the shot off without being blocked. The shooter should learn to give a ball, head, and shoulder fake before making a move cutting behind the charging defender.

- This drill should be practiced from different areas of the court with the defender coming straight on and from different directions.

- Once the shooter is confident in making the shot as well as faking and initiating a move behind the defender, the defender

Once the basic techniques involved in the drill are fully understood, the player should imagine ways to make the drill as game-realistic as possible.

should try to fool the shooter as to whether he is really trying to block the shot or if he will concentrate on the rebound.

The aforementioned steps are designed to assist the player in becoming more comfortable in judging when to shoot or drive. The shooter will also learn to relax and simultaneously focus intensely on the target in the face of a charging defender. Other possible options to practice this move to the basket include:

- Drive in for a layup from either side of the basket.
- A pull-up jump shot immediately behind the charging defender.
- Pull-up jumper eight to 10 feet from the basket using the backboard.
- Pull-up jumper from the free-throw line.
- Drive the lane and pass outside.

This drill illustrates how a player can take one drill and utilize it in many ways on his own in order to simulate game-situations.

Summary Points

Drills can be designed to teach or emphasize almost any aspect of basketball. It is up to the coach and the player to refine existing drills and develop new drills. The player can discover ways to make up new drills as he practices on his own. The point to keep in mind is to pay attention to detail, learn in stages, and make drills game-realistic.

It is up to the coach and the player to refine existing drills and develop new drills.

CHAPTER 13

Game Demeanor

The Coach as a Role Model

As a rule, coaches who are under control at all times and explain what needs to be done have teams that play better in times of stress. Players look to the coach for guidance and confidence. The coach should be positive and encouraging; negative attitudes are destructive. If things aren't going well, the players may already be down on themselves. The coach must keep their players' confidence up and put the team in situations where they can be successful. If the players are hustling on defense but aren't making the right decisions on offense, the coach should be encouraging and supportive—even if the shots aren't falling. If the coach wants the players to learn to control their emotions during the game, he must set the example.

If the coach wants the players to learn to control their emotions during the game, he must set the example.

The screaming coach is always yelling instructions to the kids as they play. The point to keep in mind is that the players can't focus on their duties if they are always looking to see what the coach is yelling. A coach who has fully prepared the team should seldom have to yell instructions to players. The yelling coach who finds it necessary to constantly scream negatives at his players should reconsider his decision to coach.

A Coach Should Know His Players and Their Personalities

A coach should know his players and their personalities if he is going to effectively manage and motivate them in difficult times or situations. Some players are very responsive to coaching when they come out of the game. With these players, it is very easy to remind them what they need to do. However, if the coach tends to get upset with the players, or if a player gets upset with himself easily, the coach should consider a policy of letting both himself and the player have time to get in a more responsive mindset before talking to the player. It is probably wise to let each player coming out of the game sit on the bench for a few minutes before instructing him on what the coach wants.

A player who is always very hard on himself may need a few moments to blow it off and calm down. It is sometimes difficult for a coach to know how to handle these players because they may appear to be mad and sulking. However, they are usually mad at themselves. After the player has had time to calm down, the coach should calmly explain what he wants, and then ask the player if he understands and can do it. Over time, these players will probably learn to respond more calmly.

Communicating With the Player Who Made a Mistake

The coach communicates with a player by his actions and his expressions, as well as what he says and how he says it. Non-verbal actions, such as turning his back toward the player, glaring at the player, or other actions demonstrating disgust, are not helpful. A player who is being pulled from the game after making a mistake already knows what he did, and he is usually upset with himself. Getting on him as he comes out will not help. It may actually make things worse.

If a player is having a hard time or if the player loses confidence easily, the coach should acknowledge the player, and show confidence and express encouragement in him. Ignoring the player as he comes to the bench should be the most anger a coach shows. The coach should insert the player back into the game in a timely manner. Before reinserting the player, the coach should ask the player what he needs to do and make any instructions or corrections at this time. Reaffirming that the player understands what is expected of him is very important. Punishing a player by keeping him out of a game for an extended period of time may make a point once or twice. Frequently taking this step over time, however, may create ill feelings, rather than a desire to excel. The following story illustrates this point:

"An inexperienced young college coach was often the brunt of fans' laughter and scorn. Her antics of jumping up screaming in anger at the players or referees astonished opposing fans and embarrassed and angered the team's parents and fans. After one game, the coach asked one of the team captains why she seemed upset. The player told her she realized the coach's job was to remind players when they did something wrong. The player stated, 'I am a smart player and I usually know immediately what mistake I made. I know it is your job to make certain that I know what I need to do. If you need to remind me, do so in the same tone and manner we are talking now. Don't yank me out of the game, get in my face, and embarrass me in front of my teammates, the fans, and parents. Making me sit on the bench for the rest of the half was bad enough, but then to go into the locker room and replay the whole scene is not the way to make me a better player. It will only make me play

The coach communicates with a player by his actions and his expressions, as well as what he says and how he says it.

worse and make me lose my desire to play. Would you like to be treated that way?"

To the coach's credit she re-evaluated her coaching techniques and became less animated each game. As the next year unfolded, she seldom screamed at the players. As a result, both the coach and the players enjoyed the game of basketball much more.

A team reflects the attitude of the coach. In a close game, the team is more likely to play well with a coach who is calm, prepared, and confident, rather than one who is overly excited and emotional. Coaches should be the kind of teacher they would want to learn from!

Handling the Shooter Who is Having an Off Night

Good shooters will have streaks during which their shots will not fall, and it will be very easy for them to get down on themselves. How the coach handles the player may determine how the player shoots in the game and could impact how he shoots the rest of the season. As such, the coach needs to be encouraging to the player, since the shooter will probably already be discouraged and be hard on himself.

If the player has proven in practice and in games that he is a good shooter, he will snap out of the streak. Is the player taking good-percentage shots as part of the normal offense? Is the player trying to do too much? Pure shooters are often streaky—they could miss five shots in the first half and make the next five. Larry Bird, one of the purest shooters in NBA history, had games in which during one half, he might be 1-for-12, but by the time the game was over, he had scored 20 or more points. In reality, it only takes a little something to let the player get the feel again. It could be a defensive steal, a free throw, or some other small feat that allows a player to regain confidence and his shooting touch. During the game the coach should:

A team reflects the attitude of the coach.

- ➢ Know that when a player is down on himself as he comes out of the game, he needs encouragement first. Instructions or corrections should be made just before going back into the game.
- ➢ Encourage the player and tell him to relax, and his shot will start to fall.
- ➢ Emphasize other skills that will help the player restore his level of confidence.
- ➢ Not tell a pure shooter not to shoot.
- ➢ Ask himself what message his body language is sending when the player looks over at him. Is it encouragement or disgust?

If a shooter had a bad game, the coach should encourage him and work with the player during practice to help him get his shooting touch back. What are the factors involving shooting touch that usually need evaluation?

- Technique.
- Rhythm.
- Shot selection. Is the player trying to do too much?

Practicing the types of shots likely to be taken in the offense can be helpful to a player who is struggling. Plays should be practiced that allow the player to get into the flow of the offense.

Do Not Overreact to Players During a Game

Basketball is like war, in that each team is trying to force its will on the other, hoping to control the game with its offensive and defensive strategies. As a result, players have to make adjustments and take what is given them. The team that does this best is the team that usually wins. Players will sometimes be instructed to do something that the opponent denies them the opportunity to do. Coaches must carefully evaluate if the players made the correct choice or whether the players did not execute properly. In the heat of the game, a coach should be careful not to overreact. Sometimes, the coach will discover he was wrong, and any damage done to a player may be difficult to repair. As a result, the player may lose respect for the coach. The following example illustrates this point:

"A high school varsity team was in a close game. The home team had been trying to score inside the key most of the time without much success. At the start of the fourth quarter, the coach instructed the team to keep working the ball inside. Each time down the court, the lane was so clogged with seven to eight players, that a good shot could not be attempted. The power forward stepped out 12 to 15 feet toward the corner, and when the defense didn't come out to challenge him, he hit four consecutive baskets.

The coach pulled the forward from the game. The home team tried to pound the ball inside and went scoreless during the last four minutes of the game. A close game had been lost because the coach wasn't attentive enough to see that the opponent had four defensive players in the lane at all times. When the forward stepped out to create an open shot, he had reacted correctly, but was reprimanded in the huddle and after the game for not continuing to post up."

Practicing the types of shots likely to be taken in the offense can be helpful to a player who is struggling.

The player had made the correct decision. The coach not only failed to realize what was occurring in the game, he made matters worse by punishing and humiliating the player. When a coach misjudges and overreacts to a situation, he will lose face in the eyes of the entire team.

Putting Pressure on the Players

Putting undo pressure on players will never make them play better. Putting pressure on a player by telling him he must have a great game if the team is to beat the next opponent puts unfair pressure on that player. It may be true, but the coach should not tell the player. The player should function as part of the offensive and defensive game scheme. If the coach wants the player to be more aggressive, he should tell him so and specifically what he would like for him to do differently. The following story illustrates this point:

> "A college player was talking about her experience the previous year. She was not happy with the coach, who at the end of the year had lost her job. The player said that since the team was struggling there had been the usual problems. They were made worse when the coach told her on several occasions that if the team was to win she would have to have a big game. The player felt it was unfair to put that kind of pressure on her when it was a team game. She said she knew she needed to play well every game, but it is more difficult to do when you are struggling. The player felt she needed encouragement and not additional pressure."

Putting undo pressure on players will never make them play better.

If a player has not been playing up to his potential during several consecutive games, he will typically be concerned and will be worried about what the coach thinks. The coach should demonstrate concern for the player and should inquire if there are any problems. No mention should be made to the player that the next game will depend upon the player's performance. If additional work is needed to help the player improve, the coach should suggest steps the player can do after practice to help. Players already have pressure on them to produce or lose playing time. Why put more pressure on them?

The coach can actually take some pressure off some players by clearly communicating his expectations. For example, a post may not be a scoring threat, but the player may be a great defensive player who is also good at blocking out. The player may believe he isn't playing well because he isn't scoring many points. The coach should tell the player not to worry about scoring, but that he wants him to continue to play great defense, blocking out, and rebounding. The player should be reassured that his scoring will improve with continued work and time. The coach should review anything from the scouting report that will help give the edge to the player during practice. A show of confidence often does wonders for a player's performance.

Coaching No-No's

The following examples reflect situations that actually occurred during games. These scenarios involved actions of average and very successful coaches on the high-school level.

- A coach yanked the player by the hair during a time-out. The player was his daughter. Another coach shoved a player rather forcefully.
- Opposing coaches got in their players' faces and screamed.
- One coach was so upset with her team that he took off his shoe and threw it against the wall behind the empty bench as he waited for his players to come to the sideline during a time-out.

The coach should ask someone to periodically videotape him during games. This person should be asked to critique the coach's game demeanor, and the coach should do the same. The two should review the critiques as they review the tape. The coach should ask himself whether he would like to be a player on a team coached this way.

Tips for Game Demeanor

A coach who wants to coach in a "positive manner" will adhere to the following factors:

- Be calm and cool.
- Be instructive and constructive.
- Be disciplined and encouraging.
- Set simple goals.
- Realize offensive lulls and defensive breakdowns will occur during a game.

Summary Points

The role of a coach can often be diverse and demanding, Not only must he be a teacher, he must also set standards of performance and behavior. At all times, the coach should act responsibly and professionally towards his players. As such, the coach should strictly adhere to the premise that the first person he should lead is himself.

The coach can actually take some pressure off some players by clearly communicating his expectations.

CHAPTER 14

Game Management

Game management is the manner in which the coach handles his team during the game as situations change. Game management begins in practice. How well prepared and confident is the team? Are they fundamentally sound as individuals and as a team? Has the team prepared for the wide variety of situations that may occur? Is the team comfortable switching offenses or defenses quickly? Is the team used to making adjustments? Detailed preparation allows a team to react correctly on the court and improves its chances of success.

Game Plan and Objectives

Game management is much easier if the coach has prepared a clearly defined game plan, accounting for special situations that might occur. It is best to have written reminders to refer to during the stressful times that sometimes occur during close games. Planning ahead of time for what you would like to do in certain situations makes it easier to make correct decisions in the heat of the game.

Game management begins in practice.

- Scouting Report

The game plan should be derived from a detailed scouting report. A number of reference books are available that have sample scouting report forms that can be modified. Generally, the scouting report should provide information on the team and its players. This information will assist the coach in formulating a game plan for his team. Specific information on players will be used in this game plan, as well as in providing the team's players with any information that they might need to get an edge. Examples of the type of questions that a scouting report might answer include:

What are the opponent's strengths and weaknesses? What offenses and defenses do they prefer and how are they run? How do our teams match-up? What will the opponent most likely do to stop us? Who are the best and weakest players? Do they have tendencies of which we can take advantage? Do they have favorite places to shoot or favorite moves? Are the players right-handed, ambidextrous, well-rounded players? How can we take advantage of them? How do we match-up? What match-ups do we want, and how can we get them? Whom do we want to shut down and how do we want to attack the other team?

After a game, the coach should review the scouting report and make notes while the game is fresh in his mind. Evaluate the game plan and the team's execution. Suggestions should be noted in case the teams play again. After reviewing the game film and the evaluation, the coach should immediately modify the next day's practice in order to work on things that need correcting.

- Match-ups

Basketball is a game of match-ups. The team that is better prepared for those match-ups often wins. The coach should know the match-ups he would like to have and how to get them. The coach should also anticipate what the opposing coach will do if those match-ups have put his team at a disadvantage. Likewise, the coach should have his players prepared to help each other if the opponent has a match-up that is in its favor.

- Adjust the Offense and Defense for the Players on the Floor

A coach should realize that some players on his team may not have the physical skills, experience, or confidence levels which allow the players to be as effective in the offense or defense as their teammates. In these situations, the coach should adjust the game plan so the five players on the court have the best chance to do as well as they can. For example, a substitute may not be quick enough to press successfully. Accordingly, if the team is asked to press, a good chance exists that the team will give up unnecessary points. This outcome would only hurt the team, as well as the player's confidence. As such, that player may be more effective playing a zone or picking up the offensive player at the three-point line in a man defense. Remember:

> The first objective of defense is to not allow the opponent to score. No one cares how you do it.
> The first objective of player development is to build confidence and not destroy it!

Basketball is a game of match-ups. The team that is better prepared for those match-ups often wins.

➤ For example:

> "Near the end of the first half, a junior-varsity coach inserted a substitute in place of a starting guard. The starting guard had been beaten down the floor on a fast break by the opposing point guard several times during the half. The substitute wasn't as fast the starter, yet the coach put the substitute on the point guard and asked him to play full-court man-to-man defense. In the next two minutes, the sub was beaten down the court twice, yanked from the game, and yelled at."

The obvious question is, 'If the fastest player on the team couldn't stay with the opposing point guard, how could a slower teammate?' The sub had been put in a 'lose-lose' situation, and his confidence was severely shaken. It hurt the team, and it hurt the player. This player would have been more effective in a defense as described above. Many other situations occur during games where a wise coach should try to effectively match-up the skills of the players on the floor with the opponent.

Managing Difficult Game Situations

Coaches should be prepared for special situations that sometimes arise during a game, such as when a team is more likely to let up or give up. Coaches also struggle with substitutions and playing time and trying to keep a balance between winning and losing and playing the subs.

- Teams Letting Up

    ➤ If the team works hard to send the game into overtime, it often relaxes and loses the momentum during the time-out between regulation and overtime. The players sometimes are so excited to catch-up, they lose their focus, concentration, and intensity. The coach has to re-focus the team. If aggressive play enabled the team to catch up, they should continue to be aggressive. The other team is probably a little discouraged if they have lost the lead, so don't let them back in the game! Come out and play intensely and smartly. Sometimes in overtime, coaches abandon what the team did well to catch-up, and the team quickly loses momentum and, possibly, the game. The point to keep in mind is to do what you do well until the other team stops you.

    ➤ Teams tend to let up after gaining a big lead. If a team has jumped out to a big lead early, it is common to let up and let the other team back into the game. Players often lose their focus and intensity in these situations, and it is often impossible to regain

Coaches should be prepared for special situations that sometimes arise during a game...

that attitude. The coach must keep the intensity up, both on the floor and the bench. He should be aware of cocky and unfocused attitudes on the bench. Players with that type of mindset will not have their mind properly focused when they enter the game. Teams usually jump to a big early lead because they are playing great defense, blocking out, and rebounding well, and running the offense correctly with good ball- and player-movement.

- <u>If Your Team Gets Way Behind</u>

Close games are the ones that many coaches love to play. Blowouts, or games in which the opponent has a large lead are the games that most coaches dread. When things aren't going right, and the team has gotten way behind, a different challenge faces the coach. Coaches should know ahead of time how they want to handle this type of situation.

> ➤ If the team gets way behind early, the players will be down, and they will look to the coach for leadership. If you coach basketball, you will sometimes have games like this no matter how good your team is. The team can't get a break, make a shot, and the other team is playing the game of their lives. How the coach handles himself, what he says, how he says it, and what his body language says will be very important in this situation in ensuring the players don't give up or lose their confidence. The following suggestions may be helpful:
>
> - Be calm and confident. The players look to you for leadership. You can be intense and can criticize a lack of effort. Don't get mad at the kids; they don't want to look bad. Substitute to make a point or to change things up.
> - Be informative. Tell the players something they can do to help, even a little. Never forget that turn-arounds start one play at a time!
> - Re-evaluate your offensive and defensive strategies.
> - Insist on hustle. Compliment a particular individual if you get terrific effort from that player.
> - Set small, realistic goals that are achievable and, upon which, your team can build confidence. If a team is way behind, the players might not believe they can still catch-up. The coach must set goals to reduce the lead by an equal amount each quarter so that the lead won't seem so overwhelming.
> - Be encouraging anytime players give an extra effort or do what you asked them to do better.

> Reminder! Every game has an ebb and flow!

In every high school, college, or professional game, each team will have a period of time during which they go without a basket for several minutes. It could be the first minutes of a game, the last minute, or anytime in between. The secret to winning is to play great, hustling defense, while avoiding turnovers and fouls. During this lull, it is important for the team that is struggling to deny the opponent easy baskets.

A hustling defense often initiates confidence and scoring opportunities. One hustling effort may be all that is needed to switch the momentum of the game. When evenly matched teams play each other, and one team, playing very emotionally, jumps out to a big early lead, the opponent can stay in the game if they remain calm, play great defense, and execute the offense. The game is played for four quarters. Convey that fact to the players.

> ➢ If a game is totally out of hand, the team will be discouraged. The players will know they can't win. To prevent loss of confidence, the coach must re-focus his team. He must help the team make something positive out of a bad situation.

The coach should not say, "Since we have already lost this game," or, "Since we can't win this game." The coach should inform the team that it is important to work on fundamentals and to make correct decisions. Emphasize it is only important that the players give a 100 percent effort and they execute the offense or defense properly. Reinforce the fact that if they do their best and give their all, the coach will be very proud of them. Be positive. Young athletes need all the encouragement they can get.

Don't be hard on the players, they will be hard enough on themselves. Acknowledge hustle, good attitude, and doing the right thing, whether it works or not. After a blowout, it is often best not to review what the team did wrong. This is especially true immediately after the game. If you feel something must be said, criticize a lack of hustle or mental mistakes, but never humiliate players by blaming them. At the next practice, you may or may not want to discuss the game. It is more important to keep the players excited about playing.

Evaluating the Effectiveness of the Offense and Defense During the Game

The effectiveness of the team is determined by whether or not the team is in the correct offense or defense, and how the players are able to execute that particular phase of the game. Every coach has his favorite offenses and defenses that he prefers to run. Those preferences should never prevent the coach from objectively evaluating their effectiveness. Sometimes this is difficult because you want them to work. The great coach will not stay in an offense or defense too long if it is ineffective, particularly if his team is well-prepared for other alternatives.

A coach must quickly answer the following questions during the game: Is the defense giving up too many easy baskets? Is the press defense giving up more points than it is generating? Is the press getting the team's key players in foul trouble? Is the offense executing well? Are the timing and spacing good? Are players standing and waiting, or are they making something happen? Is the zone offense penetrating the defense?

Remember! If it works—keep it up! If it doesn't—find something that does!

Substitutions and Playing Time

Playing time is the reward that players get for all the effort they have put forth in practice and during the off-season. It is the reason kids want to play basketball. Players will not continue to give an all-out effort in practice if they do not believe they will get quality playing time. Work without reward leads to disillusionment and dissatisfaction. The coach walks a fine line between winning games and giving the players an opportunity to play enough to improve.

• <u>The Substitution Patterns of Varsity and Sub-varsity Levels is Different</u>

If the emphasis on the sub-varsity level is on player development and winning, the program wins when every player improves. If a coach stresses winning over giving substitutes adequate quality practice and playing time, the coach is stating that he does not believe other players have a chance to improve enough to contribute later on.

As a primary rule, the emphasis on the varsity level is winning. On the other hand, on some varsity teams, seven or eight players get all the playing time unless the game is a blowout. On other varsity-level squads, the bench is strong enough that five substitutes can play giving up few points to most teams. Is this because the team was lucky to have good players, or did the program do an excellent job developing the players?

• Why Giving Substitutes Playing Time is Important

Substitutes can only develop skills and confidence and be ready to contribute if the coach has prepared them in practice and in games. Skills and confidence are "developed" in practice and "reinforced" in games. Substitutes must be developed because they will be needed in the future. Players will be lost during the season due to:

- Illness and injury
- Academics

Players will be lost year to year due to:

- Transfer to another school or city
- Academics
- Quitting basketball for various reasons:
  - To concentrate on other activities
  - Loss of interest
  - They are unhappy with the program

Substitutes expect the starters to get the most playing time. However, substitutes expect and deserve to get quality playing time. If the subs are not given adequate playing time, why should they work hard in practice? They will lose their desire, confidence, and self-esteem. The development of the team, the starters, and the substitutes is dependent upon every player giving 100 percent in practice. Quality practices are necessary if the team is to be prepared to play well against quality opponents.

Everyone wins when the substitutes are skilled enough to challenge the starters in practice. The more intense the competition in practice, the better prepared the players will be. If the starters improve much more rapidly than the substitutes, the program will lose because practices will not be as challenging to the starters. Developing a program requires believing in one of the cardinal rules of basketball: develop every player on the team to his fullest potential.

• What is Quality Game Time?

Running players in and out at the end of a game so the coach can say everyone has played is not quality game time. The coach should ask himself how he would feel if he were a sub in this situation. A coach who truly wants every player to improve to the maximum will do his best to provide every quality moment he can to his players, whether in practice or in a game. The coach knows that a player's confidence is reinforced when individual and team skills are executed successfully in game situations.

Game Management

Players on the bench should know their status and their role on the team. The coach must clearly communicate with the substitutes so they are comfortable with their role. It is important that the players know they are expected to utilize their strengths.

Substitution motto: If you practice hard, you play! Game time is the reward for working hard.

Types of Substitutions

- Planned substitutions are made to:
  - Rest players
  - Allow other players quality playing time

- Unplanned substitutions are made because a player is:
  - Making too many mistakes.
  - Not playing good defense or not executing the offense.
  - In foul trouble.
  - Not hustling.
  - Mad and out of control.
  - Injured.

• <u>Substituting for a Player Who has Made a Mistake</u>

Every coach will have to substitute for a player who is making mistakes or is having troubles. Be assured every player will make mistakes and will struggle at times. How the coach handles these substitutions may affect an individual's psyche and his play.

Never yank a player for making one mistake; it can destroy his confidence. Players can't play well and will not develop if they are afraid of being yanked from the game for making one mistake. In that situation, the player will often glance over to see the coach's response. Be encouraging! You are sending a message that you believe in the player. A player who never makes a mistake is probably playing too cautiously and is not pushing himself to the limit.

If a player is being pulled because he has made several mistakes, the coach should be aware that what he says and does will send a message to the player. No one plays badly on purpose. The player will already be upset with himself. The coach should not yell at the player or use body language that shows disgust.

Coaches handle these substitutions differently. Some prefer to let the player sit on the bench for a while, then talk to the player before he goes

Never yank a player for making one mistake; it can destroy his confidence.

back into the game. Other coaches prefer to talk to the player when he first comes out and while the ideas are fresh in the coach's and player's minds. If this is the case, the coach should be calm, cool, and informative.

If a player is pulled after two or more mistakes, whether turnovers, bad passes, or being out of position, quietly discuss the mistakes while on the bench, review with the player what was done wrong and how to do it correctly. Tell the player what you expect. Ask the player if he understands. Ask the player if he can do it. Encourage the player, and let him get back in the game as soon as possible.

If a player is pulled from the game for making a mistake, do not wait too long to put the player back in the game. The player wants and deserves the chance to prove he can do a better job. If it was time to pull the player for rest and player substitution, put the player back in the game at the normal time. However, if the player is pulled for making a mistake, be ready to put the player back into the game right away. If the player will not be able to get back in the game due to lack of time or the need to play other teammates, the coach should inform the player directly of this situation. This prevents the player from being too down on himself and wondering what the coach thinks about him.

Some inexperienced coaches subconsciously show favoritism to their best players by discussing what they should do when they go back in the game, but failing to give any suggestions to the substitutes. This type of coach does not expect much out of his subs, and they are being played only because it is mandatory. Unfortunately, these coaches probably run their practices the same way.

Player-Rotation Schedules

Player-rotation schedules are very helpful in assuring the coach does not forget to make the substitutions he had planned.

Player-rotation schedules are very helpful in assuring the coach does not forget to make the substitutions he had planned. The player rotation schedule is a written reminder the coach can refer to during the heat of the game to insure that the correct players are in the game for specific game situations and that all players get quality game time.

- ➤ The coach should work out a schedule of who starts each quarter, when the substitutions will be made, and for whom.
- ➤ The schedule is a reminder of offenses and defenses he would like to use in certain situations, as well as the players he would like to have on the floor.
- ➤ An assistant coach or manager should be assigned the duty of keeping up with the substitution schedule and the situation schedule.

If all the players have received quality playing time before the last four minutes of the game, the coach no longer has to worry about getting players in the game. He can concentrate on winning the game and having the best five players on the floor for different situations.

If the coach has rotation schedules for end-of-the-game scenarios, it is much less hectic and stressful during the game and timeouts. The coach can concentrate on giving instructions rather than trying to figure out who should be playing.

The coach should have considered possible game situations ahead of time and know what he would probably do. He should also know who he would like to have in the game during these times. The coach should have his game plan for these situations written out, along with the five players he would want on the court. The coach should also decide which substitute guard, forward, and post player will be needed and notations for each situation in case of injury or fouls. The following examples illustrate end-of-the-game scenarios that the coach might want to consider:

➤ With four minutes to go in the game, your team is either:
  ◆ Leading or trailing by eight or more points.
  ◆ Leading or trailing by four to seven points.

➤ With two minutes to go in the game, your team is:
  ◆ Leading or trailing by eight or more points.
  ◆ Leading or trailing by four to seven points.
  ◆ Leading or trailing by one to three points.

➤ With less than one minute in the game your team will:
  ◆ Be fouled quickly.
  ◆ Have to foul immediately to save time on the clock.

➤ Last-second, three-point shot plays should be executed and defended well.

The coach should have selected players for the aforementioned types of situations when the team is leading and trailing.

The following situations illustrate examples of are some combinations of styles that teams may need. Some of these situations will utilize the same players, while different situations may require players who have other abilities.

If the coach has rotation schedules for end-of-the-game scenarios, it is much less hectic and stressful during the game and timeouts.

Offensive Teams:	Defensive Teams:
• A pressing, breaking team	• A pressing team
• A stalling and free-throw shooting team	• A stall defending team
• Three-point scoring group	• A team to defend against three-point shots
• End-of-game two- or three-point play group	

These groups must have practiced these situations if they are expected to be effective.

Coach's Talks with the Team

A coach's communication with the team prior to the game, at halftime, and after the game can be very important to the team's mental focus. The team should have been thoroughly prepared to win during practice. At this point, the coach should use this time to help the players be in the right frame of mind. Each coach will develop his own style.

• Pre-game preparation

Hopefully, the team is adequately prepared, so very little needs to be discussed at the last minute. However, many coaches find it helpful to review the overall game plan with the players at an appropriate time before the game. The coach can remind any players of special assignments or special precautions before the game commences.

Pre-game speeches do not have to be enthusiasm-inspiring oratories. As a coach, you might prefer not to have the team overly emotional. Well-prepared teams that play on an emotional even keel tend to do much better. The coach may want to review the game plan one last time and ask if anyone has any questions. An important game may have the players very uptight. Sometimes, a coach may need to find a way to loosen the players up a little before the game.

Pre-game speeches do not have to be enthusiasm-inspiring oratories.

• Halftime

- ❑ Take a short break. Let the players go the bathroom, get a drink of water, and cool down. During this time, the coach has time to calm himself down and think about what needs to be done differently during the second half. If an aide has made notes, the coach should review them before going into the locker room.
- ❑ Share your feelings with the team. If the team has played well, acknowledge the play, but point out things they can still do better. If the team is playing poorly, the team should be criticized as a group. A coach must be careful before publicly criticizing an

individual. How will a particular player respond to humiliation in front of his teammates? Some players will get mad and show the coach up by playing better, while more sensitive players may lose their confidence.

There are times when the coach needs to show his emotions and intensity, especially if the players are not playing with intensity or are down on themselves. Yelling at players can be counter-productive. However, a coach may occasionally need to be emotional if the team is not giving an all-out effort or is not following instructions in the aspects of the game that are controllable. Yelling is most effective when it is seldom used.

❑ Have a plan. A coach's responsibility is to determine the basic problems and make adjustments. Keep it simple.

- ➢ The first four minutes of the second half often determine the outcome of the game.
- ➢ Clearly define what is expected, and ask the players to repeat it back so you are certain they understand what is expected.
- ➢ Encourage the players.
- ➢ Review the overall game plan for the second half.
- ➢ Save the most important parts of the adjustments until the end of the halftime.

❑ If you have special instructions or suggestions for individual players, go over these points with them privately after the halftime speech or when they return to the floor.

• Post-game Talk

❑ After an easy win. An easy win doesn't really prepare the team for the harder games to come. Teams don't learn much. Congratulate the team on the effort. However, there will be many things that a coach can point out that need to be worked on before the next game. The next few days after such a game, the players should be challenged to improve their skills and intensity.

❑ After a close win. Let the players celebrate a little. Compliment the team. The coach may want to compliment players who did what was asked of them or more. The coach should also bring the team down to earth by pointing out how easily the game could have been lost. He can mention some things the team will need to work on at the next practice.

Yelling is most effective when it is seldom used.

- After a close loss. Even if the last minutes of the game did not go as you would have wanted, blame cannot be placed exclusively on what transpired during the last minutes. Emphasize that everything that happens in the beginning of the game is as important as those things that happen in the last minute of the game. Everything is very magnified at the end of the game, since there is no time to make up for a mistake. Acknowledge the players' efforts and good play. Tell them that as long as they give their all, they are winners. Ask the players what they think they need to prevent losing a game like this again. They may know what the problems are, and they are more likely to buy into the solution if it is their idea. The next day, the coach should have the team work on what is needed.

- After the team is beaten badly. After a game like this, the players' confidence and self-esteem will be quite low. The coach needs to be a cheerleader for them. Even in a blowout, a coach can find some plays during the game that warrant compliments, whether it be for hustle or making the right decision. During the next few days, work on fundamentals, basics, and building the confidence of the players.

If your team loses, players will already be down on themselves. Getting mad, yelling, intimidating or humiliating players will do nothing but hurt the players and the team. Don't point fingers at players! They will feel bad, and you will feel bad later. If the players gave a good effort, tell them so. If the other team played better, give that team the credit. Then, make sure that the players realize that if they work harder and smarter, they can get better.

The next day, ask the players why they think they lost and what they need to do in order to become a better team. If the players come up with helpful suggestions, they will be more likely to respond correctly in the future. If the coach perceives other problems, he should clearly define the problems and go over the solutions.

Even in a blowout, a coach can find some plays during the game that warrant compliments, whether it be for hustle or making the right decision.

CHAPTER 15

There will be times when a player is discouraged or has questions and concerns. This is normal. Any player, at any level of competition, will have doubts and concerns, especially if things aren't working exactly as he had hoped. Teenagers are no different. They will question their ability, especially if they are struggling, or if they are unsure of their status. Players will seldom come and talk to the coach about their concerns, but they normally discuss them with their parents.

Coaches must understand the common concerns that players have before they can prevent or deal with those issues. This chapter addresses common questions that players ask their parents. Hopefully, you will find the following questions helpful in understanding the problems with which players often struggle. Each question is followed by an example of possible responses that parents or coaches could give to these questions.

Questions Players May Ask

1. How do I get more playing time?

Coaches love players who make something good happen and who don't make mistakes. Be a hustler, know the offense and defense, and make something happen.
- Beat your man in practice.
- Run hard all the time.
- Play aggressive defense.
- Fight for loose balls.
- Hustle to help teammates.

First, ask yourself: What am I doing to help the team? Am I making something happen, or am I just taking up space? Evaluate your game carefully and objectively. Ask the coach for his opinion. Second, go out and work hard to get better.

> **Any player, at any level of competition, will have doubts and concerns, especially if things aren't working exactly as he had hoped.**

2. How can I get faster or quicker?

Each player has genetic limits on his natural speed and quickness. Ask your coach for suggestions. Basketball is a game of sudden explosions of movement and sudden changes of direction. Irregardless of those genetic-based factors you can't change, there are things you can do to become quicker:

- Be in the best offensive and defensive positions.
- Learn to anticipate rather than to react.
- Learn to fake well and explode off your planted foot.
- Be unpredictable.
- Learn how to scout your opponent.

3. If I don't have good offensive skills yet, what can I do to get the coach's attention?

If you don't have good offensive skills while other players do, you are at a definite disadvantage. You must work extra hard on developing your non-ballhandling skills. Skills, such as playing good defense, setting screens, rebounding and blocking out, can be learned more quickly than shooting and dribbling skills.

You must work harder on your offensive skills than the other players if you want to gain a competitive advantage on them. Coaches love players who give 110 percent all the time. They also love players who pay attention and know the team's offenses and defenses well. Desire with intensity, brains, and lots of practice are the keys to improving quickly and getting the attention of the coach.

4. What is expected of me since I have been promoted during mid-season?

Ask yourself, "Why was I promoted? What was I doing well?" Then, keep doing it, and work harder to do even better. Don't be shy or tentative; be confident and aggressive!

The coach doesn't promote a player in mid-season to sit idly on the bench. The coach will expect you to play and to contribute. A coach usually promotes a player when the player can help the team, or because the player has made considerable improvement and can now improve more rapidly by playing against better players. If you have any doubts, ask the coach what he expects of you.

5. How do I get more involved in the offense?

Make certain you are a team player. Know the offense and defense well, and hustle 100 percent of the time. When you get the ball, make something happen. Quickly make a shot, make a move to the basket, or pass to an open teammate. The more aggressive players will quit looking to pass to a player if he is tentative and who never makes anything happen when he gets the ball.

Some young players hang around outside waiting for a pass while other players take the ball toward the basket or fight for a rebound. The ball is seldom passed back outside in these situations unless the coach emphasizes doing so in practice. Get involved. Fight for rebounds and loose balls. If you turn up the defensive intensity level, the players may notice a change in your attitude. Try to shut down anyone you're matched up against in drills or in scrimmages (including the "star" players).

6. I am the best free-throw shooter on the team, but I never seem to get the ball when we are in the bonus or at the end of the game. What do I need to do?

Evaluate your game. If you are only a three-point shooter, you will seldom ever go to the free-throw line. Players who are making moves to the basket are the ones who go to the free-throw line. When your team is ahead at the end of a game, the other team will be forced to foul the best ballhandlers. If you aren't a good dribbler or ballhandler, or if you aren't aggressive about going to the basket, you need to develop these skills.

If you are a good all-around player, the opposing team will try to keep you from getting the ball in these situations. You must work harder to get open if you want the ball.

7. My coach says I should anticipate better. How can I do that?

Anticipation, either on offense or defense, improves your effectiveness and "apparent quickness." You can't anticipate anything if you wait to see what happens. Anticipation requires that you understand what is likely to occur, and your mind and body are already preparing to react.

On defense, anticipation means that you realize that the offense is probably going to do something because it is available. For example, your defensive teammates have stopped the dribbler, and the other outlet pass areas appear to be well-defended. The passer will probably look to reverse the ball. If you don't realize that this is likely to occur shortly after the player looks to your side, you may be too slow reacting and will seldom intercept the pass.

On offense, anticipation is important as well. If you have hit two or three long shots, the defensive player will be charging fast to try to deny or block your shot. If he does charge, a good fake and a quick move will get you on the way toward the basket for a layup or a short pull-up jumper.

A good passer must anticipate when a teammate is coming off a screen. He must start to prepare mentally and physically to pass as the teammate approaches the screen, so the pass can be delivered to the cutter when he is most open. If the passer waits until he sees the cutter is open before preparing to pass, the defense will catch up. Players commonly make the mistake of not delivering the pass at the right moment.

8. I didn't make the junior high (ninth-grade or junior varsity) team and I really want to play. What can I do?

First ask yourself, "Am I ready to give 100 percent effort and truly work everyday to improve my skills and fundamentals?" If you want it bad enough to make a true commitment, Go For It! Visit with the coach who cut you. Tell him of your commitment and ask him for his help. In this regard, the following factors apply:

- The coach should be able to tell you what the first things you need to work on are.
- The coach can assign drills that you can work on at home and can help you find leagues to play in during the off-season.
- Keep in touch periodically with the coach, asking for his advice or tips.

If the coach sees your improvement and determination, you may have a better chance to make the team the next year if your are still a marginal player. Teachers and coaches tend to love players who give the extra effort on their own and have a true desire to work hard. Learn how to practice effectively by yourself or with one other person.

You may find that your true reward for your efforts is the improved level of self-confidence that you will gain from knowing that you can get better at anything if you work hard at it. In life, you will seldom receive great rewards unless you venture out and work hard for what you believe.

Coaches can and do make mistakes in judgment. As a sophomore in high school, Michael Jordan didn't make the basketball team. Who were the players that did make it? Subsequently, with determination, he went back and worked hard every day to improve and to prove the coach wrong. In a similar vein, many junior high, high school, and college players in all sports have been told they would never make it. However, they believed in their dream. They learned to use their abilities to the maximum through hard work and a determination to succeed. As a result, these players went on to succeed at the next level.

9. Sometimes I don't understand what I am supposed to do, and I am afraid to ask the coach because everyone else seems to understand. What should I do?

If you don't know what to do, tell the coach you don't understand. Once he explains it, he expects you to know it. A pet peeve of coaches is having to explain the same thing over and over because players weren't paying attention when they explained it a few minutes before. Remember:

- Listen and pay attention to what the coach is explaining.
- Learn what the coach wants.
- Then do it!

If you don't ask, the coach will still notice when you mess up, but he may not know why you messed up. The coach may think you are not hustling or not paying attention. Coaches tend to like players who ask how to get better. If you ask, you must work extra outside of practice to improve. After you ask, the coach will pay attention to see how you do. If you work hard and improve, the coach will notice your improvement and may be more attentive to helping you improve even further. If you don't work hard and don't improve, the coach will also notice and will assume you are all talk and no action.

10. What other things must I do if I want to be an outstanding player?

In addition to being a fundamentally sound player, you must develop confidence in your ability to score consistently in one-on-one situations and defensively to force the offensive player to take unwanted and low-percentage shots. You must give a 100 percent effort every day and in every way!

11. What is leadership?

In high school and college, a coach wants leadership to be exhibited on his team, but often the kids don't know what leadership is. Coaches expect the team's seniors to exert leadership because those players have been around the program the longest and usually have the most experience. The seniors should know what the coach expects. In some situations, seniors have waited their turn to start, but they may not be the best players or best leaders on the team. If the seniors are insecure as well as being less talented, there can be problems with team morale.

Does the leadership have to come from a senior? No, leadership can come from any player who knows the team's objectives, plays well, and gives 100 percent in practice and games. A leader leads by example. A leader does what it takes to help the team, and the leader thinks of the team before himself. The leader encourages others and sometimes challenges others if they aren't playing smart or giving 100 percent. A leader never asks anyone to do anything that he doesn't routinely do.

12. I never get the ball passed to me, what do I need to do?

If you want the ball, you have to work to get open. Inexperienced players are often open, but they are behind the play. The teammates are taking the ball to the basket, and they can't see behind them. Teammates like to pass to players who work hard, are aggressive and unselfish. Don't be a player who stands around waiting for the ball so he can shoot. Work hard to get open, learn to take the ball to the basket, and look to pass to open teammates. Learn to move without the ball! When you get the ball, make something good happen! This can be a shot, drive, or pass.

13. What should I expect if I am a younger player competing against an older player?

The older player will almost always be given the first chance to do well if players on the team are close in their skills. A young player should always expect the senior to be given the first opportunity to succeed. Usually, the seniors have worked hard for three years. The older player will have to play himself out of the position, or the younger player will have to outplay him in practices, scrimmages, and games. If the younger player wants to earn the starting position, he will have to prove to his coach and his teammates that he deserves it. Any other way may create a problem (such as jealousy) on the team.

14. What do coaches want from a player?

- Plays great defense.
- Makes few mistakes.
- Knows and executes the offense well.
- Makes something happen when he is on the court.
- Is a scorer.

A good young player should easily be able to do the first three. The other two will come with experience and hard work.

15. What can I do to get better?

Play smart:

- Learn the game.
- Improve your skills to the maximum.
- Scout and know your opponent.
- Learn to anticipate.

Play with intensity:

- Never give less than 100 percent in practice or games.
- Be aggressive.
- Don't stand and watch. Anticipate and be prepared to react quickly.
- Know the proper techniques that will make you more effective.
- Challenge on offense.
- Get back on defense quickly every time.
- Always assume a shot will be missed and be ready to grab the rebound. Follow your own shot.
- Never relax on defense. Always be ready to react quickly.

Work harder than anyone else. Work extra, but make that practice count by practicing smart. Learn to "get the edge."

16. Why am I always getting in foul trouble and sitting on the bench?

Most fouls are called on defense because the player:

- Isn't in proper defensive position.
- Doesn't play defense by moving his feet.
- Reaches or slaps at the ball.

Review several game films, and see if you can determine why the fouls were called. Don't be lazy! Good defense involves hard work and hustle. Move your feet to maintain good defensive position. If you do reach for the ball, you must not allow yourself to be beaten because you were not moving your feet or you were leaning forward. You should always go for the ball with the hand that is on the ballside. Don't reach across your body. This movement throws your shoulder into the player and gets you out of a good, balanced defensive position. If you reach for a dribble, reach from below and try to deflect the ball while it is low and close to the floor.

Offensive fouls, such as charging, are caused by not looking down at the floor. Your head and eyes should be up so you can see the play developing. Were you out of control in the air as you took a shot or passed the ball? Did you try to jump up and reach over a defender near the basket as you shot or dunked the ball?

17. Why is the coach always on my case? I can't seem to do anything right!

The coach is on your case because he believes you can do much better, and he wants to see you do well. A player should be concerned if the coach never cares enough to correct or reprimand him when he is not doing things correctly. If a coach offers constructive criticism, accept it without giving excuses. If you ever feel criticism was unjustified, work that much harder to prove to the coach what type of player you are.

18. How can a player make up for being short or slow?

A short or slow player must learn to get the edge in every manner possible if he is to out-play taller, faster players. You must learn to do the things you do better than the other players. Learn everything you can in this section and more. Develop into a complete ballplayer with well-balanced skills. Be ambidextrous when it comes to dribbling, passing, and taking short shots around the basket. Be an attacking dribbler who penetrates a defense looking to score or pass. In addition, you should:

- Learn to be a scorer. Shoot with a quick release. You cannot jump stop in the lane and shoot over players who are much taller. You need to learn to shoot the running jump shot and how to slide into the open areas on a drive. Learn to shoot with contact.
- Know your opponents (and yourself).
- Learn to use your body. Use your body as a shield to prevent a taller defender from getting to the ball.
- Learn to use your brain. A smaller player must use his brain to get every advantage he can. Pay attention to the little details. Develop good court awareness.
- Understand the game and game situations. Play smart! Learn to anticipate on defense and offense.
- Don't try to block the shots of taller players; you will get more fouls than blocks. Instead, play more aggressive defense before the player gets the ball.

➤ Be an excellent free-throw shooter. If you are an attacking ball-handler, you will shoot a lot of free throws. You must want the ball at the end of a half or the game so you can go to the line.

19. Why don't I get to play more? The starter is tall and quick but he doesn't play defense or rebound? He still doesn't know the offense (defense), and he makes frequent mistakes and turnovers.

You can't coach height or speed. Coaches will often give the taller or quicker player the first chance to succeed. The other player may have to play himself out of the starting position. Accept it and try harder to develop your strength. You have to work hard, be patient, and be ready when your chance comes.

Beat your teammate in practice. This is friendly competition so get an intense basketball attitude. Don't let anyone beat you; you beat them. Practice each scrimmage as if it were a game. Scout your teammate as you would an opponent. Look for tendencies and habits. This approach will allow you to make adjustments and anticipate better.

Understand the offense and defense your team plays! Many high school and college players learn the offense and defense very slowly. Coaches are impressed with players who quickly learn what to do. So pay attention and learn!

Don't make mistakes and turnovers. Coaches often are impressed with a player's speed, quickness, or height, even though that particular individual may not play well. These players will often get a first chance to succeed and often have to play themselves out of the position. Coaches hope they can teach the good athlete to be a good basketball player. Quite often, the athlete isn't dedicated enough to work extra hard to become a good player. Mistakes lose ball games. Because coaches know this, they will turn to the smart player who gets the job done without many mistakes. Ask the coach what you need to improve. Then do it!

20. What do I do if I lose my starting spot and my playing time is going down?

If you have lost your position, there is a reason. It is easy to blame the coach or your teammates. However, you must re-dedicate yourself to earning back your spot. Find out what you have done wrong or what you need to do better. Among the steps that you should take are the following:
➤ First ask yourself why you think a person has beaten you out. Be objective. Has the player been playing better than you have? Did you make mistakes or fail to do what the coach wanted?

- Evaluate the other player's style of play. Does your teammate play an aggressive defense, trying to harass the offense, deflecting passes and anticipating passes? On offense, is the other player pushing the ball up the floor, penetrating and attacking the basket? Adjust to the player's tendencies.
- Objectively review game films. What does the coach want? What does the other player do well that you don't do? What do you need to do differently?
- Pay attention while the coach is teaching someone else. Learn from the situation. What does the coach tell the other player he did well? What did he say the player needed to improve on? If that player beat you out, you really need to listen.
- Consult with the coach. Ask what you need to improve on, and what you need to do differently. Don't be hurt or defensive if the coach tells you something you didn't want to hear. Just say, 'thanks, I will do better.' Ask the coach if he has any drills or tips that you can use to help you improve. Then go to work.
- Develop a sound basketball attitude. During drills and scrimmages, shut down anyone you are matched-up against while on defense; offensively, be aggressive and beat your opponent.

21. What does the coach expect of me? How am I doing? What is my role on the team?

These are questions that players at all levels have struggled with. In fact, these may be the most common questions players ask. For anyone to have self-confidence and to develop as a player, he must know his status and role on the team, and the coach's expectations of him. The coach should communicate this information to each player on the team periodically. If your coach hasn't, you may need to visit with him to discover the answers.

Summary Points

For players to be focused, motivated, and free to develop to their fullest potential as individuals, they must be comfortable and free of the typical problems teenagers and teammates deal with. Before a coach can eliminate these distractions through leadership and communication, he must first be aware of and accept the fact that they exist.

CHAPTER 16

Players with College Potential

Coaching players with college potential can be a source of great joy to coaches. With such an opportunity comes different responsibilities and challenges. High school players and their parents look to the coach to lead them through these times and help the players to fulfill their dreams of playing basketball at the next competitive level.

Expectations of the Players and Parents

At a minimum, the players and parents expect the following:

- The coach to know if the player has college potential. If so, at what level of competition? What will be the likelihood of interest by college recruiters?
- The player to have a chance to demonstrate the player's strengths in the coach's offensive and defensive schemes.
- The coach to consult with the player during the year on what he needs to work on outside of practice in order to continue to improve.
- The coach to explain to the player and the parents what they should expect once the recruiting process is started.
- The coach to work hard to help his players get scholarships. The coach is expected to have contacts with other high school and college coaches.

What Responsibilities Does a Coach have to Players with College Potential?

In order to better understand the extent of his responsibilities to players with college potential, a coach needs to address the following issues:

- Does the coach have a responsibility to help the player be discovered by the colleges?

> Does the coach have a responsibility to prepare players for college athletics?
> Does the high school coach have an obligation to help the players and their families understand the recruiting process and what collegiate athletics is like?

High school coaches must answer these questions before the season starts if they have a special player. The player and his parents have probably never been through this experience before, and they will look to the coach for information and guidance.

Does the Coach have a Responsibility to Prepare a Player for College Athletics?

Yes, he does, if the player has the ability and the desire—but not at the expense of the team. If the coach believes in the cardinal rules of coaching, he is already committed to developing every player to his fullest potential. As the coach evaluates his team each year and decides on the offensive and defensive schemes, he must decide how to use these special players within the team concept.

If the team's offensive and defensive schemes don't fully utilize the player's abilities, the coach should continue to help the player develop all of his skills! He should consult with the player and explain how he is helping the team, especially if some of the player's skills aren't being used fully. This step will help eliminate the doubt the player might have if he knows he can do more.

Encourage the player. Help him be an even better player. Offer him suggestions to work on outside of practice. Consider designing a few special plays that will utilize his skills in a critical situation. These plays could prove to be very effective, since the opponents may not be prepared for it. If the player sacrifices himself for the team, the coach owes it to the player to let the colleges know of the player's true ability.

The Coach Needs to Be Involved in the Recruiting Process

If the coach feels a player has college potential, he should consult with the player and his parents. The coach should find out the player's desires and objectively inform the player of his chances of playing after his high school career has been completed and at what level. The player and his parents must be informed of the realities of recruiting, including the possibility that the player may not play in college.

Colleges often send written information during or after a player's junior year, if the college thinks they might recruit the player in the future. The high school coach should ask the player if he would like help with being recruited, if this process occurs. The player needs to have an open and honest relationship with his coach. The coach should encourage the player to visit him anytime he has concerns or just needs to talk. The coach can be of immense help to the player and his family during this time.

During a player's senior year, the player will often feel some self-imposed pressures to do well if he is hoping to get a scholarship. This feeling is especially true for those players who are college material, but aren't being recruited heavily. Tell the player to not worry about his performance, even if he has a bad game. Encourage the player to go play, have fun and enjoy his senior year. Tell him you will do everything you can to help him get the opportunity to play somewhere.

Getting Discovered Isn't Easy

Those athletes who are excellent players, who aren't blue-chip recruits or who don't fit the college coach's perception of what a player looks like, may find it hard to be discovered. Most college coaches look for the great athlete with skills who can step in and contribute now. By doing so, they often overlook good athletes—with great skills and a burning desire to improve. The truth is, some college coaches think they can teach any basketball player with great natural athletic abilities to be a great player. So, why should they take a chance on a lesser athlete? After all, they reason, you cannot coach height and speed.

In reality, college coaches often misjudge talent and potential. In fact, many college and professional athletes were overlooked by the major college programs. In fact, many college and professional athletes were overlooked by the major college programs.

Many college and professional athletes were overlooked by the major college programs.

Truth be known, very few full-athletic scholarships are available each year. For example, most NCAA Division I schools only offer, on the average, three to four scholarships per year since a limit exists on the number of scholarships allowed per team. Given the fact that thousands of individuals play high school ball, and each state only has a few Division I or II schools, the math isn't encouraging to someone who expects to be recruited.

How Do Players Get Discovered?

Years ago, players who carried their teams to the state tournament were considered the best players. Unfortunately, many good players on weaker teams were ignored, unless they had previously developed a reputation. In many respects, this situation is still true. The difference is that now reputations often are initially developed when a player is a freshman or sophomore, based on his performance on the varsity or by excelling during summer competition. College recruiters expect college prospects to contribute early in their high school careers. The player is usually expected to have established a reputation by the end of his junior year. College coaches expect to scout many of the best players at state or national AAU or BCI tournaments or in a few invitational basketball camps. The recruiters want to get a better feel of how each player will do when he is playing against the best competition available. A young player with college potential should try to get on "select teams," competing in high-level spring and summer tournaments. These organizations generally have competitions for players of all ages.

Living in a rural area may make it even more difficult for a player to get noticed unless his high school makes it to the state tournament. College recruiters and scouting services feel their time is better spent in large cities, where they can attend several different tournaments without much travel time or expense. In other words, if you are a player with college potential living in a rural area and attending a smaller school, you should not assume the colleges will discover you.

At a minimum, players should do the following to improve their chances of being discovered:

> Be a complete, versatile player.
> Work very hard in the off-season o develop new skills and perfect old ones.
> Do everything they can do to help their high school team be successful.
> Practice extra during the season, at least several times a week.
> Play high-level competition, teams such as being on AAU or BCI teams, during spring and summer months.
> In junior high, attend quality college camps. In high school, attend the highest quality college camps available.

The reality is college coaches often overlook many very good players.

What Type of Player Impresses Coaches?

Players who are exceptionally tall or fast quickly get the attention of coaches. Recruiters are looking for great athletes whom they hope will turn into good or great college basketball players. The reality is college coaches often overlook many very good players. As such, shorter and/or slower players with exceptional skills may have to work extra hard to prove themselves.

College coaches generally look first for great athletes with good basketball skills and/or exceptionally tall players, then for great athletes with average skills, and finally for average-height players with good quickness and exceptional skills.

Types of College Prospects and Their Chance of Being Recruited

As a rule, the following observations often reflect the realities of the recruiting process:

- Very tall and/or quick players on an excellent team have a very good chance of being recruited.
- Average-height players with good skills and quickness on an excellent team that makes it far into the state playoffs probably will be offered a scholarship or a grant. This is especially true if the program has a reputation of producing college players.
- Average-height players with good quickness and excellent skills on an average-to-good team are not likely to be discovered.
- Colleges easily overlook players who will need to change positions in college. These players need to get the coaches' attention by having great athletic ability or exceptional skills. Colleges want to be certain the player has the skills to make the transition. They will not offer a scholarship to an athlete unless they are certain that he possesses the skills necessary to play at the next level. For example, a tall, good-shooting point guard without blazing speed might be a shooting guard in college. An average-height low post player might be a power forward in college.

Regardless of the aforementioned observations, even if an individual is the star player on a state-ranked team no guarantee exists that he will be offered a scholarship.

Another factor that can impact the recruiting process is the fact high school players often play positions they would not play in college. Accordingly, if the high school system does not allow the player to demonstrate all his abilities, the college recruiter is forced to make judgments on what is seen on the floor. Those judgments may be wrong. The recruiter also may believe that if the player isn't from one of the largest schools, he may not have competed against enough outstanding players to prove he can play at the collegiate level. Sometimes that may be true, but some quality small-school programs schedule much larger schools in order to challenge their players to be ready for the playoffs. The following example illustrates this point:

> ...even if an individual is the star player on a state-ranked team no guarantee exists that he will be offered a scholarship.

"A small school was ranked in the state's top 10 at the end of the season and was ranked #1 in the state at the start of the next year. The team went 30-0, while defeating larger playoff-bound schools in non-district games. The team was upset by a point one game shy of the state tournament. The star was a 5'11" post player who had scored an average of 26 points a game over the last two seasons. In the coach's system, he always wanted her to be near the basket so she could use her height advantage.

The girl was very athletic and could run the floor. She had worked hard the previous two summers developing her ball-handling and outside shooting skills by playing in summer tournaments. From a recruiting standpoint, her problem was that no one knew how good she really was. Weeks passed after the end of the season, and no colleges had contacted her. Luckily, she was invited to play on a local select team in a seniors-only tournament in which she was in an offense that allowed her to show her abilities to run the floor and play a wing position. Immediately after the tournament, she was offered several scholarships."

If the star player on a #1 ranked team in the state has a hard time being discovered, how difficult will it be for other players to be discovered if they aren't as fortunate? In this instance, what could the high school coach have done? Unfortunately, there are some coaches of top programs who make no effort to assist their player in the recruiting process. Even though these players have given their heart and soul to their high school team, their coaches have failed to exert any effort on their behalf to enhance their chances of being recruited. In the aforementioned instance, for example that coach should have contacted several colleges to let them know of her abilities. In reality, parents and players fully expect their high school coach to care enough to be actively involved in getting recognition for the team's deserving players.

What Should the Coach Do If the Player Isn't Being Recruited as Much as Expected?

The coach has a responsibility to make some contacts to determine why the player isn't getting any attention. If a particular college has not evaluated the player, the coach needs to find out why not. If the player has been evaluated, the coach should ask the coaches who have done the evaluating to share their opinions. If the coach thinks the recruiters are wrong, he should work that much harder to help the player find a college that would be interested.

In either case, the coach will need to do some promoting of the player. The coach should remember to be objective in the player's evaluation, since the coach's reputation as a judge of talent is on the line. If the player turns out to be a good player, college coaches will pay attention when a player is recommended in the future. The reverse is also true. College coaches tend not to listen to high school coaches who have previously offered less-than-honest feedback concerning a player's performance.

At some point during or after the season, the coach should sit down with the player and the player's parents and share what he has learned about the player's scholarship opportunities. Most players have expectations about what recruiting will be like. If the player isn't getting much attention, he probably has some concerns. The coach should accurately assess the player's status as a potential college player, and what the player's options are concerning playing at the next level. The coach should explain what he would like and might be able to do to help the player in this regard. He should also ask the parents and the player what course they would like to pursue.

As a general rule, the truth is that the only individuals who have the best interests of the player at heart are the player's family and his high school coach. Recruiters often may show an interest early in the careers of many of the top high school players. They then maintain communication with that individual until they decide which players they want the most and have the best chance of signing. College coaches can only take a few of the many players they recruit. The other players, with their expectations soaring, are left hoping someone else will come around with an offer. On occasion, the player is never even informed that the college is no longer interested—the college just stops contacting the player.

If a player isn't being seriously recruited, the player and his coach may have to take the initiative. One option in this regard are the numerous colleges and universities at the NCAA Division II, III and NAIA Division I, II, and III level. Many of these institutions wait until after the NCAA spring signing period is over before they seriously start offering scholarships. In essence, the large programs get their pick of the players, and the smaller programs start scrambling to find the best players still available.

If a player isn't being seriously recruited, the player and his coach may have to take the initiative.

Smaller schools with limited scholarships and/or educational grants are always looking for tips about good players. In reality, schools with limited athletic budgets are often forced to depend upon tips from respected sources to help them find the best players available. They find out about quality players from other coaches, recruiting lists, high school coaches, and friends of the college or university.

A player should undertake the following steps at the end of his junior year either if he has received recruiting letters or inquiries or if he would prefer to play at a smaller school:

- Take the SAT or ACT college entrance exams during his junior year or early that summer.
- Get a copy of his high school transcript and class ranking, if available.
- Verify his compliance with the NCAA academic eligibility requirements (i.e., anticipated completion of the core 13 courses with a 2.5 GPA).
- Compile a highlight tape demonstrating his skills against quality teams.
- Along with his family, decide on the academic institutions that he would prefer to attend. Attend camps for advanced varsity players at these schools if available. These camps provide an opportunity for the player to learn about the school and the coach, and for the coach to evaluate the player.
- Have his high school coach call the college coach and follow up with a letter of recommendation for the player. A description of the player's skills, height, stats, and overall abilities should be provided. The player's ability to play other positions, or other attributes of the player that may not be obvious on video or in a scouting report, should be discussed in the letter. If the player is a smart, quick learner, and a leader on and off the court, his coach should be sure to mention it. Appropriate academic and eligibility information, along with a highlight tape featuring the player, should be mailed with the letter. The same protocol can be followed during the player's senior year if needed.

Scholarships and Grants-in-Aid

Scholarships and grants-in-aid are important to the player's family. NCAA Division I colleges offer full athletic scholarships. Smaller colleges and universities offer partial scholarships and/or grants. Scholarships and grants do not have to be repaid. To receive federal grants-in-aid, the player's family must meet the eligibility requirements that are based on income. Low income and low-middle income families with several children may qualify for different state and federal grant programs that will pay for their children to attend college. All factors considered, players from middle- or upper-income families will have little chance of getting grants-in-aid.

Most NAIA and NCAA Division II and III colleges and universities depend heavily upon government grants to subsidize a student's education. Many of these institutions utilize grants as a primary source of tuition income for their athletes. The first question the college or university often wants to know during an official visit is whether your family qualifies for federal or state grants. If so, there's no problem. In these situations, a middle-income family may have difficulty affording the cost of college unless the child qualifies for academic scholarships. The only other choice would be student loans that have to be repaid.

High school coaches should always remember that scholarships and grants-in-aid are very important to the economic security of these families. Securing financial assistance can severely reduce a family's financial hardship for years to come.

When a Player Gets a College Scholarship

If a player gets a scholarship, the coach needs to visit with the player and his parents to inform them of what to expect in collegiate basketball. College basketball will be much different than high school. Among the more notable differences are the following:

- College basketball is a business.

College coaches are under the pressure to win now. The player will be asked to work harder than he has ever worked, both in the weight room and on the court. In reality, the collegiate level is stocked with many excellent players. As a result, coaches look to the players who can contribute now; often, they do so at the expense of other players. With the coach having limited practice time and a pressure to win, he may not be willing to spend extra time developing a player if there are other players on the team who can do the job at this point in time. Coaches expect the player to work extra hard to catch up if he wants playing time.

- First impressions are very important.

The player must be ready to compete. Therefore, when the player shows up on the college campus, he should be ready to take full advantage of his opportunities. In that regard, he should:

> Get in great physical shape.
> Be attentive.
> Work to quickly learn the offense and defense.
> Hustle, hustle, hustle!
> Play great, hustling defense. Coaches love an all-out defensive effort.
> Be confident. Freshmen can contribute.

High school coaches should always remember that scholarships and grants-in-aid are very important to the economic security of these families.

➤ Be prepared to possibly play a different position in college. Start working to develop the skills necessary to play at the next level as soon as the high school season is over.

• <u>The college game will be more physical and faster-paced.</u>

The college game involves more of an emphasis on the player's level of physical condition. As a result, the college player will have to do much more running and weight training than in high school. So, he should get in shape before he arrives on campus. He must also learn to play quicker. The college game is considerably faster than the high school game. Everyone is faster, the lanes close more quickly, and the defense is much better.

• <u>Confidence is Critical.</u>

When high school stars become substitutes getting very little attention or encouragement from the coach, the player can easily get down on himself. This circumstance is a common problem for freshmen who have never been substitutes. They do not know how to handle the situation. Such a player, who may never have suffered from self-doubt, will need the coach's expertise and encouragement. Will the player get it? Hopefully, the coaching staff is supportive, but the player should not count on it. The player's primary support system will be his family and friends, including his teammates. The player should visit with his coach and find out what skills he needs to improve.

All College Coaches are Not Created Equal

Players and parents often think that a college coach must be much better than the players' high school coach or he would not be coaching at the collegiate level. This perception is not necessarily true. In fact, many great high school coaches exist who could be great college coaches. For various reasons, they just didn't get the opportunity to excel at the next competitive level. By the same token, some college coaches are far from all that they could or should be.

Players should not expect every college coach to be what they want in a coach. As such, they should ask questions during the recruiting process. Talk with team members in private. Get a list of all recent graduates, both starters and non-starters. Visit with them about their experience with the coach. Would they choose the coach and the school again? A marginal coach, or a system that doesn't fit the style and strengths of the player, can ruin the collegiate basketball experience for which he has worked so long.

CHAPTER 17

Dealing with Parents

One of the great fears that many junior high and high school coaches have involves the problems they have dealing with parents. Is this fear justified? If you coach a child, you have a relationship with the parents. The parent-coach relationship can be whatever the coach wants: informative and supportive or intimidating and confrontational. Which would you prefer?

Parents want the best for their children. It would be unnatural for them to be otherwise. Parents entrust their children to the coach, believing that he will try to improve every player on the team to the fullest. This belief implies that each player will be given quality practice and game time. Parents are looking to the coach not only for teaching basketball, but also for the expertise in recognizing and dealing with the problems that may arise with the players and the team. Parents believe the coach will have great interpersonal and communication skills. The coach is expected to effectively communicate with his players and their parents in a way that problems are prevented (or at least minimized).

At the initial team and parents meeting, the ground rules for a successful relationship should be laid down. It is important for everyone to know each other's expectations and desires. At this meeting, the coach should have the parents vocally agree to his philosophy and rules. If the players and parents are part of establishing the rules for the season, they are more likely to be more supportive when difficult times arise. (A more detailed discussion of coach-parent communication can be found at the end of the chapter on communication.)

If the coach communicates poorly with the parent and child, the parent will become more protective and assertive if the player is struggling. If a parent feels his child is not getting a fair and equal opportunity, the parent will usually be quite unhappy. The coach should count on it! On the other hand, if the parent knows the coach is coaching by the cardinal rules, the parent will be more likely to be very supportive of the

At the initial team and parents meeting, the ground rules for a successful relationship should be laid down. It is important for everyone to know each other's expectations and desires.

coach, because he will have first-hand knowledge of how hard the coach works to help every player.

Classification of Parents

Basically, the coach will encounter four types of parents:

• <u>Concerned parents.</u> These parents know little about basketball. They trust that the coach will teach their child everything he needs to learn. They only become involved if a crisis occurs.

• <u>Concerned and involved parents.</u> Some of these parents are extremely knowledgeable about basketball. They will look at the game and player management with a critical eye. On one hand, these parents can be the best supporters of the program and a great help to the coach. On the other hand, they can be a pain if they feel the coach doesn't function by the cardinal rules or doesn't know basketball as well as he should.

• <u>Disinterested parents.</u> Disinterested parents are not interested enough in their children's activities to show up for meetings, scrimmages, or games. How terrible their children must feel. The coach can be an important part of these children's lives. Some of these parents do not even pick up their children when the team arrives at the school after a late-night game. A distinction must be made between disinterested parents and those parents who have honest conflicts. Some parents work unusual shifts or work several jobs to support the family.

• <u>Interfering parents.</u> These parents may or may not know much about basketball. They are concerned either only about winning at all costs or that their child is given preferential treatment. These parents try to influence the coach by complaining or causing other distractions. Interfering parents are the individuals who tell their child to disregard some things the coach has told the players to do. An interfering parent is also the obnoxious parent who yells and degrades the coach and the referees. The parent who tries to coach his child from the stands is another example of an interfering parent.

The Parent from Hell

Occasionally, a team has a parent from hell. In reality, every profession has to deal with difficult individuals. The coach should take it as a challenge to his interpersonal skills. The parents at the initial team meeting of parents, players, and coaches should have agreed upon what is acceptable behavior by the parents. The key is to have everyone to be aware of and agree to what constitutes acceptable behavior prior to the beginning of the season. All factors involved, the parent feels more pressure when he has previously agreed to what is acceptable. This self-imposed agreement to abide by the rules set by the coach, but accepted by the players and the parents, places a strong feeling of peer pressure to comply. If a problem with a parent does develop, the coach should address it the very first time it occurs. He should not wait to deal with the problem. The coach must fulfill his promises and those expectations to which he agreed, or he may give a parent an excuse to not comply.

Tip for parents: Don't be a parent from hell! It will embarrass your child and may affect his play.

The key is to have everyone to be aware of and agree to what constitutes acceptable behavior prior to the beginning of the season.

When a Parent is a Coach's Boss

Undue pressures can be placed on a coach when a parent is a school board member, a school administrator, the school's principal or a faculty member. When the parent is the coach's boss, the coach must treat the player as he would any other child. Most parents in these positions are usually very supportive parents. Occasionally, however, a very enthusiastic parent holds one of these positions. This situation creates a very uncomfortable situation for the coach, whether intentional or unintentional. Insecure coaches may even feel a self-induced pressure for the child to be successful. A veteran coach knows it is best to deal with this potential conflict before a problem ever arises.

In reality, the parent who is the coach's boss should take the lead in addressing any potential problem before the child enters the program. On the other hand, if the subject has not been addressed before the season, the coach should consider broaching the subject. The coach can address the subject by saying that, in these situations, he always likes to make sure that everyone is on the same wave length, in order to ensure that no other parents will feel that any player will get preferential treatment. If he is asked how he would expect to handle the situation if a particular player wasn't good enough to be a varsity player, a starter, or in need of discipline, the coach can say, "I am sure you would want me to treat your child as I would any other child, isn't that correct? In these situations, I feel that we should be in agreement before I start coaching. You agree, don't you?"

In reality, the parent who is the coach's boss should take the lead in addressing any potential problem before the child enters the program.

• <u>The Parent is a Member of the School Board</u>

This situation is more of a problem in small rural school districts than in large metropolitan districts. Smaller districts don't have an administrative buffer zone, and the board members within these school systems are used to dealing with many of the day-to-day problems within the school district. As such, parents may interfere directly with the coach or indirectly by what they say to others. As a rule, small towns have few secrets, and rumors get back quickly to the coach. School board members who are parents of players should remain at arm's length. Any pressure on the coach, whether intentional or unintentional, is unfair to the child, the coach, and the team. The following is a true story and is probably played out many times a year across the country:

> "The seventh-grade basketball coach was being fired because a school board member did not like that he turned a relative in to the principal for disciplining. The nephew had been asked to leave a junior high gym because he was loud and abusive. Upon leaving, the student cursed at the coach and made an obscene finger gesture to him.
>
> After visiting with the coach and getting his permission to discuss his situation, a parent made an appointment for the following afternoon with the superintendent. That evening, the parent received a call from a junior high school teacher. The teacher said that in the 20 years she had been teaching in the school district, she had never seen anything upset the staff as much as the handling of this situation. The teacher said many loyal teachers were very concerned, and she hoped the superintendent could be urged to change his mind.
>
> The superintendent was well-thought of, with a reputation for fairness. The parent stated that he was concerned about the situation. First, because of his daughter's concern and, second, because of the call he had received the previous evening. During the course of the conversation, the superintendent stated the coach's contract was not being renewed for the following year, but they had already found him a job in another area of the state.
>
> The parent rephrased what he thought he heard. 'You are firing a good teacher and coach, against whom there have been no complaints by parents or other teachers. If he has violated no policies, why is he being fired? You think enough of him to already have him another job lined up. His only mistake was disciplining the nephew of a board member. No wonder the faculty is concerned! How could the board have made that decision, if the board has not yet convened?' The superintendent said the decision had been made.
>
> After further discussions, the superintendent promised he would relate the parent's concerns to the board as accurately as possible. The school board met on Monday, and the subject of not renewing the contract was not brought before the board. There was a collective sigh of relief among the faculty when they heard the news. The coach remained at the school for several years before moving to another city."

Unfortunately, situations like the aforementioned example occur every year, often with the result of the coach being given the choice of resigning or being fired. Coaches should never be submitted to this kind of pressure.

Summary Points

When a person coaches a child, he has a relationship with the child's parents. The coach will determine the type of relationship he wants to establish with the parents of his athletes. This relationship should be based on the needs and best interests of his players, his team, and his school, and should reflect his coaching philosophy and communication style.

When a person coaches a child, he has a relationship with the child's parents.

SECTION II

Fundamentals of Basketball

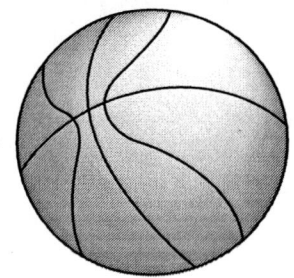

"The eight laws of learning are explanation, demonstration, imitation, repetition, repetition, repetition, repetition, and repetition."

— John Wooden

No player or team can be good if not fundamentally sound. There are many books on basketball that describe how to dribble and shoot or how to execute an offense or defense. This section of the book addresses fundamentals with a slightly different perspective, sometimes making suggestions that often aren't discussed elsewhere, such as ways to execute those skills better, how to practice smarter, and how to get a competitive edge.

The chapters in this section review the basics of basketball. Concepts that are not often stressed are discussed, such as how to teach an offense, how to teach a player to play quicker, or how to initiate a half-court offense.

Much of this section is intended not only to teach fundamentals, but also to assist the coach in teaching the player how to "get an edge" (i.e., how to do the little things that are so important in success). Players also need to learn how to practice intelligently on their own, scout their opponents, and utilize their time on the bench.

During the season, many high school teams are so busy working on offense and defense that they spend very little time on fundamentals. The coaches of these teams claim that there isn't enough time to get everything done. The more limited time is, the more critical it is to have fundamentally sound players who can learn offenses and defenses faster.

How can a team improve if the players don't become more fundamentally sound? Have you ever seen a team that was too fundamentally sound? Basketball is a team game that is dependent on players using their individual skills within the confines of an offensive or defensive team concept. Many of the parts of the offense or defense depend on the coordinated use of small-group skills. In reality, basketball can be broken down into individual skills, small-group skills, and team skills.

A lot of Individual skills include dribbling, passing, shooting, rebounding, and blocking out. Small-group skills involve two- or three-man games, such as the give-and-go, the pick-and-roll on offense, and helping out a teammate on defense. Team skills involve employing the combined and coordinated skills of the five players on the court in an offensive or defensive scheme.

The fastest way to improve fundamental skills is to utilize well-designed drills, especially if the drills are also designed to duplicate the skills and moves necessary in the offense or defense. Every player should strive to be a fundamentally sound and well-rounded ballplayer, knowledgeable about the game of basketball.

With the advent of the three-point shot, the importance of sound fundamentals has never been greater. Offenses are currently more likely to use posts further from the basket, and a tendency exists for more motion offenses in which posts are asked to have more wing skills and guards are asked to be scorers, not just spot-up shooters. As a result, all players should develop their fundamental skills to the maximum, since no player can ever be certain what skills he will need in the future if he is to get playing time.

Individual Skills

The basic offensive skills in basketball include catching the ball, pivoting, and then shooting, dribbling, or passing. Most players don't have to be encouraged to work on the dribbling and shooting skills. However, the other skills that are just as likely to win a ball game are often ignored. Players seldom think about defensive skills; they just play defense. If a player wants to develop to his potential, he should work to improve each of the following skills:

- Offensive non-ball skills:

  - Vision
  - Communicating
  - Faking
  - Offense without the ball:
    - Moving without the ball
    - Faking
    - Keeping the defender busy
  - Screen or picks:
    - Setting up a screen
    - Setting the screen
    - Using the screen
    - Resetting the screen

- Offensive ball skills:

  - Dribbling
  - Passing
  - Catching the ball
  - Pivoting
  - Faking
  - Moves
  - Shooting
  - Free throws
  - One-on-one skills

- Going-for-the-ball skills:

  - Getting open without the ball
  - Cutting
  - Catching
  - Rebounding

- Defensive skills:

  - Defensive position
  - Sliding
  - Sliding with pivots
  - Defending the ballhandler
  - Overplaying the defender
  - Beating the defender to the spot
  - Off-the-ball defense
  - Blocking out

- Seldom-taught skills:

  - Anticipation
  - Knowing your opponent
  - Setting up your opponent

- Two-man games:

  - Give-and-go
  - Screen (pick) and roll
  - Inside-outside game

Team Skills

Team skills involves coordinating the movement of the players in an organized manner so that the players know where and when to use their individual skills. An offense cannot function well either if the players are out of position or if they don't know when to cut or move. Defensive team skills require teaching the defenders to use proper technique and positioning so they are in position to defend their man and to help a teammate. Players need to understand the following team concepts:

❑ Offensive team concepts:

- Fundamentals of offense
- Transition offense
- Fastbreak offense
- Man-to-man offense
- Zone offense
- Press offense
- Out-of-bounds plays
- Special plays

❑ Defensive team concepts:

- Transition defense
- Man-to-man defense:
  - Denial defense
  - Help defense:
    - Sagging defense
    - Rotation defense
- Defending screens
- Zone defense

The chapters in this section discuss the fundamentals of basketball. They do not, however, try to explain how a player should bounce a ball or shoot a jump shot. Rather, this section presents information that may allow the player to improve greatly on the basic skills and on his knowledge and understanding of the game of basketball.

CHAPTER 18

Great teams must bond together. The players don't have to be great friends, but they must like and respect each other, and want each person to succeed. Teams will have players from different classes and with different friends and interests. The coach and the team captains should set the tone by trying to bring everyone together. The coach must set the tone of teamwork in practice. He should teach the team captains to encourage group extracurricular activities to assist in the bonding of the players. Players don't have to be great friends, but they do have to be great teammates!

THE ROLES OF THE PLAYERS

Most great teams have only two or three great scorers. The other players are role players who are critical for the success of any team. These players aren't expected to score a lot of points, but they are expected to fulfill their roles well. Every team needs a defensive specialist who can dog the lane or shut down the opponent's best player. Excellent rebounders who can play solid defense are special assets. An outstanding point guard is expected to be the quarterback of the team and have a good assist-to-turnover ratio.

Players need to know their role on the team. It is critical that every player understands what the coach expects of him. The coach should clearly define those expectations, along with the concept that if the player's skills improve, his role on the team may change.

The players don't have to be great friends, but they must like and respect each other, and want each person to succeed.

THE FIVE POSITIONS ON THE BASKETBALL TEAM

Through the years, the terminology used to designate the five players on the court has changed, as has the style of play. Even today, coaches on different teams may use different terminology for the same positions.

Years ago, most teams had two guards, one post or center, and two forwards. Teams that were lucky enough to have two tall players might use a two-post offense and one forward. Today, teams may have a variety of offenses, including one or two posts, no posts (i.e., three guards and two forwards), and other combinations. Generally speaking, most teams today have a point guard (No. 1), a shooting guard (No. 2 guard), an off-guard or wing (No. 3 guard), a power forward (No. 4 position), and a post or center (No. 5).

❑ The Point Guard

The point guard is the quarterback of the basketball team and is critical to the success of the team. A point guard doesn't have to be a great scorer to be a good point guard. However, the point guard should possess the following attributes:

- Ballhandling skills
- Passing skills
- Court awareness
- Knowledge of the offense and defense

A great point guard should also have the following characteristics:

- Is a threat to shoot or pass.
- Looks to fast break after a steal or a rebound.
- Beats the press with the dribble and attacks the basket immediately.
- Controls the tempo of the game.

Young players sometimes don't appreciate the importance of a good point guard. They feel they are being asked to play point, because they are small or because they don't have the physical abilities to play other positions. The point guard does not have to be a great scorer, but the team will be stronger if he is. The point guard has to be a smart player who truly understands the game of basketball. The point guard is responsible for taking control of the team on the floor.

• <u>What are the duties of the point guard?</u>

- The point guard is the ballhandler who must be able to get the ball up the court against intense pressure by very quick defenders. The point guard must become ambidextrous dribbling the ball and become used to intense defense, so that he is relaxed as he performs his other duties.
- The point guard is responsible for getting the ball up the court and initiating the offense by dribble penetration or passing the ball.

- The point guard should be the player the coach depends on to make smart decisions and to take charge on the court.
- The point guard must understand basketball well enough to quickly recognize the opponent's defense and can set up the appropriate offense. The point guard may have to remind his teammates where they need to be to initiate the offense.
- The point guard must vary the offense to avoid predictability.
- The point guard must be able to recognize special game situations, such as:
  - √ A teammate is hot and can't miss a shot. Feed him the ball! The offense should be run to take advantage of a particular player's hot streak until the defense stops the player or he cools off.
  - √ A particular play or a part of the offense is resulting in easy baskets. Keep doing it until they stop it.
  - √ If a dominant opposing player is in foul trouble, the point guard may want the offense to challenge the player in order to get another foul and get the player out of the game. If the opponent is playing conservatively to avoid another foul, he may let up on defense. The point guard should recognize this and attack.
- Clock awareness by the point guard is very important, if the team is to take advantage of every scoring possibility. One lost opportunity to score may decide the game. Clock awareness is very important at the end of a quarter, the first half, and the end of the game. The point guard always needs to be aware of the time on the clock as these situations approach. If the team has the ball in one of these situations with eight seconds or more, the point guard should expect the team to get a high-percentage shot or a foul, with a chance to go to the free-throw line.
- Controlling the tempo of the game is another important skill of the point guard.
  - √ If the team is running up and down the court and not scoring because of turnovers, or taking poor-percentage shots, the point guard must slow the game down and get the team back into a sound half-court offense.
  - √ If the team needs to play a more up-tempo game, the point should take charge.
  - √ At the end of the half, the point guard may need to slow the game down in the last minute, so the team gets a good opportunity to score and not leave enough time for the opponent to score if the shot is missed.
  - √ If the team is ahead near the end of the game, the point guard must realize that it may be more important to eat up the clock than to shoot.

√ In a close or tied game, the point guard may want to look for a transition or fast-break basket if the opportunity presents itself. This option may be most effective if the team doesn't usually play a transition game, and the opponent has come to expect the offense to walk the ball up the court.

• *Statistics to evaluate:* Point guards are often measured not by how many points they score, but by their assists and turnovers. This measure is usually considered separately or as an assist-to-turnover ratio. A ratio of 3:1 or higher is good. In other words, the point guard should have many more assists than turnovers. The point guard must always be aware of the fact that turnovers lose ball games.

❑ Shooting Guard (#2 Guard)

• *Skills needed:* The shooting guard should be a good shooter who is not afraid to take the big shot. The shooting guard should be a good three-point shooter.

• *Job description:* The shooting guard is usually the team's best outside shooter. He is not usually the best ballhandler, and he often gets open by using screens. The shooting guard is ready to immediately shoot, drive, or pass after coming off a screen. The shooting guard should be ready to rebound or get back on defense. Many players trying out for the team will compete for this position, since a spot-up shooter of average height and speed can play this position.

A great two guard normally possesses the following qualities:

> Is a great three-point shooter who can alter the opponent's defense.
> Is a scorer who can drive the lane, score or pass.
> Is a good ballhandler.

> **Point guards are often measured not by how many points they score, but by their assists and turnovers.**

• *Statistics to evaluate:* points, assists.

❑ Small Forward (#3 Guard)

• *Skills needed:* The #3 guard is a tall, athletic player who has the height to play inside and the ballhandling and shooting skills to play a guard position.

• *Job description:* The small forward must be an aggressive player who looks to rebound and take the ball to the basket. A small forward should be a good outside shooter and scorer who looks to score in the lane when driving. The forward should be a good mid-range jump shooter from around 14 to 16 feet. However, if he can also shoot the three-pointer, he will be a special asset.

A great small forward is characterized by the following attributes:

- Looks to be a scorer and a rebounder.
- Should be aggressive and want to take the ball to the basket.
- Should be a good free throw shooter, since he will frequently be fouled when he drives to the basket.
- Should possess post-up skills.

• *Statistic to evaluate:* triple-doubles (points, rebounds, and assists).

❑ Power Forward (#4 Position)

• *Skills needed:* The power forward is usually a tall, powerful player who is a cross between a post and a wing or small forward. This player should be a good rebounder and a scorer in both the lane and along the baseline.

• *Job description:* The power forward is an aggressive rebounder and has the offensive-post skills to score inside, as well as the facing the basket skills to score outside. He should be able to score at least fifteen feet from the basket.

Years ago, most offenses ran a two-post offense. Today, most teams run a one-post offense, and the other post has become a power forward who can run the floor. The power forward is expected to be an aggressive defender, both inside and outside.

A great power forward has the following attributes:

- Is a good rebounder.
- Is a scorer in the paint and along the baseline.
- Can shoot outside and drive to the basket.
- Sets and uses screens well.

• *Statistics to evaluate:* rebounds and put-backs.

❑ Post (Center or #5 Position)

Posts are usually the tallest players on the team, and often are not very good ballhandlers. The post has to be physical and aggressive. The post

The small forward must be an aggressive player who looks to rebound and take the ball to the basket.

The power forward is usually a tall, powerful player who is a cross between a post and a wing or small forward.

must be able to post-up well and catch the ball in a crowd, while being pushed and shoved. Defensively, the post is asked to clog the lane and prevent drives to the basket. The post is expected to be a good rebounder and a shot blocker. In years past, the post would be tall and slow and would seldom stray very far from the lane area.

In today's game, with the three-point shot and given the larger, faster players who are playing, the role of the post is changing. Today, many offenses require a mobile post. Many times during a game, a post may be asked to set or defend screens near the three-point line, either at the top of the circle or in the wing area. A post should possess good pick-and-roll skills. A post who can shoot from outside is an especially valuable player to an offense, since he will require the opposing post to come out to defend, thereby opening up the area under the basket.

- <u>What should a player work on if he is a post?</u>

Obviously, the player should work on the skills necessary for the offense or defense being run. In addition, the post should:

➢ Learn and analyze the offense to determine what types of skills are necessary to get open, to make a shot against a good defense, and to get a rebound.
➢ Recognize which shots are usually open in the man-to-man and zone offenses the team runs.
➢ Develop several complementary basic moves from the low-post area.

- <u>Posts need to be versatile.</u>

While players are learning the skills necessary to be successful at the post position, they should never limit their future potential by assuming they can and will only play this one position in the future. Young players in junior high should realize that they may grow at different rates and for different durations than their peers. As such, a tall player in the seventh grade, may not be considered tall when he is in the twelfth grade.

Players should continue to work on all the basic basketball skills and not just those used by the post. If enough time doesn't exist in practice, a player who wants to excel in the future should take it upon himself to work extra outside of practice. Most high school and college coaches are looking for the tallest and most talented players for every position. As a consequence, even if the player remains a post, he will be much more effective if he is a complete player.

- What skills are necessary to be a good post?

  ➤ Offensive post skills: A post is more effective if he has both low-post and facing-the-basket skills. A post who can shoot well further from the basket will draw his defender away from the lane. This scenario opens the floor up for the post and for his teammates to drive or cut to the basket.
    √ *Low post skills.* When a player posts up at the low-post position, he has established a position on the block near the basket. The player has his back to the basket as he establishes his position and prepares to catch a pass. Most low-post moves are initiated while the post has his back to the basket.
    √ *Facing-the-basket skills.* When a post is away from the basket, he can score more easily if he catches a pass and pivots to face the basket. Facing-the-basket skills are the same skills that a wing or forward needs. The player must be able to make a jump shot from 15 feet, pass, fake, and drive to the basket.
    √ *Ability to shoot freethrows.* The post should be a good free-throw shooter! A post who is an excellent free thrower is a special asset to the team. Posts have more free-throw opportunities because they are fouled more than any other player. There is no reason that a post cannot be the best free throw shooter on the team! Shooting is a learned skill, and the post must make a commitment to improve his free-throw accuracy.
    √ *Ability to shoot and rebound while being fouled.* Once a post has developed confidence in his shots and moves, he should participate in drills where he is jostled, bumped, or fouled. Basketball is often a very rough, "non-contact" sport. In reality, many bumps and fouls are not called, especially in the lane area, where the posts and forwards are usually positioned. A player must get used to a little rougher play, so when such play happens in a game, he has learned how to power through the foul and still make the shot, or at least get the shot off.

The great post has the following attributes:

  ➤ Dominates the lane defensively.
  ➤ Is a great rebounder.
  ➤ Is a great passer.
  ➤ Screens well.
  ➤ Possesses a variety of shots and moves.

- *Statistics to evaluate:* Points, rebounds, and blocks or altered shots.

- <u>Common mistakes that posts need to avoid.</u>

  ➤ Unnecessary dribbling is a cardinal mistake for any basketball player, but for a post, it is a sure way to lose the ball. While shooting at home or at practice, young players frequently get in the habit of dribbling the ball one time before they shoot, even if they do not move from their position. A dribble should be used only to quickly get a post to a more open area. Any unnecessary dribble will give the defense time to swarm the post.

  ➤ Not being ready to catch a pass. Some posts have a problem catching a pass cleanly without bobbling the ball. There are few excuses for dropping a good pass in practice or in a game. The two most common mistakes posts make are not being mentally and physically prepared to catch the ball. The player must have good court awareness and anticipate the likelihood of a pass and the type of pass it will probably be. If the player not only anticipates the pass but the possibility that the pass might be less than perfect, then the player will bobble fewer passes.

  ➤ If a post is standing around, especially when he is on the offside of the court, his defensive opponent will find it very easy to help his teammates. An offside post should find ways to keep his man occupied and worried about him. He should not make it easy for the defense; he should keep them busy. The coach should teach the post what he should do so he is ready to block out, rebound, cut, or screen at the proper time.

  ➤ Bringing the ball down low after getting an offensive rebound. If a post gathers an offensive rebound in scoring position, he should never bring the ball down low. Doing so allows shorter, quicker players the opportunity to steal the ball. After getting the rebound, the post should keep the ball above his head and quickly make a shot or pass.

  ➤ Not immediately looking to make an outlet pass after getting a defensive rebound. Some posts routinely rebound and bend over, protecting the ball while looking down, or pivot a couple of times before looking around to pass. The transition offense depends on a quick, accurate outlet pass.

  ➤ Being a "black hole" post. The term "black hole" refers to the astrophysical term describing an area in space where gravity is so strong that when any object, even light, enters the area, it never comes back out. On some basketball teams, when a guard passes the ball inside to a post, the post shoots every time he gets the ball, even if it is a poor-percentage shot, and even if the player is double- or triple-teamed. The ball is never passed back out. These teams have a problem. There are no two- or three-man games, and no true team concept. The post is concerned only with scoring points himself. The other players will eventually resent this attitude. The coach has the responsibility of making certain there are no "black hole" players on the team. It should be corrected in practice, and the importance of two- and three-man games and ball movement should be emphasized.

- <u>Coaches need to spread the ball around.</u>

Coaches at the sub-varsity level who are concerned only with winning often instruct the other players to keep feeding the post. In this situation, the other players will not develop their skills and confidence. As a result, they may have trouble when they go to the next level.

For example, if a junior high coach always wants the ball to be passed inside, the guards and wings will never develop shooting and other offensive skills. A player should not be forced to wait to get to the varsity before learning how to be a shooter or scorer.

So You are a Substitute?

Substitutes are critical to every team's success. The stronger the substitutes are, the more they can challenge the starters in practice, and the better the team will be. Being a substitute can be very difficult. Substitutes must be very encouraging and supportive of their teammates, while they are waiting their turn to get quality playing time.

Everyone wants to play. Who wants to work hard in practice if they have no chance of getting playing time? The truth is that if a player is tall and quick, he will get the attention of the coach. If two high school players are equal in talent, the player who is the upper classman will get first chance to play. He has paid his dues by working hard in practice. In both of these situations, the starters will have to play themselves out of the starting position, or the substitutes will have to beat out the starters.

Substitutes are critical to every team's success.

Sometimes, a player knows he can do as well as the starter if he can get the chance. What must he do to get more playing time? Among the steps that he can take in this regard are the following:

- Be a good teammate to everyone.
- Learn how to get the edge.
- Pay attention to the coach.

- Know what the coach expects.
- Observe what the starter is having trouble with.
- Be prepared when he gets the chance.
- Beat his opponent. An opponent is any player against whom he is competing, even in practice.
- Play with intensity! Dive for loose balls, and hustle to save balls from going out of bounds. Play aggressive defense.

❑ When You're on the Bench

How can you ever expect to get better and get more playing time if you aren't prepared when your time comes? Many high school players are not focused on the game while they are on the bench. Playing time is a right you earn through hard work in practice and by being prepared to do a good job. Failure to focus on the game may stop a coach from putting you in. If you are on the bench, stay focused on the game. The actions you need to undertake when you're on the bench include:

- Study the opponent. Figure out the opponent's offensive and defensive strategies.
- Evaluate what your team is doing and not doing successfully.
- Scout your individual opponents against whom you are likely to play.

❑ When You Get in the Game:

When you finally get into the game, make something good happen, either offensively or defensively. But, be a team player. Execute the offense and defense the way the coach wants them run.

❑ If You Make a Mistake

Once you are in the game, play smartly and intensely. Make every minute count. Basketball cannot be played without making mistakes. If you make a mistake, forget it and play ball. Learn from your mistakes. If you lose the ball or throw the ball away, get back and play good defense. Don't hang your head, complain to the referee, or look at the bench to see the coach's response. Coaches don't like mistakes; mistakes lose ballgames. Coaches love a player who hustles and gives 100 percent. If you make a mistake by being out of position because you were confused, admit it to the coach. Then work hard to correct the mistake before the next practice or game. Everyone makes mistakes. A mistake gives a player the opportunity to improve. Consistently making the same mistake will result in more bench time. Mental mistakes are caused by:

- Not knowing what to do.
- Not recognizing situations.
- Carelessness.

Coaches hate mental mistakes. Mental mistakes demonstrate that the player isn't prepared, isn't focused, or doesn't have a desire to excel. Mental mistakes will put you and keep you on the bench. Mental mistakes can be eliminated through hard work and by learning the concepts of the game of basketball.

Summary Points

If you are a substitute, work as hard as you can during and outside of practice. Your role on the team may change during the course of the season as you gain more experience and confidence. The coach may take awhile to realize what you can do or what your teammate cannot do well consistently. At all times, be a positive and encouraging teammate to everyone, especially the players against whom you are competing for playing time.

Mental mistakes will put you and keep you on the bench.

CHAPTER 19

Basketball Attitude

A player with an appropriate basketball attitude is aggressive, confident, and believes that he will outplay any individual opponent. The player becomes even more determined to do well if an opposing player shows him up, especially in a one-on-one situation. The player wants to win so badly that it hurts when the team doesn't.

How Does a Player Demonstrate a Basketball Attitude?

All coaches want a player who:

- Cannot stand for another player to outplay him. It makes the player play that much harder.
- Says to himself and executes skills on the floor that demonstrate the attitude that:
  - You can't beat me!
  - You can't get the ball!
  - The ball is mine!
  - One player can't stop me!
  - I can score!
- Believes that teams win and individuals lose.
- Plays with intensity.
- Plays fair, but plays to win.
- Is serious about getting better and uses his time effectively in practice trying to improve.
- Shows respect to the coach:
  - The player tries his best to do what the coach asks him to do.
  - The player listens when the coach is speaking, even to another teammate. The player does not dribble or bounce the ball when the coach is speaking.
  - The player learns from what the coach is telling other teammates. This prevents wasting the coach's time repeating the same thing over and over.

A player with an appropriate basketball attitude is aggressive, confident, and believes that he will outplay any individual opponent.

- The player never talks back or argues with his coach.

Coaches look for players who respond to a challenge. In that regard, what is your response if:

➤ The coach gets on you?
➤ Your spot on the team (or starting line-up) is challenged?
➤ You are benched?
➤ You are matched against a better or more athletic player in practice or in a game?

Proving Yourself

There will be tough times when a player isn't getting playing time, gets demoted, or is constantly being harped on by the coach. During these times, it is easy for a person to get frustrated and feel that things aren't fair. Every player should keep in mind that all factors considered, life isn't fair. As such, players should realize:

➤ If the coach is on your case, it is because he wants you to be better! You should be concerned only if the coach doesn't care enough to get on you if you make mistakes or do not improve.
➤ Coaches are human. They make mistakes in judgment, just like everyone else. Every coach makes mistakes when trying to evaluate the players' potential. It is impossible to measure the desire and determination some players have when they haven't yet shown it.
➤ Coaches challenge players who they feel aren't working hard trying to improve. Coaches may challenge players by getting on the player in front of the team, demoting a player, or removing a player from a game at a critical time when he usually plays.

Coaches want players who have pride and a desire to excel.

Don't Pout or Complain

If you truly want to be a basketball player, make a commitment, be determined, and prove yourself. Some players get mad when the coach gets on them and are determined to prove that the coach is wrong. Guess what? That is exactly what the coach wants. This determined attitude to prove one's self is the winning attitude a coach wants. These players refuse to lose; they are winners. Do you want to be a winner? Coaches want players who have pride and a desire to excel.

Develop a Basketball Attitude, Not Just an Attitude

If a player wants to be good and wants to be on the good side of a coach, he should develop a basketball attitude, not just an attitude. Having an attitude implies you have a "bad attitude" and is one of the surest ways to stay in the coach's doghouse.

CHAPTER 20

Ambidextrous Players

To be an outstanding player, a player must be totally comfortable using either hand in any situation. Likewise, even though the player may have favorite areas of the court, the player must be comfortable operating from any area of the court.

As a rule, everyone favors his dominant hand and tries to avoid his weaker hand if he can get away with it. Players must become equally effective with either hand while dribbling, passing, and even shooting short shots.

Coaches should encourage and insist that their players develop skills from different areas of the court and from different distances. Offenses are less predictable if they are designed and run from either side of the floor. All drills must be designed and run equally for either hand and for either side of the court. The coach should be alert to players who keep reverting back to their dominant hand, when they should be using their other hand.

When Should a Player Be Taught to Use the Off-Hand?

Ambidextrous skills are much more natural if a young player learns initially to perform them, using either hand. As soon as he starts playing basketball is the best time for a player to develop his ability to do things ambidextrously. Do not expect the off-hand to develop as quickly as the dominant hand. Be patient, it may take several years until the player no longer favors one hand. The time to learn to use the off-hand is not at the high school junior varsity or varsity level. It is hard enough for a player to learn to compete and to get playing time at this level. A well-rounded player has a better chance of being successful at the more competitive level.

What if a talented player who can only use his dominant hand makes it to the junior varsity or varsity level? As soon as the coach realizes that a problem exists, he should consult with the player and explain what

The time to learn to use the off-hand is not at the high school junior varsity or varsity level.

extra effort will have to be taken in this regard. Drills should be assigned to the player to perform outside of practice. For example, in the off-season, the player could be required to only dribble with his off-hand for a month or so. The player should later be required to not favor the dominant hand in any fashion. Some players have been known to dribble home after practice using only the weaker hand. The coach should be imaginative. The following story of an extremely gifted young athlete who led her team to the state championship can help illustrate the value of being ambidextrous.

> "She was a great kid and an unselfish team player. During junior high school, she was a post, since she was taller than the other kids were, and she could really jump. After the season had started in her sophomore year, she was moved up to the varsity as a wing. The problem was she had no guard skills, so she had to start learning them quickly. She progressed at an amazing rate and by the end of her junior year she had turned into a potential college prospect. She had one flaw. She was a one-handed player! She would seldom ever use her left hand, and when she did it was for only one or two bounces. She was so much taller and faster than everyone else she got by with using only one hand.
>
> The college she signed with was usually ranked in the NCAA Division I top 10. She was the college's fastest and quickest player, but she was easily defended by her teammates in practice since they were fast and defensively skilled players who knew how to defend a one-handed player. The player had to learn to use her off-hand if she was to become the player she wanted to be. The coach decided he had more skilled all-around offensive players, so he decided she would be the team's defensive specialist. She did a great job, but she was never able to utilize her offensive skills. What would have happened had she been required to dribble only with her off-hand for a month or two prior to her junior and senior seasons in high school? No one knows, but we can imagine!"

Being ambidextrous when it comes to dribbling, passing, and shooting short shots will improve the players' chances of doing well.

Summary Points

Being ambidextrous when it comes to dribbling, passing, and shooting short shots will improve the players' chances of doing well. The ability to be comfortable executing those skills successfully from any area of the floor can make the players even more effective.

CHAPTER 21

Basketball is a Game of Quickness

Quick refers to how fast someone performs a task. If speed was the only requirement to be a player, the sprinters on the track team would be the basketball team. Basketball is a game of quick cuts and acceleration. Good fakes accentuate the quickness of moves. Playing quicker makes any player better. A slower player can be successful if he has good skills and executes them quickly and efficiently. Anyone may play quicker by undertaking the following:

- Knowing the habits and tendencies of the opponent.
- Anticipating your teammates' and your opponents' moves. This requires court awareness and a knowledge of the offenses and defenses.
- Maintaining flexed knees at all times so you can quickly react by cutting, jumping, or accelerating.
- Being in proper position and using good technique.
- Being unpredictable in the way you play. Make it hard for the opponents to anticipate your next move.
- Being versatile. A player who can play inside or outside, shoot three-pointers, or drive to the basket is much more difficult to defend than a one-dimensional player.

From a quickness-standpoint, it is beneficial for a basketball player to have:

- A quick first step
- A quick shot
- A quick release
- A quick change of direction dribble
- A quick cut or acceleration
- Quick jumping ability

A slower player can be successful if he has good skills and executes them quickly and efficiently.

A quick first step is critical if a ballhandler is to beat his man in one-on-one situations. In this regard, the player must:

- Explode off the opposite foot.
- Take a quick, long stride past the defender.

A quick cut is intended to get the player open for a pass, shot, or dribble. Players must explode off their opposite foot as they take the first step. Many young players do not understand the concept of pushing hard off the back foot on a cut or their first step. These players just lean and step in the direction. No explosion occurs off the opposite foot. Quick acceleration after a cut allows the player to maintain any advantage he gained.

A quick shot should be taken at a speed and rhythm with which the player is confident. As a player learns to shoot, he should increase the speed of his shot until he is shooting at game speed. A slow, deliberate shot allows a defender time to recover. After some players have learned the correct shooting techniques, they continue to practice slow and deliberate shots. These players will often have difficulty getting their shots off in a game. As a result, they may lose confidence in their shooting. Players must learn to shoot at game speed once they have developed the proper technique. Initially, the player may feel uncomfortable as he learns to shoot more quickly. The point to remember is that the player must learn to shoot quickly, but not hurriedly.

A quick release allows a player to successfully get the shot off faster, because he is ready to finish the shot as soon as he reaches the top of his jump. There is no pause in the shot once the ball is brought into the shooting position. This situation is in contrast to players who try to hang in the air before shooting the ball. A player appears to have a quick release when he eliminates any delay or unnecessary movements prior to the shot.

Jumping quickly will allow the player to rebound more effectively and to get his shot off more quickly. Players can learn to jump more quickly by paying attention to the following suggestions:

> **As a player learns to shoot, he should increase the speed of his shot until he is shooting at game speed.**

- The player must be in proper body and foot position in order to be ready to spring upward.
- The player should try to land simultaneously with both feet in a good jumping position.
- The player should not overflex when jumping. His knees must be slightly flexed, and he should also flex slightly at the waist. Overflexing will not increase the height of his jump, but slow down how quickly he can jump.
- The player should practice learning to jump quickly. In this regard, among the steps that he can take are the following:
  - Jump rope every day.
  - Practice repetitive jumping drills emphasizing the above principles.

- Jump high as quickly as he can.
- Ask his coach for drills to utilize.

The ability of a player to learn to play quicker is developed by using intelligence, paying attention to details, getting the edge, and lots of hard work.

Exercise and Weight Programs

Players want to improve their quickness and jumping ability. As such, players are looking for guidance in ways to increase their quickness, jumping ability, explosiveness, and strength. Weight programs can be very helpful in this regard. Unfortunately, many young players do not understand the importance of a good training program. The player who wants trying to get the edge and wants to be as good as he must understands and adheres to the principles involved in a sound developmental program.

Unfortunately, the player may not know exactly what he should be doing. The player needs reassurance that what he is doing is the right program. Many players know how to exercise to build strength, but they want to be certain that they will improve their quickness, jumping ability, and flexibility. The players and their parents want to make certain that they are doing what is best for them, especially if the athletes are working hard to improve.

Several excellent books are currently available that detail weight training and exercise programs that are designed especially for basketball. In addition to increasing their jumping ability and quickness by exercises and weight programs, players must also learn to increase the quickness level that they are able to execute their skills.

Learning New Skills

As a new skill is learned, the player is usually slow and deliberate as he learns the technique. First, the player learns the footwork, and then the rest of the basic move or shot is practiced. Once the player is comfortable with the basic skill, he should increase the quickness of the skill until he is performing it at game speed.

Players must be able to execute skills at a quick, game-speed tempo, while being under control and unrushed. Some players never practice a skill at game speed. Instead, they continue to practice their shot or a particular move at a slower and more deliberate tempo. Not surprisingly,

The ability of a player to learn to play quicker is developed by using intelligence, paying attention to details, getting the edge, and lots of hard work.

when these players get in a game, everything moves so fast that they feel rushed and uncomfortable. The result is the player becomes frustrated, unsure of himself, and loses self-confidence.

Other Ways a Player Can Appear Quicker

If a player has good court and situation awareness, he should be quicker because he is anticipating and is ready to react. He will know the location of the defenders, as well as his teammates, before a pass is made. As a result, the player is mentally and physically ready to react. The player will be in the proper position to receive the pass and quickly drive, shoot, or pass, since his body is ready to react quickly.

Examples of how court and situation awareness can make a player appear quicker are illustrated in the following situations:

- The low post pins the defender with a drop step with the leg closest to the baseline as the ball is being caught. The post immediately spins around the defender and makes the basket.
- When the ball is reversed to the weakside, the wing anticipates the sagging defender will charge toward him, and the low post defenders will be adjusting from an overshift to the opposite side. As the wing is catching the ball, he is simultaneously springing on his back foot. As soon as the ball is in his fingertips, the wing explodes off his back foot and is immediately dribbling around the charging defender. The player goes in for a layup or takes a pull-up shot.
- The defender anticipates that the opposing team is going to reverse the ball to the weakside wing. The defender is flexed and ready to spring forward to intercept the pass. Furthermore, the player should be in the ready position so there is no wasted motion or time.
- Some guards or wings have developed a habit of delaying the shot after catching a pass. The players catch the ball, pivot to square up, and then step backward slightly with one foot before starting their jump shot. Any delay in executing a shot will allow the defense time to deny the shot. Instead, the wing should be comfortable pivoting either right or left to square up to the basket. The player's legs should be flexed as he pivots so he can immediately jump once his shoulders are squared up to the basket. In other words, the jump shot is initiated immediately as the trailing foot squares up; no additional movements are necessary.
- The player should never rest and stand up straight on the basketball court unless play has been stopped by the referee. When

a player is standing straight up, his legs are fully extended and he cannot react quickly. He must flex his legs before a quick movement can be made.

- The player should learn to jump quickly. Players who must take a deep knee flex to jump are slow jumpers. Players who can spring upward when their legs are flexed slightly will be much quicker jumpers. This advice is especially useful for posts and forwards who are expected to rebound. Quick jumpers have an advantage around the basket. To learn to jump quicker, players should work on drills that stress quick leg extension.

Anticipation vs. Reaction

A player who reacts to a situation is slower than he should be, because he waits to see what happens before deciding what to do and then reacting. His reaction time will be delayed enough to allow an opponent to take one or two steps.

A player who anticipates a situation is already prepared mentally and physically to respond quickly. For example, a good rebounder is already in a flexed position, ready to spring when the ball hits the rim, and he has an idea where the ball will go if it misses. Anticipation is a learned skill that makes it easier to make the big play. (The ability to anticipate is discussed in greater detail in the next chapter, Getting the Edge.)

Summary Points

Basketball is a game of quickness. The quicker an individual can perform any skill effectively and under control, the better the player will be. The point to keep in mind is that every player can learn to play quicker.

A player who reacts to a situation is slower than he should be, because he waits to see what happens before deciding what to do and then reacting.

CHAPTER 22

Getting the Edge

Getting the edge means doing the little things that give the coach and his players an advantage. It means paying attention to the smallest details and incorporating them into the players' style of play. Getting the edge means learning seldom-taught skills that every player should know, but for various reasons, are seldom taught or emphasized at the junior high or high school levels. These factors are very important in helping players develop to their fullest potential.

Know Your Opponent

One of the best ways to get the edge is to know your opponent better than he knows himself. If a player wants to gain an advantage over another player it is much easier if the player knows his opponent's strengths and weaknesses, as well as his opponent's tendencies in different situations. With this knowledge, the player is better able to make adjustments that will enable him to gain an advantage on his opponent.

❑ Who is the Opponent?

An opponent is anyone a player is competing against at that moment, whether in practice or in a game. When a player steps on the court, he must have the basketball attitude that he is going to beat anyone against whom he is paired. Each player's obligation to the team is to play as well as he can every day in practice. Players are competing against teammates for a spot on the team and for playing time. Healthy competition between teammates can make both players and the team better.

In friendly competition, players compete as hard as they can, while encouraging their teammate and acknowledging his good play or outstanding effort. This approach maintains friendship and helps build team spirit.

When coaching young inexperienced players, the coach should be very alert to a player against taking competition personal. At the beginning of the season, the coach should communicate to his team that he expects every player to give 100 percent in practice, and that friendly competition should not affect friendships off the court. The coach should also be alert to make certain that players never carry their personal feelings onto the court or off.

❏ Knowing Your Opponent Means Studying Your Opponent

A player should always be studying any player he is playing against in practice or games. Once you know your opponent, you have the ability to better anticipate his every move. It is then easier to deny desirable shots or floor position.

In practice, it is common for a player to be matched against the same two or three players most of the time in drills and scrimmages. Know your teammates. Use that knowledge to get the edge or advantage. How a player does in practice will usually determine who plays and how much they play. Do you want it badly enough to go the extra distance? If you learn how to properly scout your teammates, you will also know how to scout your opponents in games.

Players should study their opponents before the game, as well as during the game. Studying opponents before the game means learning the opposing team's offensive and defensive schemes. As a rule, the coach will work on these during practice. Pay attention!

❏ Teach Players to Scout the Opposing Team

Young players will typically not know how to scout their opponent. As a result, coaches need to teach players how to scout opponents in person and with game film. They should also teach their players how to scout their opponent during the game, whether they are playing or sitting on the bench.

A player should always be studying any player he is playing against in practice or games.

• *Pre-game scouting in person and/or with game film.* It is common practice for football players to study game film. For some reason, however, pre-game scouting is seldom done in basketball. What's the difference? The objective is to identify (and, therefore, be better prepared to respond to) the tendencies of the opponent.

If you have the opportunity to watch a future opponent, scout that opponent and the players against whom your team will likely be matched. Take notes. You can't remember everything you see on film. Don't be embarrassed if you are the only person making notes. If you are successful, other teammates will soon be doing the same thing.

If you can get game film of the next opponent, study it. Be careful to notice your opponent's tendencies, especially against the types of offenses and defenses your team will employ. If your team has already played a team earlier in the season, be sure to study that film.

• *Scout the opponent while you are playing.* Pay attention and learn as you play. Don't be a robot running up and down the floor and never using your head. Know what the opposing team is trying to do offensively and defensively. Know your individual opponent's tendencies. What are they having success doing? They will probably continue doing whatever they are currently doing until your team stops them.

• *Scout the opponent while you are on the bench.* Many players sit on the bench and watch the game; but only a few special players study the game. It is easier to get an overview of what the opposing team is doing if you are watching carefully. If you are a substitute, you need to know everything you can to help you play well when you finally get the opportunity to get in the game. The better you do in the game, the more playing time you will get in the future. Playing time is earned; make your time count. Take advantage of the opportunity. Don't socialize and joke around. Such behavior should be saved until after the game.

Playing time is earned; make your time count.

❑ Know your opponent's characteristics:

- Strengths and weaknesses
- Favorite shots and moves
- Favorite area on the court to shoot or initiate a move
- Passing tendencies
- Other general tendencies. Is there anything a player always does before a shot, move, pass, or defensive action? Some habits are keys to what the opponent is likely to do.
- Defensive tendencies. Is the opponent aggressive and always trying to steal the ball or block the shot? Does he lean or reach for the ball? Does he always overplay? Can he be faked easily? Does the opponent sag off or play denial defense?
- Ability to fight through the screen, switch, or go over or under the screen
- Rebounding skill. Does the opponent charge the boards? Does he block out? Does your opponent get up the court slowly after a turnover or a basket?

Deny Your Opponent's Strengths

❑ Test Your Opponent Early.

Once a player feels he knows what the opponent is likely to do, he should test the opponent early in the game. The objective is to challenge the opponent early in the game to determine whether the scouting report is correct or if modifications are needed. For example, if a player believes his opponent has a weakness dribbling with his left hand, the player should overplay his opponent to completely deny the right-hand dribble. If the opponent responds by driving well with his left hand, then the player knows to slightly overplay both hands. By quickly affirming the strengths and weaknesses of his opponent, the player is now on his way to getting an edge.

❏ Deny Your Opponent's Favorite Position, Shot, or Move.

Players usually have a limited number of moves or shots if their favorite move or shot is taken away. If the offensive player is having difficulty, continue and intensify your efforts. If the player has well-rounded skills and is ambidextrous, play the offensive player more normally. In this situation, it is usually best to force the player to take longer shots, since his shooting percentage will usually be lower from further out. Other steps that you can take to help minimize the effectiveness of a player's favorite position, shot, or move include:

➢ If a player is thought to be only a spot-up shooter, deny the shot and challenge the player to drive by overplaying slightly to his dominant hand. If the player doesn't look to drive, then play closer to him to deny the outside shot and do not worry about a drive until the player starts driving.
➢ If the player isn't a threat to score from outside, sag off and play more help defense than normal when on the off-side of the court and sometimes on the ball-side.
➢ If the opponent is an all-around scoring threat and shoots or drives from any area of the floor, play him honestly and do not overplay too much.
➢ If an offensive player believes his defensive opponent is too aggressive trying to block shots, that player will want to fake and shoot or make a move to the basket.

Never be satisfied with your play—room for improvement always exists.

Scout Yourself

Critically scout game film or filmed scrimmages of yourself. Be objective. Look for the positives, but also look to find things you could have done better. Never be satisfied with your play—room for improvement always exists. Don't wait until the next practice to work on specific skills if you can practice before then. Film doesn't lie, and it may allow you to see yourself as the coach and the opponents see you.

Be a Well-Rounded Player

Develop all-around basketball skills. Don't be dependent on only one skill. Having complementary skills and being unpredictable are two ways to ensure an advantage over your opponent. It is much easier to beat your opponent when they don't have a clue what you are going to do next until it is too late.

❏ Develop Complementary Skills.

- ➢ Having complementary skills can provide you with an invaluable competitive edge. For example, a spot-up shooter is easier to defend than a good shooter who also likes to drive to the basket. If the defender knows you are not a threat to drive and score, then it is easy to guard you while sagging off and helping on defense. Make the defender play honest. A post's moves are more effective if he also passes and fakes well.

In today's game, the post is often at the three-point line setting a screen or waiting for a pass. A post who can shoot from 15 feet or further out is more effective than a player who can only shoot from four or five feet from the basket. If the defender has to come out to defend the post, because of his threat to score from long range, the lane to the basket is opened up. The post can drive to the basket or pass to teammates cutting free under the basket.

- ➢ Develop complementary shots or moves. These moves or shots may initially start out the same, but result in an entirely different move or shot, often in a different direction.
- ➢ Learn to use both sides of the court equally well. Every player has a favorite spot to shoot. However, some players are only effective shooters from that particular spot. A player should develop confidence shooting from all areas of the floor. This attribute will take work outside of practice.
- ➢ Learn to be ambidextrous. A guard who dribbles with the same hand all the time is very easy to defend. Force yourself during the off-season to work extensively on becoming a more proficient dribbler. A post is much more effective if he can use either hand for the short shots, thereby always using his body to shield himself from the defender.

Some players will only make a move to the basket if they are on one side of the court. For example, a right-handed wing may feel comfortable driving to the basket only when he is on the left side of the court, since

Don't be dependent on only one skill.

he can shield the defender with the body as he dribbles with his favorite hand. Learning to dribble well enough with his left hand and practicing one-on-one moves while using the left-handed dribble will help an individual become a much more complete and effective player.

❑ Be Unpredictable.

Once the well-rounded player knows his opponent, he should further confuse his opponent by being unpredictable. Scout yourself as you would an opponent. What are your tendencies? Are you too predictable? Do you have any keys on which an opponent can focus? Do you have a favorite shot, move, or favorite spot from which to shoot? Do you fake every time?

Practice being unpredictable. Being unpredictable does not come naturally. It must be practiced until it becomes second nature. We all tend to fall back on things that are easy. We must first think about being unpredictable.

Anticipation will make it easier to be unpredictable. If a player is having a good game and knows what the opponent's weaknesses are, it will be easy to anticipate what he is likely to do differently this time. For example, if you have made several shots, the opposing coach will then make certain that someone will challenge you. If you are open and receive a pass, the defense will charge out to get on you quickly. By anticipating this response, you should be ready to fake and drive by the player.

Use Your Body

Using your body to shield the ball from an opponent will allow you to compete effectively against a taller or faster opponent. In this regard, the following steps can help you:

> - Dribble low and fast when guarded or in a crowd. Vary the dribble from high to low as you go to a cross-over dribble.
> - Keep the ball in front of you when you shoot near the basket and the defender is behind you. If you bring the ball above your head to shoot, it will be blocked from behind. Instead, keep the ball in front and slightly forward of your normal shooting position.
> - While driving the baseline to the basket, square up and bank the shot when possible. This action allows your body to shield the defenders, by keeping them behind you. Keep the ball in front of you as previously recommended.
> - Learn to shoot a hook or jump hook. These shots allow you to

Being unpredictable does not come naturally.

use your body as a shield so that the shot can get the elevation needed to get over a taller defender.
- Go straight toward the basket if you have an open lane, but shift back slightly in front of the defender to keep him behind you, and to deny a recovery angle.
- As you slide around a defender on a move near the basket, quickly move or lean around the defender and reach toward the basket to shoot or finger roll the ball. This subtle move to the basket puts the defender behind you, where it is more difficult to block a shot and easier to be called for a foul.
- Shoot short shots around the basket with either hand so that you can shoot with your left hand on the left side of the basket (for the right-handed player). This ability will give you a better angle than a right-handed shot would in the same situation. It also allows you to keep your right hand up and in the way of the defender. In this scenario, it is actually easier for you to make the shot, even though you may be getting fouled.

Anticipation vs. Reaction

As was discussed in the previous chapter, a player who reacts rather than anticipates is slower because he waits to see what happens before deciding what to do and responding. His reaction time will be delayed by the amount of time it takes to decide what to do and the time it takes to get into the proper position. This delayed reaction time is enough to allow an opponent to take one or two steps.

A player who anticipates a situation is already prepared mentally and physically to react quickly. For example, a good rebounder is already in a flexed position, ready to spring when the ball hits the rim, and he has an idea where the ball will go if the shot is missed.

❑ Anticipation

The ability of a player to know and to be ready for what another player is about to do can make the player appear quicker. Anticipation is a learned skill that makes it easier to make the big play. A player who is good at anticipating must first accurately recognize the situation and then realize what he would do in that situation. Anticipation is improved when a player has good court and situation awareness.

Situation awareness refers to the ability of a player to understand what his team should do in a situation, as well as what the opponent's situation is and what the opponent is likely to do. A player who is situationally aware also understands game situations, such as amount of time remaining, and the foul situation, including when there are fouls to give at the end of the game or when an opposing player is in early foul trouble.

Every player on the team should have good situation awareness. However, it is a particularly critical skill for a point guard, since he controls the offensive tempo of the team and often calls the defensive signals as well. Winning is often determined by the players who do the smart things in special situations.

Examples of "special situations" in which a smart player can have a greater impact than normal include:

- Times occur in a game when your team or opponent wants to get the ball to a specific player because of that player's free-throw shooting ability, a player is in foul trouble, or a mismatch exists. In these situations, the following guidelines apply:
  - If the other team's best player is a post and is in early foul trouble, it is smart to attack the defense through your post before the opponent can be taken out of the game. The referee is subconsciously aware that the post fouls, and is watching him more closely. Your offensive player should challenge the post to try to get another foul or an easy basket, if the post is playing passively to avoid another foul.
  - If an individual mismatch occurs in your team's favor, the team should take advantage before the opponent can help or switch back. If your team is at a disadvantage because of the mismatch, someone must help out right away.
  - The coach may want a specific player to handle the ball more at the end of the half or game if the other team is fouling and your team is in the bonus.
- Times occur in a game when the momentum is about to change. Usually, both teams want to take advantage of the moment. They often turn to their "go-to" player, because of his ability to make something positive happen.
- A team with an adequate lead at the end of a game may find it is more important to use up some of the clock than it is to score two more points. The clock is the enemy of the team that is behind. Sometimes, rather than driving to the basket, a player may be wise to pull the ball back out and move the ball around to eat up the clock.
- The end of the quarter or half is near. In this situation, the following scenario may exist:
  - The coach wants a player to take charge and get a good shot off without leaving enough time for the opponent to score.

Winning is often determined by the players who do the smart things in special situations.

- The opponent may have only six to eight seconds to get the ball across midcourt and get a shot off. A guard should apply enough backcourt pressure, without fouling, to eat up enough of the clock so a good shot cannot be taken.

Court Awareness

Special players who always seem to do the right thing have excellent court awareness. Court awareness is the knowledge and recognition of where all players, both teammates and opponents, are on the court. It is knowing when and what they are likely to do, thereby allowing the player the opportunity to make an exceptional play. Court awareness allows the player to be ready to make the right move, cut, pass, shot, or defensive play.

Court awareness on offense occurs when the player has:

- Vision beyond the defender
- Knowledge of the offense—position, timing
- An understanding of where the defenders are and what they are likely to do
- Good peripheral vision

Vision beyond the defender and peripheral vision are two concepts that are seldom emphasized or taught. Both attributes are essential traits for the player who wants to excel.

❏ Vision Beyond the Defender

The ability to look beyond a defender while dribbling or preparing to make a move enables the ballhandler to anticipate more effectively. Since the offensive player already knows the defense being played, he can visualize the position of the defenders, player movement, and where the openings in the defense are. When developing a player's ability to see beyond his opponent, the coach should be mindful of the following:

- A player must first develop his ballhandling and faking skills so he has confidence enough to look beyond the defender.
- An inexperienced player often has a hard time breaking the habit of looking down at the ball as he dribbles.
- Once the player starts keeping his head up, he still tends to be focused on his defender.
- The coach should work with such a player to look beyond the defender and see the whole court, while still being aware of the person defending him.

➢ The coach will have to continually remind the player about the need to have "vision" beyond the defender. He may utilize drills to help develop this desired habit in the player. Initially, the drills may be one-on-one drills that stress ballhandling and moves to the basket. Subsequently, variations to the drills can be incorporated that require the player to pass to the open cutter.
➢ With time, the player will develop confidence and will be comfortable seeing down court, while being aggressively defended.

- Head up and eyes forward

Players cannot have court awareness while looking at the floor. Unfortunately, too many players have developed the bad habit of looking down as they dribble, pick up the dribble, fake, or initiate a move. Not only will these players lack court awareness, any fakes they execute will be less effective than they could otherwise be. For example, a fake made by a player who looks down at the floor will not sell to the defender. As players learn fundamental skills, attention must be given to a player's eyes.

❑ Peripheral Vision

Peripheral vision is a person's ability to see what is on each side, while focusing straight ahead. The great passers seem to have the ability to see where people are without looking in that direction. Coaches love players with good peripheral vision, but most never teach anyone how to improve his natural ability.

People seldom develop their full range of peripheral vision. Most individuals focus straight ahead, thereby narrowing their focus of vision. When they want to see laterally, they simply turn their head. Players need to improve their lateral focus of awareness. With practice, a player can develop better peripheral vision. In this regard, a player should initially concentrate on seeing out of the corner of his eyes, while looking in another direction. With time, it will come more naturally. Drills can help develop this skill. All players should work on this skill.

With practice, a player can develop better peripheral vision.

Improved peripheral vision will enable the offensive player to see the floor better, thereby:

➢ Allowing a passer to recognize open players more easily.
➢ Allowing a passer to pass while not looking directly at his teammate.
➢ Facilitating the player's ability to see screens, traps, and double teams earlier, thereby allowing time to react.

On defense, court awareness occurs when the player has vision of both the ball and the floor. In this regard, the following factors apply:

- If the defender is guarding the ballhandler (i.e., on-the-ball defense), the defender's vision of the court is limited. Good peripheral vision will allow the defender to focus on his man, while being more aware of the immediate area around him.
- Defenders who are off-the-ball (i.e., guarding players who do not have the ball) should be in a position to always see the ball, the opponent, and see the play develop. They should anticipate as the play develops and be ready to react immediately.

Players should never be so busy denying a pass or maintaining floor position that a ballhandler is allowed to drive toward the basket. Some inexperienced defenders may still be tightly defending their man, while the ballhandler drives by and goes in for a score. All players should always adhere to the following defensive principles:

- Never allow an uncontested drive or shot!
- Play help-defense!

Team Defense

A defender must thoroughly understand his role in the defense, as well as how he can help a teammate. The player should know how his team's defense functions. This knowledge should include being aware of where the offensive players are and what they are likely to do.

Good defensive players always have a great understanding of the game as it develops.

- The defensive player must know the offense being used by his opponent.
- Which players are likely to score most of the points, their favorite moves and shots, as well as where on the floor they are likely to make a move, shot, or pass.
- The defender must also realize if a teammate is having a difficult time defending his man or area.
- The defender should know if the other team's offense is trying to attack a certain part of his team's defense.
- The defender should know if one of his team's best players in foul trouble, and whether the other team is trying to attack that player to get him out of the game.

Good defensive players always have a great understanding of the game as it develops. They are always in good defensive position with good vision of the ball and the floor so they can anticipate and react quickly.

Other Seldom-Taught Skills

Some essential skills, although important, do not always receive the attention that they deserve or should merit. If executed properly, these seldom-discussed skills will help give the player an edge.

❑ Setting Up Your Opponent

Players can be more effective if they set up their opponent. The player can gain the advantage if his opponent is faked or decoyed. The following examples illustrate just some of the ways that a player can set up his opponent:

- The player decoys his defender so he doesn't see the screen coming.
- The defender lays off an offensive player to encourage a pass to his man.
- An offensive player doesn't appear to be involved in the offense, prior to cutting suddenly toward the basket or a screen.
- The dribbler sets up the defender for a change-of-pace dribble or cross-over dribble.

❑ Keeping the Backside Defender Busy

In a half-court offense, an important skill is the ability to keep the backside defender so busy that he cannot play good help-defense. If an offensive player is standing around waiting for another part of the offense to develop, it is very easy for his defender to give backside help and clog the lane. The defender should be kept busy, so he will not have the time or the proper position to help out.

The off-the-ball defender should be kept so busy that he might not see a screen being set. By keeping the backside defender busy, the player is faking the defender until it is the time to rebound, look for a pass, cut around a screen, or screen for a teammate.

Quick, sudden changes of direction or speed are critical in basketball if a player is to get open or to gain an advantage.

❑ Exploding Off the Opposite Foot

Quick, sudden changes of direction or speed are critical in basketball if a player is to get open or to gain an advantage. Accelerating quickly on a player's first step or cut is a skill that cannot be over-emphasized.

- **The first step.**

The first step is the most important step in basketball. An explosive first step enables an offensive player to gain enough separation for the player to get open. On defense, the quick first step allows the defender to gain and maintain proper defensive position.

Many players initiate the first step by simply leaning as they step with their lead foot. No explosive movement occurs. A quick first step requires a balanced body position. The player must be in the ready position with his knees slightly flexed and his weight is on the balls of the feet. A quick first step requires the player to explode off his back foot as he steps with his lead foot. His leg is flexed, and he pushes very hard on the ball of his back foot. He then finishes by pushing off with his toes.

How can players get a quicker first step? Players will have to work outside of practice to improve quickness. The coach or the individual assigned to be the conditioning coach may be able to help the player with suggested exercises or activities. For example, jumping rope is a good exercise to increase stamina. When jumping rope, the emphasis should be on the player staying on the balls of his feet, and improving quick-foot movement and quick jumping. He should make side-to-side, forward, and backward movements while jumping rope.

First steps appear quicker when they follow a short, quick fake in the opposite direction. The fake is designed to get the opponent to lean or step slightly in the opposite direction.

- **Cutting.**

Players often simply step in the direction to which they want to go. This movement often results in a slow, rounded change of direction that is readily recognized by the opponent. Cutting, on the other hand, is a sudden move made by pushing hard and quickly off the foot opposite to the direction the player wants to go.

A sudden change of direction and an increase in speed are only attained by using proper techniques. The technique is identical to making a quick first step. The player should have his weight on the ball of his back foot, with his knee slightly flexed. As the player lifts his lead foot to step forward or in another direction, he should explode off his back foot by pushing hard and very quickly off his toes.

- Knowing when to cut to an open area.

Cutting to an open area is a basic premise in basketball. Offenses are designed to create open areas. Knowing when to cut is just as important as the actual cutting movement. Cutting at the wrong time may result in the ballhandler being unable to deliver the pass, or the cut may upset the timing of the offense. Young players are sometimes frustrated when they do not receive the pass after cutting to an open area. They are focused on cutting to the area, not when to cut. Sometimes the ballhandler cannot see the cutter or get the pass off at that moment.

For example, a sophomore had been invited to play on a summer league team with seniors. After the first game, the young player said the seniors would not pass the ball when she made a cut to the basket. Game film showed that every time the player cut to the basket, the ballhandler had pivoted and was looking in another direction, and therefore was unable to see the cutter.

The cutter and passer should learn to make eye contact before the cut is made. Even if the ballhandler sees the cutter, the defense may be in good enough position to prevent the pass from being made. If so, the cutter may need to break in another direction where the pass can be made. This factor is especially true if a player is being double-teamed and is in danger of getting a five-second count and losing the ball. The following examples illustrate ways of breaking to an open area:

> Breaking high to low. If a player is being double- or triple-teamed on one side of the low-post area, a teammate near the top of the circle will often be open if he fakes and breaks into the lane toward the basket. The player being double-teamed passes the ball to the cutting teammate for an easy shot.

> If a teammate is shooting from the side or wing area, a rebounding lane is often left open in front of the basket. If a player breaks from the high-post area toward the front of the basket or the weak side of the lane, he will often find a rebounding area.

> Cutting the baseline. If the post is at the high-post area and an open lane to the basket exists along the baseline, a teammate should cut to the basket. A teammate can also make a back-door cut from the wing position when the low-post area is open.

Knowing when to cut is just as important as the actual cutting movement.

- Drift to an open area. If the cutter finds there are no large open areas, he should drift a few steps to a more open area when his defender sags off to play help defense. This subtle movement will open up the player for a good shot.

Summary Points

Getting the edge involves learning the little tricks or techniques that enable a player to come closer to his potential. Getting the edge means playing smart!

CHAPTER 23

Few young players make the commitment necessary to play great defense. If a defender can shut down the best offensive player on the team in practice, he will get the attention of the coach and more playing time. Coaches tend to love players who play aggressive, hustling defense. Defense wins games and championships! Believe it and achieve it.

What is the purpose of defense? The basic goal of defense is to prevent the other team from scoring. Among the other goals of sound defense are the following:

- To prevent the opponent from penetrating the defense by dribble or pass
- To create turnovers
- To make the offense work hard for a basket
- To deny desirable offensive position. This step not only helps achieve the first three goals, but also sends a message to the opponent that this contest is going to be a battle. If indecision, doubt, or frustration creep into the mind of the opponent, then the defender has gained another advantage.

Who Can Play Sound Defense?

Almost any player can play good defense if he has the desire, uses good technique, works hard, and gives a 110-percent effort. The difference between the first and second team is often the level of their offensive skills, not their defensive skills. Many substitutes can contribute significantly in a game by playing great defense and not making turnovers on offense. Subs who can play a few minutes per game and help maintain a lead or not allow their team to get further behind are very valuable to the team when a key player is in foul trouble, fouls out, gets hurt, or is just having a bad game.

Almost any player can play good defense if he has the desire, uses good technique, works hard, and gives a 110-percent effort.

Defense and Offense Are Equally Important

Defense is as important as offense, although fans, media, and statistics overwhelmingly tend to emphasize offense. Not every player is a scorer, but every player can be a good defender. Every team needs role players. Seldom are players recognized for their steady defense or rebounding. Yet every winning team has to have unselfish players who are happy to work hard in practice and games. Defense is hard work. It takes desire and determination.

Physically, it is much harder to play defense than it is to play offense. The coach and players should acknowledge defensive effort and hustle in practice and in games. Players who deny a pass, prevent a shot, or deny the offensive player his preferred offensive position or favorite shot are playing defense, as well as the player who steals the ball or blocks a shot. When an opponent has to work harder to get into the flow of the game, he not only tires out, but doubt and frustration often enter into his mind. Thwarting key players in an offense may upset the psyche of the whole team. A defender who has the heart and determination to give 100 percent on defense can be very important to the team. Players need to ask themselves if they have the desire.

Defensive Skills Are Learned Faster Than Offensive Skills

Since it takes longer to develop individual offensive skills and coordinate an offensive scheme, coaches usually spend more practice time on offense than defense. By emphasizing the importance of defense on the first day of the season, the coach stresses to the players how important defense is to the team's success. He also provides the less-skilled and less-confident players something they can quickly grasp. These players can feel that they are contributing to the team's success. They will then have the confidence and desire to continue to give a full effort in practice, even if they don't get as much quality practice time. Remember, an average player who plays smart and hustling defense and effectively scouts his opponent can play great defense against a more talented player.

Not every player is a scorer, but every player can be a good defender.

If the coach truly wants to emphasize the importance of defense, he should start every practice with man-to-man drills, as well as other defensive drills. Execution and effort are essential in defense. The coach should insist on it in practice.

Players Should Play Good Defense in Every Game!

Offensive execution fluctuates from game to game and even from minute to minute within the game. Defensive execution, on the other hand, should never falter. Every game has one or more periods of time, ranging from a couple of minutes to several minutes during which one team has trouble scoring. How well each team plays defense during these offensive lulls often determines the winner of the game. Consistent and excellent defense is necessary every minute of every game, if the team is to perform well during an offensive lull. Players should never rest on defense. No excuse exists for having a bad game on defense. Excellent defense gives every team a chance to win.

Team defense will not be any better than the effort of each individual defender to fulfill his role as intended. One player slacking on his job will result in overall poor team defense. Defense is truly a team effort.

Defense is Played with Your Head, Heart, and Feet!

• *A smart defender knows his opponents.* Offensive players are often predictable because they have favorite moves and shots. Every defensive player should learn his opponents' tendencies, strengths, and weaknesses. Since a defender may be matched against several different offensive players during a game, a smart defender will scout several of the players on the opposing team that he is likely to be matched against. If a defender is asked to double-down to help on defense, he should study the moves of the post that he will help double team. A defender should ask the following questions and adjust his defense accordingly:

> ➢ Is the offensive player quicker than I am? If so, play a full step away so that good defensive position can be maintained.
> ➢ Is the offensive player a good shooter? What are his favorite shots and moves, and where is he effective in making those shots. Adjust your defense to deny these.
> ➢ Does the offensive player have any apparent weaknesses? Most players have weaknesses in their offensive game. If the opponent is forced to his weaknesses because the defense is denying his strengths, the defense must capitalize on that weakness.
> ➢ How effective is your team's defense? If the offense is exploiting the defense, what are they doing successfully? If the defense is effective, what will the opposing offense try to do differently to get an open shot?

• *A smart player anticipates.* The defender should be prepared and ready to anticipate the offensive player's move.

• *A smart player plays defense with his heart.* A great defender does not have to be the fastest player, but he has to have a big heart. He has to

One player slacking on his job will result in overall poor team defense.

have the desire to play good defense. Unfortunately, too few players choose to have that desire.

• *A smart player plays defense with his feet.* This concept is so important that it should be emphasized the first day of practice. Defense is played with the feet, much more so than with the hands. The key to great defense is to move the feet quickly to maintain proper defensive position, even though the offensive player may be trying every trick to get the defender out of position. The defender is beaten if he is out of position by half a step. A defender who is out of position is more likely to be called for a foul. Therefore, a player who is in foul trouble must hustle and play defense with his feet—not his hands—if he wants to stay in the game.

A simple drill to emphasize the movement of the feet is to create a narrow lane from the end of the court to halfcourt. A ballhandler will try to dribble to the other end while staying in this lane. The defender puts both his hands behind his back. The objective is to prevent the ballhandler from getting to the other end. A turnover, a dribble that is picked up, or stepping out of the lane are considered defensive stops. The coach may want to set a time limit on getting to the other end. This drill is designed to teach the importance of foot movement and hustling defense, while emphasizing to the dribbler the importance of taking advantage of any opportunity (however small or large) to drive past the defender.

Finish the Defensive Effort

If the defense has worked hard for 30 to 40 seconds and has forced the opponent to take a poor shot, the defense must finish the effort. Why give the offense another chance to score? Finish the defensive effort by blocking out and getting the rebound.

> Defense is played with the feet, much more so than with the hands.

The Defensive Position

In the basic defensive position, the player has his weight evenly balanced on the balls of both feet. His feet should be separated slightly more than the width of his shoulders. His head and the chin should be up. His knees are bent, his back is straight, and all joints are flexed. When his man has the ball, he focuses his eyes on his opponent's midsection so he isn't faked out easily. His hand on the ballside should be low to deny a dribble or a bounce pass. His other hand should be high to deny a pass. He should switch hand positions as the ball is changed from one side to the other. He should slide his feet. He should never cross his feet unless he is beaten, and he has to run to catch up.

Any player defending away from the basket must be prepared to react and move quickly to prevent the offensive player from cutting or driving around him. When the defender is guarding a player close to the basket, the greatest threat is a shot, not a drive. For that reason, the defender will stand a little more erect. The defender must still play defense with his feet, but he must play "taller" so that it is more difficult for the offensive player to shoot over him.

When Your Man Doesn't Have the Ball

Defense is much easier if the defender plays aggressive and smart defense before his opponent gets the ball. Most of the time, your man will not have the ball. There are five players and only one ball. You must be determined to deny the offensive player what he wants. Deny his strengths and make him depend upon his weaknesses. When your man doesn't have the ball (i.e., off-the-ball defense) you should:

- Prevent your man from catching a pass, while going toward the basket.
- Prevent your man from catching a pass in a position where he is a threat to shoot, drive, or make a move.
- Learn your man's favorite moves and shots, as well as his favorite place to receive a pass.
- Be alert. Continue to think and anticipate. Don't straighten up or relax on defense.
- Be ready to avoid a screen, slow down cutters, or play help-defense if a player is free in the scoring zone.
- Block out your man when a shot is taken, and then go for the rebound.
- Be ready to help a teammate.

When Your Man Has the Ball

An offensive player is most dangerous when he first catches the ball because he can pass, shoot, or drive. This is called the "triple-threat" position. As the defender, you should do the following when defending a player who has just caught the ball (i.e., on-the-ball defense):

- Stay between the ball and the basket.
- Get in the basic defensive stance. Stay low and be ready to move your feet.
- Overplay by a half step to the offensive player's strongside or favorite move. The ballhandler's lane to the basket is blocked. Maintain your position.

Defense is much easier if the defender plays aggressive and smart defense before his opponent gets the ball.

- Deny penetration into the lane by either a dribble or pass.
- Focus your eyes on the player's chest or belly button, not on his eyes.
- Keep your hands ready and in position to deflect a dribble, pass, or shot.
- Anticipate the ballhandler will change directions by crossing over or picking up his dribble.
- If your man picks up his dribble, immediately get in his face with a tight defense to prevent a shot and make a pass more difficult.

Going for the Ball

A player can spring forward faster than he can reach. Therefore, when a player anticipates a pass and goes for the ball, he can react more quickly by springing for the ball and reaching simultaneously. If the player is in a balanced defensive position, on the balls of his feet with his knees flexed, he is then ready to spring into the passing lane. Any time a player reaches for the ball, he should remain in a balanced stance so he can react quickly. If he leans forward so much that his weight is no longer evenly balanced, he will not be able to react quickly if the opponent attempts to drive by him.

Stealing the Dribble

If you are attempting to steal the ball, you should:

- Flex your knees a little more so you can get lower to the floor. From this lower position, you may spring and/or reach forward to deflect the ball. Remain in a balanced defensive position. Do not lean forward.
- Try to steal the ball as it approaches the floor or bounces off the floor. By reaching a little lower, a better chance exists of getting the ball and less a chance of being called for a foul.
- Reach with your hand closest to the ball. Do not reach across your body to go for the ball. By reaching across your body, your reach is restricted. Furthermore, your stance is no longer balanced. Your shoulder and body are thrown forward toward the opponent, thereby increasing the likelihood of a foul being called.
- Do not slap down at the ball if you are trying to steal the dribble. A foul will be called. Reach laterally or upward.

Deflections

Deflections are a sign of an active, hustling defense. Many high school and college coaches keep stats on the number of deflections a player makes. A defender who can't get in position to steal the pass can still create havoc for the offense by deflecting the ball. The deflection may result in a turnover or upset the timing and flow of the offense. The point to remember is that if you can't steal the ball, deflect it.

Deflections are a sign of an active, hustling defense.

Intercepting the Reverse Pass to the Backside (Offside)

In zone and man-to-man defenses, the defender on the backside has the responsibility of sagging down toward the lane to help on defense. This positioning leaves the offensive player open. Zone defenses may offer more opportunities for interceptions on the backside. Only a few players instinctively have the knack of being able to intercept the pass when the ball is reversed to the backside player. However, players can learn to anticipate and intercept the reverse pass. The following examples illustrate ways that you can use to enhance your chances of achieving such a goal:

- Analyze the opponent's tendencies. Are the passes crisp when the ball is reversed? Are they bounce or chest passes? Does the passer fake the pass? Does the offside player step aggressively to meet the ball, or does he wait on it?
- Know the situation. Is your team's defense denying all scoring and passing opportunities on the offside of the court? Is the player about to be called for a five-second violation? Is the ballhandler having trouble finding an open teammate? If so, the ballhandler will look to reverse the ball to the opposite side of the court if the teammate appears to be open.
- Set up the passer. Defenders can set up the offense into thinking a player is open when, in reality, the defender is waiting to jump into the passing lane and intercept the pass. If the defender has not attempted to steal the pass before, he may play a half step closer to the ballhandler the next time so his teammate still appears to be open.

Zone defenses may offer more opportunities for interceptions on the backside.

The defender may also decoy the offense by acting as if he isn't paying attention to the passer. The defender may have his head turned slightly in another direction, while he is really focused on the ballhandler. The defender may also hide behind offensive players in or near the lane, so when the passer glances to that side he does not see a defender close by.

➢ Explode to the ball. Watch the eyes of the passer. Is he focused intently on the player? Anticipate the pass. When the passer's hands or arms pull back slightly to coil and get more power on the pass, the defender's body should be coiled and ready to explode into the passing lane as the ball is released! The defender should try to intercept the pass one or two steps inside the offensive player, so they will not collide if the offensive player steps toward the ball. Watch the ball into your hands. Take the ball quickly in for a layup.

If the ball cannot be caught cleanly, the defender should try to deflect the ball so it falls slightly in front of the defender. He can quickly gain control of the ball without chasing the ball down.

Man-to-Man Defense

Shutting down your man is not enough; each player on the court must be ready to play help defense. Each defender must have good court awareness and know where the ball is and what is happening on the floor. Court awareness and anticipation help good defensive players become great defenders.

❏ Man-to-Man Defense is Played One of Two Ways

With regard to man-to-man defense, coaches will teach their players to play denial defense and/or help defense, depending upon their defensive philosophy:

Court awareness and anticipation help good defensive players become great defenders.

• *Denial defense.* The objective of denial defense is for each defender to guard his man so tightly that he can never receive a pass. Every defense tries to prevent an offensive player from getting the ball close to the basket. In denial defense, the guards are hustling to prevent a pass to his man, even at the three-point line or beyond. Offensive teams can cut back door against denial defenses if the low post area is vacant.

• *Help defense.* The objective of help defense is to prevent your man from scoring, then to be ready to you're your teammates when your man does not have the ball, or he is not in easy scoring position. As a defender, you are more concerned with sagging off your man and helping teammates prevent a score than denying your man the ball.

In reality, every man-to-man defense plays both denial and help defense to varying extents. The difference is whether the coach places the emphasis on denying the ball everywhere or clogging the lane.

❑ Backside Help Defense

When the help defense comes from the offside defender, it is called backside help defense. Shutting down the lane requires great backside help defense. When the opponent is trying to feed a player near the basket, the defense has three choices: play behind the offensive player and allow him to catch the ball; play beside the player and try to deny a pass to the player; or front the player and attempt to prevent an easy entry pass to the opponent.

The instant a pass is made to a player near the basket, the offside defender must immediately help defend the player and prevent a shot or move to the basket. The backside defender should be in good defensive position before the offensive player gains control of the ball. The backside defender and the offensive player's defender then trap the offensive player. Another defensive teammate must then rotate over to cover the backside defender's man.

❑ Rotation defense

Rotation defense is an improvement on the basic help defense. In a help defense, the defender is responsible for helping a teammate, before recovering quickly to defend his man. If the opposition passes the ball well, the basic help defense may allow too many outside shots.

Rotation defense involves rotating over and covering for any teammate who has left his man to help a teammate on defense. The rotating player is covering a player who is most likely to receive the next pass. The more times an offense is forced to pass the ball to find an open man, the more likely a turnover is. Rotation defense is employed by many high school teams, college teams, and quite frequently in the NBA. Rotation defense involves a total team concept. Any one player not hustling and doing his part will cause his defense to fail.

Rotation defense involves a total team concept.

Another example of a rotation defense being employed involves a situation when the weakside, low-post defender goes across the lane to help double team. Another player on the offside needs to sag down to defend and front the offensive low post, who was left unguarded on the offside. The objective of this rotation is to deny all shots close to the basket and force the offense to shoot the lower-percentage outside shot.

❑ Basic Man-to-Man Defensive Rules

The following basis man-to-man defensive rules apply, according to the situation specified:

- When your man doesn't have the ball (i.e., off-the-ball defense). In help defense, the defender is defending both the player he is guarding and the ball, while sagging down toward the lane. The defender should step back one or two steps toward the lane and be prepared to help a teammate, intercept a pass, or quickly hustle back to defend his man. In denial defense, the defender stays between his man and the ball at all times.

- When your man has the ball (i.e., on-the-ball-defense). On-the-ball defense is played in the same manner as in help and denial defense. The defender stays between the offensive player and the basket in order to prevent a move to the basket or a shot. First, deny a drive or pass toward the basket. Then, deny the shot. If your man is in his scoring area, deny the shot before the drive.

- When the ballhandler picks up his dribble. In this situation, the ballhandler only has two options—to shoot or pass. As a result, the guard should immediately defend the player very tightly and aggressively without fouling. The objective of the defender is to make it difficult for the ballhandler to make a good pass, since the aggressive defense will also make it hard for him to get a good view of the floor and to deliver the pass on time. The defender should remember that the offensive player can still pivot and make a move near the basket. At all times, the defender should keep one hand immediately in front of the ball as it is moved around by the passer in an effort to find a way to get the pass off. This seldom-taught skill of shadowing the ball can easily be improved in practice by working on a shadow drill with another player.

- If a dribbler gets by you and drives toward the basket. Do not chase the ballhandler. Instead, beat the ballhandler to the spot where he is headed. Remember, a straight line gets you there faster. If you are beaten, you must hustle and either try to deny a shot or anticipate a pass if your teammate has helped out. If a teammate left his man to help stop your man, the ballhandler is likely to pass to the player who was left open. Hustle to intercept the pass by breaking into that passing lane.

- When your man has passed the ball. In this situation, you should block the path of the opponent to prevent him from immediately cutting to another area or sag back toward the lane to establish a defensive position where you can watch the ball and your man.

The Guard in a Man-to-Man Defense

A guard playing on-the-ball defense must keep a basic low-defensive position, since his man (i.e., an offensive guard) is a very real threat to drive toward the basket. The defensive guard should:

- Not allow his man to beat him with the dribble.
- Not allow an uncontested shot.
- Deny his man's favorite moves. Force the offensive player to the weakest part of his game.
- Not allow a dribble into the lane. Force the defender to the side of the court.

A guard (or forward) may double down after his man has made an entry pass to a forward or post. Before doubling down, the defender must first prevent a cut to the basket by the passer. If the passer stays outside or drifts slightly laterally, the defender may then double down. If the passer is a great shooter, the defender may not want to double down and leave him open for an easy shot. The defense must always adjust to the offense's best scorers.

The defender who has sagged down should never lose sight of his offensive man, since the player will often drift to an open area when the defender looks away. This movement creates more time to get the shot off if the ball is passed back outside by the player being double teamed. A guard playing off-the-ball defense has two ways to play defense:

If the offensive player being guarded is a scoring threat, the best defense may be to deny the player the ball. This approach is referred to as denial defense. The defender plays tight, aggressive defense and plays the passing lanes. The object is to make it difficult to pass to his man. If a defender is playing an aggressive denial-defense, the offensive player can easily cut to the basket (the backdoor cut) if the defender looks away for a second.

If the offensive player being guarded is not a scoring threat or likely to drive to the basket, the defender may want to sag off a little more than usual so he can play help defense. The defender will look to help pick up a penetrating dribbler or help double team the person with the ball. The purpose is to get one more defender in the lane to help his teammates. If the ball is passed to his man, the defender must hustle to cover him.

- *Post defense by guards.* Any offensive player in a man-to-man offense may post-up a defender near the basket, if the offensive player thinks he can score on him. Guards may post-up if they have a size advantage, or if they are good post-up players.

Defending in the post is different than defending on the perimeter, because the offensive player's back is to the basket. Once the player has the ball, he will shoot immediately or fake and make a move. A player who is being posted-up should follow the same principles as previously discussed for the post, as well as the following:

➣ Use quickness to his advantage if the defender is smaller and quicker.
➣ Play defense with his feet. Quick changes of good defensive position are effective.
➣ If a mismatch in height occurs near the basket, the defender must play between the player and the basket while hoping for teammates to double team.

- *The guards' role in the transition defense.* Young players do not understand the concept that their responsibility is different in the transition-defense than in the regular man-to-man defense. In transition-defense, they sometimes mistakenly leave the ballhandler unguarded, when they go to find their man. Since guards and forwards are usually out near the top of the circle on offense, they are the first ones back on defense. In transition defense, the first defenders upcourt must stop the ballhandler and any opponent to whom he may pass. The guards should only worry about their man once other teammates have assumed the role of defending the ballhandler or the lane.

In transition defense, the first defenders upcourt must stop the ballhandler and any opponent to whom he may pass.

❑ The Forward in a Man-to-Man Defense

The forward in a man-to-man defense must first deny his man a basket or a path to the basket. His next responsibility is to deny the pass to the post.

When the opposing forward cuts to the foul line, keep the opponent in front of you, so he can't back cut to the basket. Do not allow the forward the opportunity to go high-to-low after faking in the opposite direction. When playing forward in a man-to-man defense, use the same techniques as guards use. If you have scouted your opponent, you should know the offensive player's moves around the basket, as well as whether or not he fakes before shooting.

When an opponent comes out to the three-point line, the forward should be ready to step out to defend a screen or tightly cover a good-shooting offensive player. If the offensive player is not a threat to score from outside or drive to the basket, the defender can help his teammates by playing his man looser.

When defending a player on the offside, the forward must be ready to play help defense. This factor is especially useful in shutting down the lane. Rotation defense is useful in these situations. When the forward has gone to help on defense, the off-side guard will rotate down to help cover the forward's man.

Forwards are expected to be good rebounders. The last aspect of a good defensive play is to box out your man when a shot is taken and then rebound.

❏ The Post (Center) in a Man-to-Man Defense

Defensive centers often need help in shutting down their man. If they are beaten, an easy shot or dunk will usually result. Since little time exists for the defense to help after a post player is beaten so close to the basket, his teammates should help prevent the offensive center from getting the ball or an easy shot. Either the guards or forwards should help double team the center.

A double team by the defense can easily be beaten by a center who is a great passer, but as a rule, few centers ever develop great passing skills. They are usually only concerned with getting their shot off. A great passing center can create havoc with a defense.

As a post (center) playing defense, you should:

➢ Deny the offensive post the opportunity to get the ball in a desirable low-post position. Forcing the opposing center to shoot two to five feet further out will result in a poorer percentage shot. Meet the offensive player at or above the free throw line; move your feet to make the offensive post work to gain his position.
  • Keep your forearm on the post's lower back. The space created by your actions makes it difficult for the post to use a spin move. Spin moves by a post are more effective when the offensive post is close up against the defender.
  • Hustle to beat the opponent to the spot where he wants to go if he has initiated a move.
➢ Deny the passing lane to the post.

Forwards are expected to be good rebounders.

- Not react to a ball fake.
- Keep your arms straight up over your head when defending a shot. Do not reach out toward the opponent. Never slap at the ball.
- Not try to block the shot if you are in early foul trouble. Maintain verticality and do not jump.
- Block out your man anytime a shot is taken, and then go for the rebound.
- Step out to defend a player who has beaten a teammate and is driving to the basket. Make the defender pick up his dribble and look to pass. Deny a pass to your man. You should get backside help on your man.

Since posts are used frequently to set screens at or near the three-point line, they should learn how to properly defend those screens. A post can prevent an opponent from having a good scoring opportunity if he defends screens well. (Refer to chapter 25 for more information on screens.)

• *Blocking Shots.* The post is usually the best shot blocker on the team. The primary objective of blocking the shot is to prevent the score and to gain possession of the ball. In today's game, some players think the purpose is to intimidate the opponent. They swat the ball as hard as they can, causing the ball to usually go out of bounds. This "macho attitude" hurts the team because the opponent is then given another chance to score. Blocking the shot is intimidation enough. No need exists to showboat. For example, the player making the block should not dance around as if he had never blocked a shot before. The good shot blocker simply deflects the ball enough so that he or a teammate gains possession of the ball. As a shot blocker, you should:

Blocking the shot is intimidation enough. No need exists to showboat.

- First establish good defensive position.
- Understand your opponent's favorite moves.
- Don't be so anxious to block the shot that you take your man's fake.
- Wait for the shooter to start his jump before you go for the block. Maintain the principle of verticality.
- Block the ball. Do not slap at the ball, or the referee will call a foul.

• *Defending the Backscreen.* Backscreens are often used around the lane to get posts open in the lane. Backscreens are best defended as a team. Rather than switching on the backscreen, which may result in a mismatch close to the basket, the backscreen should be defended in the following manner:

- The defender of the offensive player setting the backscreen should step out to the side and block the progress of the cutter, until the cutter's defender has regained his defensive position.
- The defender of the player setting the screen should then hustle to get back to guard his man who may also be open.

Zone Defense

In a zone defense, the defender is not assigned to defend a specific player. Instead, the defender is responsible for defending any player in his assigned area of the court. A zone defender tries to deny passes, make steals, and guard players tightly when they have the ball. When the ball is on the opposite side of the court, the zone defender will sag back into the lane as he would often do in a sagging man-to-man defense.

Why would a team play a zone defense? Every team should have at least one or two zone defenses they can effectively run, in addition to their man defenses. The defense dictates the style of play of the game. The primary objective of any defense selected is to attack the opponent's weakness, while trying to deny the opponent's strengths. The following reasons help explain why a team might play a zone defense:

- To force the opponent to shoot outside, either when they face a poor outside shooting team, or when they face a team with a strong inside game.
- If the defense is not athletic or fast enough to match up well in a man-to-man defense.
- To change the tempo and style of play. Teams get in an offensive rhythm. Changing the style of play sometimes gets a team out of their rhythm and creates doubts.
- To force the other team out of their man-to-man offense and into a zone offense if the opponent has a good man-to-man offense.
- If one of the defense's key players is in foul trouble.

A zone defense must define who the shooters are.

A zone defense must define who the shooters are. Even though defenders in a zone defense do not have an assigned man to guard tightly, the defense is designed to deny shots by the opponent's best shooters. Therefore, it is imperative that the defender is always aware if a shooter is in his area. The defender should play this man almost as tightly as if he were playing a man defense.

The defenders guarding players who are not scoring threats will sag off slightly more than usual, unless the scoring threats are near the basket. These offensive players should prove they are a scoring threat before the defense should guard them more aggressively.

Zone defenses can be modified from game to game or even during a game to adjust to the other team's offensive strategies and match-ups. The team should practice making these adjustments while scrimmaging, so the defense will be comfortable and confident making them during a game.

❑ Types of Zone Defenses

• *2-1-2 zone.* The 2-1-2 zone is designed to give zone coverage to all potential scoring areas of the court, rather than concentrating on one area. It allows for good defensive coverage in all areas, including the free-throw area, and against teams that like to work the ball inside. It allows for good rebounding and fast-break positions.

The weakness of the 2-1-2 zone is that it is difficult to cover good shooters from the wing and corner areas. Shots can be made from the top of the circle. It is also vulnerable to good baseline shots and moves.

• *1-3-1 zone.* The 1-3-1 zone is intended to force the opponent to take the shot from the corner. If the opposing point guard is a great penetrator with the dribble, this zone may be ineffective. This defense is very strong in the foul-line area and against any post offense. It supplies good coverage in most of the dangerous jump-shot areas. It neutralizes much of the overloading against a zone. It forces the offense to make adjustments to its normal zone offense.

The weakness of the 1-3-1 zone is its vulnerability to good corner shooters. It does not cover the rebounding areas as well as some zones, so it is not quite as good for a fast-break offense as is a 2-1-2 zone. It is vulnerable to short baseline shots if the offensive players are positioned well. From this position, the defense must react quickly to prevent a shot after a pass from the close-baseline area. This is the area at which the offense will attack the defense.

The weakness of the 2-1-2 zone is that it is difficult to cover good shooters from the wing and corner areas.

• *2-3 zone.* The 2-3 zone is designed to defend against a dominant offensive post. The 2-3 zone allows such a player to be surrounded by at least two or more players at all times. This defense covers the corner and the baseline, and it puts the defenders in good rebounding positions.

The weakness of the 2-3 zone is that it is vulnerable in the free-throw and high-post areas. Concentrating most of the defenders in the paint makes the 2-3 zone vulnerable to a good outside shooting team, especially if the opponent has a great inside-outside game. The front areas of the zone can be easily overloaded.

- *3-2 zone.* The 3-2 zone is very strong against good outside shooting teams, but is weak against an outstanding post offense. This zone is very good at applying pressure to inexperienced or poor ballhandling guards. Three quick guards and two large, but slow, posts could play this defense. It could be effective at initiating a good fast-break offense.

The weakness of the 3-2 zone is that it offers poor coverage to the corners and rebound areas. It is also weak, once the front line is penetrated. It is vulnerable in the free-throw area for a pass and a quick shot. It is also vulnerable to good baseline shots and moves. This offense can be overloaded in the deep area where scoring is easier.

- *Match-up zone.* The match-up zone is a combination zone and man-to-man defense. In recent years, it has become much more popular than it had previously been. It allows the defense to play aggressive man-to-man defense within a zone concept. The concept can be modified to fit various zones and situations.

Special Defenses

Special defenses are typically used sparingly in games. When one is employed, it is seldom for the entire game. Special defenses are usually instituted when the opponent has a single dominant player. They are intended to create situations for which the opponent has not prepared. Any time that a defense can create doubt or frustration in the mind of the opponent, the defense has a better chance of controlling the game.

The box-and-one defense is played when the opponent depends heavily on one player for a disproportionate part of the offense and other aspects of the game. For example, the player may be their best defender, best ballhandler, rebounder, or free-throw shooter. The intent of the box-and-one defense is to apply intense man-to-man pressure on this player every second of the game by rotating fresh defensive players. The defense wants to:

> Deny the offensive player the opportunity to score his average points per game.
> Make the player work very hard to receive a pass, get the ball up the court, or get a good look at the basket.
> Frustrate the opposing player and create doubt in his mind.
> Tire out the player so he is less effective in the latter stages of the game.

- *Box-and-one defense.* In a box-and-one defense, four defenders play a two-two zone in the lane, while one defender plays an aggressive,

Special defenses are usually instituted when the opponent has a single dominant player.

in-your-face, man-to-man defense all over the floor. If your best defender is also one of your best scorers, another defender may need to play the man-to-man defense. Whoever guards the other team's dominant player is likely to get in foul trouble. If two or three players rotate on the man, the fouls will then be spread among the players. One or two of the rotating players from the second team are often the best players to use in this situation, so that other starters are not at risk of getting in foul trouble. Every coach should remember the importance of having substitutes who play great defense.

• *The triangle-and-two defense.* In the triangle-and-two defense, three defenders play a zone in the paint. A guard is just above the free-throw line and two posts or forwards are down low near the blocks. These three players form a triangle zone. The other two defenders play man-to-man defense on their assigned players. This defense should be used only for a short time. For example, it can be employed in key situations to catch the offense off guard. Once the offense figures out how to beat it, a team should switch back to its normal defense.

Since this defense is used infrequently, the offensive strategy to attack it is seldom discussed. Among the ways to beat the triangle-and-two zone defense are the following two options:

(1) Attack the tip of the triangle:

- Isolate the two players being guarded man-to-man on one side of the court. One of these two players should be the ballhandler.
- The other three players will be on the weakside. For example, a player may be at the top, one at a wing, and one on the low-post area.
- The ballhandler drives toward the lane, and passes to a player coming off a screen on the weakside.
- The weakside wing should be open for a jump shot if the guard at the top and/or the weakside post have screened the defender at the free-throw line (i.e., the top of the triangle);

(2) Attack the base of the triangle:

- Another possibility would be to have a weakside wing and a low post. The third weakside player should be a good shooter stationed in the corner. The two players being guarded man-to-man are on the other side of the court. The ballhandler, being guarded man-to-man, dribbles into the lane and passes to a teammate in the opposite corner. The low post has screened the low-post defender nearest the weakside, and the wing has screened the guard at the triangle. No defender is free to get out to the shooter in the corner.

- *The press defense.* The press-defense is designed to create turnovers. The press is used after a basket is made, whether a field goal or a free throw. If a team presses, the coach should expect more fouls than normal. A pressing defense is used against the following types of teams:

  ➣ A slow team
  ➣ A team with poor or questionable ballhandlers
  ➣ A poorly conditioned team

The press may be needed late in a game, if the team is behind. A pressing defense should be discontinued if the opponent is getting more easy baskets off the press than the defensive team is. If the coach feels the opposing team has no depth on the bench and they are likely to tire later in the game, he may choose to continue the press.

- *Transition defense.* When a defensive team gets the ball from a turnover or rebound, the offensive team must quickly make the transition from offense to defense. The objective is to prevent an easy shot if the opponent pushes the ball upcourt.

What should an offensive player do when a defensive player gets a rebound or a turnover? To prevent an easy transition basket after the defense gets a rebound or a turnover, offensive players must:

  ➣ Defend the basket. The players nearest the top of the key must get back down court to protect the lane and the basket. Their first responsibility is to stop the ballhandler before finding their man.

  ➣ Deny the outlet pass. If a player is out-rebounded by his man, he should not allow the rebounder to immediately make an outlet pass. The defender should keep his arms high and get in the face of his opponent.

- *End-of-game defenses.* Situations at the end of the game may necessitate the defense to alter its normal defensive scheme, since the offensive team is normally changing its strategy. The defense should practice these situations at least once a week for a few minutes throughout the season to ensure the players are comfortable and confident switching defensive tactics. Unless the team has practiced switching defenses, they may have the normal defensive concepts so ingrained that they do not

The press-defense is designed to create turnovers.

A pressing defense should be discontinued if the opponent is getting more easy baskets off the press than the defensive team is.

quickly make the necessary mental adjustments. It only takes one player out of sync to disable the defense. Defenses must be comfortable in the following late-game situations:

➣ The defensive team is behind:

1. The offense stalls in the last several minutes of the game.

    - Against a stalling team, each defender must play intense denial defense at all times, or he will leave his man open for an easy outlet pass.
    - The offense will have spread out over the entire halfcourt. The guards will be trying to dribble and pass from near the mid-court line to near the free-throw line. The natural tendency is for defenders to sag off their man, immediately after he has passed.
    - Teams that have not practiced a stall defense will waste a lot of time before finally understanding what is expected and why. This wasted time may be the difference in winning and losing.
    - The defense must also look for an opportunity to trap. If a player is trapped, the other defenders must rotate quickly to cover the unguarded player and prevent passes to the closest players. The open player should be far from the basket. Players should be alert to anticipate this player cutting toward the ballhandler.
    - The coach may need to remind the team during a stoppage of play to be ready to play a stall defense.
    - Stall defenses must be practiced.
    - Stall defenses must practice fouling specific players, not the best free-throw shooter.

2. If very little time is left (only a few seconds), the coach may instruct the players to press full-court.

    - The first objective is to get a five-second inbounding call.
    - The second objective is to intercept the inbound pass.
    - The third objective is to immediately foul the first offensive player to catch the ball. Be careful to not be called for an intentional foul. Make it look as if you are trying to slap the ball away.

➣ The defensive team is ahead:

When the defensive team is ahead, the players must be prepared to adjust quickly to the current game situation. During the last several minutes of play, the opponent's offensive strategy will change according to the score and the amount of time remaining.

1. In the last couple of minutes of the game, if the defensive team is ahead by at least five or six points, the team should continue to play the current defense. The defenders should be a little more alert to the other team's best shooter and/or hottest player, who is probably looking to score. The team may also look for the three-point shot.

2. If the defensive team is ahead by three points or more in the last thirty seconds of the game, the defense should anticipate a three-point shot and adjust accordingly. For example, the defense should switch on all screens at the three-point line and stay very close to any player with the ball.

In this situation, the offense will normally try to get a shot by:

- Passing back to the inbounder.
- Passing inside then back outside.
- Screening at the three-point line to free either a ballhandler or a cutter looking for a pass.

Defensive Considerations for Coaches

A coach's responsibility in developing a defense involves:

- Putting players in a defense they can play successfully.
- Having each individual playing the position that is best suited for his athletic abilities and skills. It only takes one player being out of position to ruin the effectiveness of a defense.
- Choosing a particular defense based on the skills of the five players on the floor. One combination of players may play full-court, man-to-man defense well. Changing one player may result in a group who would be better suited playing a zone or picking up in a man-to-man defense inside the three-point line.

The coach will not always have players with the athletic ability or skills to do some of the things that he would prefer. Coaches need to adapt their scheme to the strengths of the players in the program that particular year. If the players are fundamentally sound, they can adapt easily to different variations.

❏ The Defensive Plan for the Year

The players with which you, as the coach, have to work should dictate the style of defense that the team should use throughout the year. Never insist on playing a defense because you like it. Your players must be able to execute the defense properly, or you should use a different defense.

An accurate evaluation of the strengths and weaknesses of your players and the team early in the year is critical if you are to be able to select the defense that best fits the talent of your players. Later, if the talent level changes and the players have improved significantly, a different defense can be incorporated into your defensive strategy.

❑ Evaluating the Defensive Effort of the Players

Spectacular defensive plays excite the crowds; steady, effective defense excites a coach. Players who deny a pass, prevent a shot, or deny the offensive player their preferred offensive position or favorite shot are contributing just as much as the player who steals the ball or blocks a shot. Quite often, a player on the team who has given a great defensive effort is not recognized. The "ground-bound" player who gets a fingertip on a shot, causing a miss, is no different than the defender who skies and stuffs the ball with authority. Both players have done their job. Basketball has statistics for steals and blocks, but none exist for the many other things that go unnoticed.

The coach has the responsibility of determining the defensive job done by each player by carefully observing and evaluating the efforts of each player during the game and by reviewing game film so that his players can be recognized for doing the little things that often go unnoticed.

For example, the coach may want to evaluate how often the players block out or fail to do so; how often they get beat off the dribble; the number of times they provide backside help on screens, as well as when they fail to do so. Aggressive defense that leads to a poor pass or a turnover is also noted. The coach should also look at the number of points each defender allows and determine if those shots were challenged or unchallenged. Other defensive considerations may be the number of times a player goes for a rebound, how many times a player is blown by, and whether or not the player plays good help-defense and defends back-door cuts. The defensive stats which might be kept include:

> Points allowed while defending. The number of points a player's man scored with that individual defending him. The minutes played should also be considered.
> Turnovers caused. A player can play great defense and get few steals. A defender who is challenging an offensive player may cause turnovers by causing the player to be out of position, unable to control the ball, or generally making it difficult to make a good pass or catch a pass.
> Deflections of the ball. A defender may get few steals, but he may create havoc by deflecting passes. Good anticipation, prop-

er defensive position, hustle, and desire are needed to deflect passes. A player who deflects a pass not only creates a potential turnover, he also upsets the timing and confidence of the offense. Deflections are a sign of a hustling defense. The team with a relatively high number of deflections usually wins the game. The coach may want one of the managers to keep a chart on deflections. This situation is another opportunity for the coach to notice the little things, and it is also another opportunity to praise a player who is working hard.

- Blockouts. Blocking out on the defensive end for rebounds.
- Blow-bys. Getting beat off the dribble defensively.
- Helps. How many times a player comes over and plays good help defense.
- Step-outs. A step-out refers to when a defender steps out because his man is setting the screen. The purpose of the step-out is to slow the progress of an opposing player who is cutting around a screen and to allow time for a teammate to recover.

❑ Defensive Considerations at the Junior High and Youth Level

Younger players need to learn where most points are scored before they reach high school. The most points are scored on fast-break layups either after turnovers in the half-court offense or after turnovers caused by a pressing defense. Most other points are scored within six to eight feet of the basket. Among the steps that younger players could take to reduce or eliminate some of these points are the following:

- Play smart offense and avoid turnovers, a scenario which is, in fact, the "best" defense.
- Play good transition defense against the fast break. Make the ballhandler pick up his dribble or force the dribble away from the basket. If the opponent is forced to make one or two passes, he may make a turnover.
- Make it hard for any player to get an easy basket. Play help defense. The defender's first responsibility is to prevent a score.

In junior high school and youth leagues, the defense should deny the layup and the short shots, thereby forcing the offense to pass the ball back outside where scores are more difficult.

The junior high or youth league coach must also control the style and tempo of play. If the coach allows his teams to engage in a racehorse style of play, streaking from one end of the court to the other, the team may win games, but the players on those teams will not develop the offensive and defensive skills necessary to be successful when they go on to the next level. The coach must control the game so the players are forced to learn the necessary skills, even if the team risks the chance of losing the game. The entire program will profit in the long run.

❑ Defensive No-No's Often Encountered at the Junior High or Youth League Level

- Never leave a player who has the ball if they he is in a scoring area. Inexperienced players are sometimes so concerned with getting to their assigned man or area of the court (in a zone) that they leave the ballhandler, thereby leaving him unguarded.
- Never allow a player to shoot the ball without being challenged, even if it isn't your man.
- Leaning and reaching for the ball.
- Going for a steal near midcourt on a fast break. Instead, move your feet and force the defender to the side if possible. Protect the basket.
- Watching a dribbler's eyes instead of his stomach.
- Watching the ball after it is shot, instead of blocking out your man and rebounding.
- Trying to defend an offensive player in a tight full- or half-court defense when the player is much faster than you are. He will not score from midcourt. Get down court and play him tighter the closer he gets to his scoring area.

Defensive Tips

Copy this section, cut it out, and mount it where you will see it every day.

❑ Basic Fundamentals of Defense

A player should:

- Have the desire to be a good defender. Few players want to be great defenders. Coaches love players who love to play defense.
- Have a basketball attitude. Be intense and determined to dominate your individual opponent. If he beats you, be even more determined, but never be out of control.
- Be aggressive.
- Always remember that maintaining proper defensive position is the key to good defense and avoiding fouls.
- Play defense with the feet. Keep moving.

If the coach allows his teams to engage in a racehorse style of play, streaking from one end of the court to the other, the team may win games, but the players on those teams will not develop the offensive and defensive skills necessary to be successful when they go on to the next level.

- Never cross your legs on defense, unless you're sprinting to catch up.
- Don't be caught standing straight up or flat-footed.
- Never rest or relax while playing defense—even for a second. The second a you relax, the offensive player will make a move.
- Know your opponent and anticipate his moves.

☐ Defending a Player Without the Ball:

- The best defense should be played before your man gets the ball. Deny favorable position and the ball. Eighty percent of the time you are defending a player without the ball.
- When your man doesn't have the ball, keep both the ball and your man in sight at all times. Focus more on your man and less on the ball.
- Always be ready to help a teammate on defense. Defense is a team game!
- The farther your man is from the ball, the farther you may be from him.

☐ Defending a Player with the Ball:

- Overplay your man to deny his strengths or favorite moves.
- Make the ballhandler commit. Never charge toward a ballhandler who has not used up his dribble. Establish a basic defensive position and advance toward the ballhandler. Be ready to slide right or left, and to deny a move to the basket.
- Do not lean forward and reach for the ball, or the ballhandler can easily drive by you.
- Force the dribbler toward the side, corner, or a congested area.
- Cut off all baseline drives and force the ballhandler to pick up his dribble or cut back toward the middle where the defensive help is.
- When your man passes, quickly back up two steps toward the basket, but be prepared to get in his path if he cuts to the basket.
- Stay between your man and the basket when your man has the ball, but stay between your man and the ball when he is near the basket without the ball.

☐ Defending a Player when a Shot is Taken:

- Block your man out and then go for the rebound.
- Maintain verticality, even if you go for the block.
- Do not jump to block a shot until the offensive player leaves his feet.

The best defense should be played before your man gets the ball.

Defense is a team game!

- Try to block the shot and catch the ball if possible.
- If you can't block the shot, try to obstruct the shooter's vision.

❑ Defending a Player if the Ball is Lost:

- If you lose the ball, do not fret or pout; hustle back on defense as fast as you can. At the other end of the court, avoid a senseless foul made in anger and frustration. Not hustling back immediately or making a senseless foul are reasons for the coach to put you back on the bench.
- If a teammate loses a ball, sprint back and deny a lane to the basket.

❑ Defending Screens:

- Fight through screens.
- If your man is the screener, communicate and step out to slow down the offensive player coming around the screen.
- Never switch on a pick-and-roll or on a screen-and-roll.

❑ Important Factors in Defense

The three most important factors in defense, in order of importance are:

- *The ball.* The defense must stop the ball from being taken to the basket by any player. Do not allow any player to be uncontested if they are in the lane or near the basket.

- *The defender's position relative to the ball, the basket, and his man.* The defender should be in defensive-help position and have good vision of the floor so he can anticipate and play good help-defense.

- *The defender's man.* With good position and technique, the defender can properly defend his man.

❑ Why Emphasize the Ball First?

- If the team emphasis is on the ball, the team will have maximum help, thereby allowing less athletic players to compete effectively against more talented opponents.
- If defenders are overly concerned in denying their man the ball, even when they are not in the scoring area, they will not be able to give adequate help defense. A denial defense requires terrific

athletes. The truth is that even squads with terrific athletes will meet teams against whom they must be comfortable playing help defense.

Summary Points

Defense is a TEAM game. Praise and encourage your teammates as they give outstanding efforts. Defense wins games and championships. Believe it and achieve it!

Defense wins games and championships.

CHAPTER 24

Getting Open

Many young players don't understand that if they want the ball, they have to work hard to get open. They stand around wanting someone to pass them the ball so they can shoot. Great shooters have to work hard to get open because their defenders are working hard to deny them the shot. "Break to an open area" is a basketball maxim that always holds true. If in doubt about what to do, break to an open area looking for a pass or the opportunity to screen for a teammate. An offense is designed to get players open if it is run correctly with the proper spacing, timing, and good screens.

Helping Teammates Get Open

Helping a teammate get open is a vital skill that every offensive player should possess. Among the ways that a player can help a teammate get open for a pass, move, or shot are the following:
Helping a teammate get open is a vital skill that every offensive player should possess.

> *Helping a teammate get open is a vital skill that every offensive player should possess.*

- ➢ Maintain proper spacing. A player shouldn't be too close to a teammate, or his defender will easily be able to help defend both teammates.
- ➢ If a player sets a good screen, he opens up a teammate for a pass or a drive to the basket.
- ➢ If a player makes a move, beats his man, and attacks the basket, another defender either has to step out to stop his move or allow an easy shot. As the ballhandler penetrates the defense, he looks to see from where the help defense is coming and passes to the open teammate in that area.
- ➢ One of the best ways to get a player open outside is to penetrate inside the lane with a pass or dribble, followed by a pass back outside. This scenario is called an inside-outside game, and it can be very effective. The most basic inside-outside game has

the guard passing to a post, who quickly passes back out to the guard. The guard has drifted to an open area and is open for a high-percentage shot. Penetrating a defense with a dribble or pass is an important factor in breaking down either a man-to-man or zone defense.

- Against a sagging defense, the offensive players must often make the extra pass to find a player who is open. If a defender sags down to help double-team in the lane, the defense may rotate another defender over to cover the outside player who has been left open. This rotation of players is called a rotation defense. Against a rotation defense, with one or two quick passes from the original open player, a player is often found open for an easy shot, usually at the top of the circle or on the opposite side of the court. The first pass is usually to the teammate the rotating player left behind. This player is often somewhere near the top of the circle. If the player is covered, the ball is rotated to the opposite wing or corner where the open player has moved.
- A player near the basket creates or maintains a lane to the basket for his driving teammate when the player screens or pins his defensive opponent, preventing him from stepping out to block the drive to the basket.
- When a player is double-teamed in the low-post area, the player can dribble one step toward the sideline, and the defenders will follow. This subtle movement away from the basket will open the lane for a cutter to the basket from the high-post area or from the top of the circle.
- A cutter or trailer may inadvertently prevent the defender from being able to go with the teammate as he moves by a teammate. The cutter/trailer must not try to set a screen if he is moving. The player must continue on without hesitation. Getting in the way for just a moment is enough to help the teammate get open.
- If a good ballhandling teammate is bringing the ball upcourt against a full-court man-to-man defense, the other players should get upcourt, thereby taking their defenders and denying them the ability to trap the ballhandler.
- Once a press is broken, and the offense has an advantage (two-on-one; three-on-one, etc.), attack the basket. Quickly drive straight into the lane looking to score, but be ready to pass to the open teammate if the defense commits.
- Create a passing lane by drifting to an open area. Do not stay behind and close to the defender. If your defender commits to help double-team another player, or to stop your driving teammate, cut to the basket or move a few steps to a more open area and create a passing lane, for example:

The cutter/trailer must not try to set a screen if he is moving.

- The wing's defender sags down to double-team a player in the lane. If the lane is congested, thereby preventing a cut to the basket, the wing should drift to a more open area. This is usually accomplished by taking a few steps toward the corner or toward the top of the basket.
- The wing's defender on the offside sags into the lane to help defend a player driving from the opposite wing area. The offside wing drifts several steps toward the corner while maintaining an open passing lane. The player must remain in the line of vision of the ballhandler, while maintaining eye contact.
- If your defender is stepping out in the lane to stop a driving teammate, create a passing lane by moving slightly to one side. Be certain to maintain a good scoring position.

How to Get Players Open for a Three-point Shot

❑ The Inside-Outside Game:

- The guard passes the ball inside to the post or a forward. The guard drifts to an open area as his man sags down to double-team the ballhandler, who then passes out to the open guard.
- A ballhandler, usually the point guard or a wing, penetrates inside the defense with a dribble move toward the lane. If another defender sags to help stop the drive, the dribbler passes to the open teammate at the three-point line, usually on the opposite of the court.

❑ Using screens at or near the three-point line:

- A cutter looks for a pass and shoots immediately after coming around a screen.
- A dribbler shoots a three-point shot after driving around a screen set at the three-point line.

❑ Pass the Ball Quickly:

- Pass the ball quickly while reversing and rotating the ball, until an open teammate is found against zones and sagging help defenses.

❑ In a Transition (Fast Break) Offense:

- In the fast break offense, the opposite wing is often left open for a three-point shot if the ballhandler drives slightly toward the lane to make the defenders commit to stopping the drive.

Getting Open on a Fast Break

On a fast break, the offense should fill the three lanes as the basket is attacked. Most coaches want good perimeter shooters to fill a position outside the three-point line between the wing and corner positions. On a fast break, the defense's first objective is to prevent the lane from being driven. The guards are usually the players defending the basket, thereby leaving a three-point shot open. In a fast-break offense, the ballhandler should attack the defense in order to make the defense commit. The ballhandler first looks for open teammates near the basket. If no one is open, he quickly passes to the open teammate, usually at the three-point line.

On the fast break, when the player in the wing area receives a pass and is not tightly guarded, he can shoot, make a move toward the basket, or pass to open teammates, who are usually on the ballside corner area or the opposite wing or corner areas. If none of these initial options are open, the ballhandler should look for the two trailing players (usually posts) to become open as they cut down the lane toward the basket.

If none of the initial fastbreak options are open, a ballhandler at the top of the circle or in the wing area can use a trailer to get open. If the trailer cuts near the wing area on his way to the low-post area, the ballhandler fakes toward the baseline and scrapes off his defender by quickly driving just behind the trailer. The trailer must not try to set a screen if he is moving; getting in the way is adequate.

On a fast break, the defense's first objective is to prevent the lane from being driven.

Getting Open Against a Man-to-Man Defense

Getting open against a man-to-man defense requires hard work. Four of the five players on the court do not have the ball. They must work hard to get open to receive a pass in a desirable position. A player must have good one-on-one skills to beat his man when he has the ball.

Getting open against a man-to-man defense requires hard work.

Getting Open Without the Ball

Moving without the ball is the best way to get open. Players who stand around wanting someone to pass them the ball will seldom be open to receive a pass. Moving without the ball is one of the hardest things to get players to do properly. If you want the ball, you must work hard to get open and help others do the same. Among the steps that you can take to get open are the following:

> - A change of speed with a sudden, hard cut will create a separation from the defender for a moment. Because this is the ideal time to receive a pass, you need to be ready.

- Faking-out defenders is one somewhat easier way to get open. Several ways exist to fake-out defenders, including:
  - Fake hard in one direction and break in the opposite direction to the open area.
  - Fake one way to set up your defender for a screen.
  - Fake the defender into thinking you aren't involved in the play, before breaking hard to the open area or around a screen to the open area.
  - Keep your fakes simple and sudden.
- Come back toward the ball if a teammate is having a hard time finding anyone to whom he can pass. The player opens himself up by coming back toward the player with the ball.
- If your defender goes to help a teammate, cut to an open area or to the basket.
- If your defender turns his head to look for the ball, break for an open area, preferably toward the basket or another area from which you are confident scoring.
- If you do not have a low post on your side:
  - And you pass the ball, cut to the basket.
  - If you do not have the ball, break to the basket when your defender turns his head. This is called cutting backdoor. The backdoor cut is usually made against an aggressive defender who is trying to deny a pass to the player as he pops out near the three-point line in the wing area. The defender will slip to the inside of the offensive player, looking to intercept the pass. As the defender turns his head to look for the ball, the offensive player cuts backdoor toward the basket. Another way to set up a backdoor cut is for the offensive player to relax as he reaches the three-point line if a pass isn't being made. The defender will relax and stand more erect. This is a perfect time to cut backdoor because the defender is not ready to react quickly.
- If the low-post area is congested, and your defender sags away to help on defense, drift or break to an open area. Drifting to an open area is seldom taught, but it is a very effective way to get open if a player can't cut to the basket.
- If the low post area is open on one side of the lane, cut down the lane after passing to a teammate. For example, a player near the top of the circle may pass to a teammate just outside the lane. If the other low-post area is open, the player should cut to the basket looking for a return pass. This move is called the give-and-go.

Getting Open When You Have the Ball

Getting open when you have the ball in a half-court, man-to-man offense is more difficult, since the defense is always focused on the person with the ball. A fake usually initiates a move. A well-executed offense with proper spacing and timing will create lanes for moves to the basket by the offensive player. Against a man-to-man defense, players must have the skills and confidence to beat their defender in one-on-one situations.

A screen set by a teammate will also free up the ballhandler. The ballhandler should keep the defender busy so he doesn't see the screen until it is too late to avoid it.

The give-and-go is the simplest and oldest move in basketball, yet it is still very effective. If a player passes the ball, he will quite often be open for a return pass if he quickly cuts for the basket or an open area.

You should be unpredictable in your moves to get open. The defender should be trying to determine your favorite moves.

Take Advantage of Getting Open

If you work hard to get open and get the pass, make the opportunity count. Catch the ball and make something happen. You should be in a ready position, anticipate a bad pass, and be in a desirable scoring position. This step seems so simple, but many teams have lost games needlessly because of these simple mistakes made after getting open.

It will hurt the team if you don't catch the pass, or if you are too far under the basket to shoot. Sometimes a player receives the pass one step too far toward the baseline, and he can no longer shoot a bank shot. Instead, his positioning forces him to take the lower-percentage shot from the side. For best results, you need to be in position and ready to score.

Freeing the Point Guard Against a Full-Court Man-to-Man Defense

A full-court, man-to-man defense against the point guard will attempt to harass, frustrate, and tire him out, as well as disrupt the timing of the offense. In college, where a 30-second shot clock is employed, defenses hope to reduce the amount of time their opponents will have to run their half-court offense. This defensive tactic is often used even when the defense is not guarding any other player full-court.

An offensive post can help get the point guard open more easily. The other three players quickly get upcourt and take their defenders with them so the ball can be advanced without any traps. The post inbounds the ball to the point guard and goes upcourt. He then sets a screen for the point guard. It is important to set the screen near the middle of the floor so the point guard isn't easily trapped, as he could be if he were near the sideline. Usually, the defensive post is not guarding the offensive post tightly, so an effective screen will easily free up the point guard. If the defensive post switches players, the point guard should quickly dribble around the post and attack the basket.

How to Get a Wing Open to Initiate the Man-to-Man Offense

An aggressive defender, playing denial defense, can make it very difficult for a player to get open to receive a pass from the point guard. The wings cannot just step out and wait for the pass. The defender must be kept off-guard if the wing is to get open and initiate the offense. The team, especially the point guard and the wings, must become comfortable initiating the offense against intense defensive pressure, or they will have difficulty against an outstanding man-to-man defense. Among the steps that wings can take to get open are the following:

> ➣ Fake in and pop out. The wing fakes a move toward the basket and quickly pops back out. Several ways exist to fake in and pop out, including:
>   - A jab step and pop out.
>   - Several quick steps toward the basket, then pop out.
>   - Break toward the basket, use a screen by a post or forward, and break to the open area.
>   - Break around the screen by the post or forward before stopping, and reversing back out to the three-point line, as a teammate sets a backscreen.
> ➣ Pop out toward the three-point line from a screen in a stacked alignment.
> ➣ Have the two wings crisscross as each goes to the other wing position. The wings simultaneously break toward the low-post position and then scissor by each other; or one wing may stop and set a screen for the other wing.
> ➣ Cut backdoor if the defender is overplaying to deny a pass, and the low-post area is open. However, if a teammate is in the low post, the wing can use the backdoor cut to get open by breaking around his screen on the way to the other side.

An aggressive defender, playing denial defense, can make it very difficult for a player to get open to receive a pass from the point guard.

Getting the Post Open in the Man Offense

The post has to work hard to get open and maintain that position. Since the low-post area is typically crowded, a post usually gets open for just a brief moment. Quite often, getting open doesn't mean losing the defender, but it does involve knowing which side of the post the defender is favoring. The defender seldom plays directly behind the post; the defender usually overplays the post in order to deny or deflect a pass to the post. The post should use his body to know where the defender is and to keep the defender in a poor defensive position, thereby creating a passing lane.

A player "posts-up" by establishing a good low-post position to receive the ball, while keeping the defender away. Having the post position involves establishing a wide base by spreading your legs, bending your knees, and keeping the defender at bay with your back, hips and elbows. Be ready to catch the pass cleanly. If the pass is from the wing area, it is often a bounce pass, so be prepared to catch it low. With an entry pass to the post, the post may have to break contact with the defender to get open and catch the ball cleanly.

The working area for posts is the free-throw lane. Posts should learn to use all of this area. Many young posts think that they should simply get down near the basket and wait for the ball. If you want the ball, you have to work for it. If the post is at one of the four corners of the lane and nothing happens, move to one of the other three corners. As the post, your options include:

- Moving directly across the lane to the other high- or low-post area.
- Crossing diagonally across the lane to the opposite post area (move low-to-high or high-to-low on the opposite side of the lane).
- Sliding up or down on the same side of the lane (either high-to-low or low-to-high).

If you want the ball, you have to work for it.

Look to set screens while moving to another area, then establish your position in the next area, wait three seconds, and then move again. Some coaches require the post to move in a triangular area between the two low-post areas and the free-throw line. As a post vacates an area, he creates a lane for a drive by the ballhandler or a cut by a teammate. Movement of the posts is critical, not only in helping to get open, but also in creating a lane to the basket for teammates when they make a move.

If the offense being run doesn't allow the post to follow the moves previously described, the player should run the offense according to its design. However, the basic concept of moving in the paint area is applicable to most offenses. Coaches should have their players perform drills to reinforce movement and screening in the lane area, as well as emphasizing catching the ball cleanly and immediately making a move.

Against a good defense, the post may find it hard to simply go to the low-post area and be open. For example, the defense will usually be geared to prevent a pass to a player who is a scoring threat in the low-post area. The post can often get open as he breaks from another area, such as the opposite side of the lane or from the free-throw line or elbow areas.

In recent years, many offenses have been designed to use the post further out from the basket. These offenses have the post popping out to the top of the circle to initiate the offense. High-post screens out near the three-point line are commonly set by the post in an attempt to free up a teammate for a shot or drive to the basket. These offenses employ high-post screens in all areas of the court. In these situations, the pick-and-roll is a valuable offensive threat if the post has good shooting skills away from the basket.

The post can be valuable as a passer. From the top of the circle, the post can reverse the ball to the opposite side or pass to teammates cutting under the basket, since the lane is now more open. The post should also be able to score as he receives a pass, while breaking from the high-post to the low-post area. In today's game, a post is much more valuable if he has the attributes of a power forward.

Getting Open Against a Zone Defense

Getting players open against a zone defense requires team effort.

Getting players open against a zone defense requires team effort. A zone offense has less offensive player movement than a man-to-man offense does, but fast and accurate ball movement are essential.

Openings in a zone can be created by:

- Quick ball movement
- An inside-outside game
- Ball reversal to the opposite side of the floor
- Varying the directions and types of ball movement
- Dribble penetration, which can break down the zone defense

Screens can be set against a zone defense to prevent a defender from getting to his defensive position in time. A properly set screen can either create an opening for a shot or force another defender to leave his zone. These screens are most effective on the weakside, when the screen is set as the ball is rotated from the other side of the court.

A team that catches passes before looking and deciding where to pass will never beat a good zone defense. The objective of quick ball movement is to quickly pass the ball inside-outside and from side to side, so the defensive players are being worked back and forth until either the zone defense is not coordinated, or a player is out of position or is slow getting back where he needs to be.

Quick-passing drills should initially be run without defenders. As the drills are being performed, proper player movement, quick passes, and the importance of players changing where the ball is passed each sequence should be stressed. As this drill is first practiced, the players will think they are catching and releasing the next pass quickly, until they are pushed to make the passes more quickly and more accurately. Bobbled or dropped passes should not be tolerated. The drill should then be run against a defense. (The zone defense should be taught to the defensive players on the floor at this time.)

The point guard should not be the only player responsible for ball reversal and inside-outside ball movement. Each player should have the responsibility to vary his passes. The coach's responsibility is to have the team so comfortable doing this that it becomes second nature. The ball should be passed in all directions against the zone. The inside-outside game means the ball is inside to a post or forward, who shoots immediately or quickly passes back outside or to any other open player. Quick ball reversal to the other side of the court is critical if a zone is to be beaten as the ball is being passed around the three-point line. The point to remember is to be unpredictable.

The ball should be passed in all directions against the zone.

❑ Dribbling Against a Zone Defense

Young players often make the mistake of trying to beat a zone defense with a dribble. In reality, they just can't do it! A zone is best beaten by quickly passing the ball.

An excellent dribbler, however, can occasionally find a crease in a zone. The ballhandler will normally not be able to find a crease as the ball is initially brought down court, since the defense is keyed on the ballhandler. After the ball has been passed to one side and is quickly reversed to either the top of the circle or the opposite wing area, a defensive player may be a step slow rotating over. This situation can create a momentary crease in the defense. A sudden move into the crease will draw several defenders toward the dribbler, who then dishes the ball to an open teammate, either closer to the basket or out near the three-point line. This scenario is called breaking down the defense with dribble penetration.

Getting Open on Inbound Passes or Plays

Inbound plays or passes cannot be successful if the players do not work hard to get open. Too many players do not give 100 percent effort in these situations. On in-bound plays, turnovers often result because players are sloppy in executing screens, or they simply do not hustle.

To get open for an inbound pass or play, players:

- Must break at the proper time.
- May fake one way before breaking quickly in another direction.
- Should break hard and quickly; go quickly to the open area.
- Should set and utilize screens correctly.

Who is the most dangerous scoring threat after inbounding? The inbounder is often open after he passes the ball. As a result, many coaches often have a good shooter inbounding the ball under the offensive basket if he thinks the player can get open for a shot.

Summary Points

Players must work hard to get their teammates open.

Players must work hard to get open if they want the ball. More importantly, players must work hard to get their teammates open. In this regard, setting screens is one of the best ways to get a teammate open.

CHAPTER 25

The purpose of a screen is to free an offensive player from his defender. When a screen is set, the defender is run into the player setting the screen so the defender is forced to either stop, go under the screen, or follow the offensive player around the screen.

A screen may also be used to create a mismatch if the defenders are in the habit of switching men, rather than fighting through screens. For example, a guard may set a backscreen in the low-post area so the offensive post can make a move to the basket, while he is guarded by a shorter player. If the defenders switch men, the post is now being guarded by a smaller player.

Screens are an integral part of all man-to-man offenses. Screens can also be occasionally used in a zone offense. Screens are set for:

- Players with the ball (i.e., on-the-ball screens).
- Players without the ball (i.e., off-the-ball screens).

Screens are also important in today's three-point game, where posts are often used further from the basket in contemporary offenses. They are used to free guards for three-point shots or moves to the basket. Posts often screen out at the three-point line, and then roll to an open area looking for a pass. Post players who are proficient passers and three-point shooters can be extremely effective in opening up the defense.

A screen may also be used to create a mismatch if the defenders are in the habit of switching men, rather than fighting through screens.

How to Set a Screen

The player who sets the screen should establish a wide base, with his feet spread far apart. His arms should be against his body. Some coaches prefer the player to have his arms folded at chest level. The screener must be completely stationary or an offensive foul will be called. A foul will also be called if the screener leans his shoulder or knees out as the defender comes around the screen.

Setting Up the Screen

A screen is much more effective if the defender has minimal advance warning that a screen is coming. Offensive players need to learn a variety of ways to fake and keep the defender busy, prior to cutting to the screen. Offensive players should be unpredictable. Fakes and cuts in the opposite direction should be used to divert the defender's attention away from the direction of the screener. The cutter or dribbler should cut toward the screener. Ideally, the defender should be able to turn and take one step before running into the screen.

Rubbing Off the Screen

The offensive player coming around the screen, whether the ballhandler or cutter, should be so close to the screener that their shoulders rub. This positioning prevents leaving a space for the defender to squeeze through.

If the defender is in an ideal defensive position, he will not allow the dribbler to get close to the screener. In this regard, the defender will squeeze between the screener and the offensive player, while maintaining good defensive position. A fake before cutting to the screen will give the offensive player a half-step on the defender, so the offensive player now controls the angle of entry to the screen.

The direction of the offensive player's first step should be directly toward the screener. If he steps slightly to the outside of that line, he will create an opening that allows the defender to squeeze by while maintaining his inside position. This is a common mistake, even at the college level.

Carelessness and poor technique cause players to swing too wide around screens. The most common reasons that ballhandlers do not rub the defender off includes:

> - The ballhandler has not gained a half-step advantage, so he cannot go directly toward the screener.
> - The dribbler does not initially step directly toward the middle of the screener's body.

Passing to a Cutter Coming Around a Screen

A pass arriving at the moment that the cutter is most open allows the player the maximum time to make a move or take a shot. If the passer waits to see if the cutter, who is coming around a screen, is open before getting ready to pass, the pass will be late arriving. The passer must focus on the defense, visualize the screen developing, and anticipate if and when the cutter will be open. In this regard, the following steps must occur:

- The passer must determine:
  - if the screener's defender is going to step out to slow down the cutter.
  - if the cutter's defender is going to be scraped off.
  - if the cutter will come around the screen or stop behind the screen.
- The passer should anticipate and release the pass just as the player starts to become open, so the ball will arrive at the precise moment the player is most open. The pass will be late in arriving if the passer waits until the player is open before initiating the pass.

After a screen has been set for a ballhandler, the ballhandler's options are to:

- Drive around the screen toward the basket.
- Flair to an open area and shoot or pass.
- Shoot behind the screen.
- Execute the pick-and-roll (this move is discussed in the section on two-man games.)

The screener's options are to:

- Pick-and-roll toward the basket.
- Pick-and-flair to an open area.
- Set a backscreen behind the ballhandler's defender.
- Move to another area to set a screen for a teammate.

Resetting a Screen

Once an offensive player has gone around a screen, the screener can pivot in that direction and reset the screen so the defender is screened if the offensive player reverses directions. Resetting the screen will sometimes free up a teammate more than the original screen.

❑ Resetting a screen at the three-point line.

A screen is sometimes reset to get a dribbler free for a three-pointer if a post or power forward sets a screen for a guard and the defender fol-

A pass arriving at the moment that the cutter is most open allows the player the maximum time to make a move or take a shot.

lows. The screener may reset the screen. (This type of screen is commonly referred to as a backscreen). The guard doubles back, scrapes the defender off the backscreen, and either shoots a three-point shot or drives to the basket.

Practicing Screens

All aspects of screen play must be practiced from different areas on the floor. Since screens are set for players going in all directions, the cutter or dribbler must be comfortable pivoting and shooting in any direction. Many players make the mistake of practicing screens only in one direction. Right-handed players practice screens as they go to the right, catch a pass from the right, pivot, and shoot. If the player is going to his left, or the pass comes from a different direction, the tempo will be much different.

❑ Where should screens be practiced?

Most people think of screens usually being set out near the three-point line. However, screens are set in all areas of the floor to get players open. Screens in the lane are an effective way to create an opening to deliver a pass to a teammate. Therefore screens should be practiced in the areas that your offense uses screens. To be a complete player, screens should be practiced:

- At three positions around the three-point line (the top of the circle, and both wing positions)
- Several feet inside these three positions
- At the free-throw line and both elbows of the free-throw lane
- In the lane near both low-post areas

Passes should be made from all different positions and angles to cutters coming off screens from these areas.

Passes should be made from all different positions and angles to cutters coming off screens from these areas. It is important for the cutter coming around the screen to be comfortable pivoting and starting moves to the basket from different positions and with different pivot feet. The cutter should practice doing one of the following things immediately after catching a pass:

- Accelerate to the basket
- Drift to an open area for a shot
- Shoot behind or just beyond the screen

Defending Screens (Picks)

❑ Know your opponent:

The defender should always know his opponent's strengths, weakness, favorite shots, and areas from which he prefers to shoot. For example, does the offensive player like to shoot behind a screen?

If the player is a threat to shoot behind the screen, the defender should always fight through the screen and never step under the screen, thereby leaving the player to shoot an uncontested shot. If the offensive player is not a good shooter or is not a threat to shoot from that area, the defender may cut under the screen.

❑ Communicating on screens:

Defending screens requires communication between teammates. Often, a defensive player cannot see a screen that is being set. Therefore, it is critical that the teammate defending the screener should communicate that a screen is being set. The defender of the screener is also the player who should determine how the screen should be played. His actions will determine whether his teammate should fight through the screen, go under the screen, or switch defensive assignments. He should also yell "switch" if he wants to switch men.

❑ Choices for the defender of the screener:

- The defender of the screener can step out to stop or slow down the offensive player if he thinks the player is an immediate threat to score or drive to the basket.
- He can step back to create a lane for his teammate to cut under the screen if he feels the offensive player coming around the screen is not an immediate threat to score.
- He can stay tight against the screener if he thinks his teammate is in excellent defensive position, and little chance exists of a score.
- The defenders can switch men if he does not think it will create a mismatch. The defending screener should be the player to call for a switch, since he can see the play developing. The coach should instruct the team whether switching is acceptable and in what situations.

If the player is a threat to shoot behind the screen, the defender should always fight through the screen and never step under the screen, thereby leaving the player to shoot an uncontested shot.

❏ Stepping out on screens:

The player defending the person setting the screen should step out to halt or slow down the offensive player enough so that the defender being screened has time to re-establish good defensive position. The defender who stepped out must immediately hustle back to defend his man. Stepping out on screens can be done either when the offensive player is a cutter trying to get open to receive a pass, or when he is the ballhandler. For example, this defensive move is very effective in the low-post position when the opponent is setting backscreens to get players open who are coming from the offside to the ballside. This defensive tactic is also very effective in defending against either the screen or the pick-and-roll.

❏ Slipping the screen:

The player defending the screener must be aware that the screener may slip the screen if the defender is overly aggressive while stepping out to stop the drive. The screener may slip a screen when the defender steps out beside the screener a little early. The screener immediately rolls to the basket or an open area before setting the screen. In essence, he fakes setting a screen and rolls to the open area.

❏ Options for the player defending the screener involving the cutter or the ballhandler:

➤ If a cutter coming around a screen is a scoring threat from that area, the defender should step out on the screen. If he isn't, the player defending the screener may step back one step to create a lane for his teammate to use.
➤ If the ballhandler is coming around the screen and is within scoring range, the player defending the screener should step out on the screen. The screener's defensive man should never allow a ball-handler to drive around him and go uncontested toward the basket!

❏ Choices for the defender being screened:

➤ Fight through or over the screen
➤ Go under the screen
➤ Switch players

The player being screened will usually fight through most screens. However, he must be ready to respond to different situations. The defender should focus on his man, the screener, and what his teammate who is defending the screener is doing.

- *Switching or fighting through screens?* Generally, it is better to fight through screens, not switch. Fighting through a screen involves working hard to maintain good defensive position or extremely close contact with the offensive player, even if the defender is forced to follow the offensive player around the screen. The defensive player must hustle to immediately re-establish good defensive position.

If players often switch on screens, it becomes relatively easy for the offense to establish a mismatch under the basket. If the defensive player is mismatched under the basket, he should front the offensive player immediately in order to make it more difficult to make an entry pass. Other teammates should immediately recognize the mismatch and give backside help.

- *Going under the screen (scissoring under the screen).* In this move, the player defending the screener steps back to create a lane for his defensive teammate if he feels there is no immediate threat of a shot or drive to the basket. Going under the screen is not recommended if the defender is guarding the ballhandler. The player defending the ballhandler should go under the screen only if the offensive player is absolutely no offensive threat to shoot from behind the screen.

If a defender has been scraped off by one or more screens, the defender may take the most direct route to the spot the offensive player is trying to reach. If a teammate has switched and taken the defender's man, the defender should pick up his teammate's man. As the defender switches to take his teammate's man, he should play the passing lane, being alert to intercept any pass.

❑ Defending an on-the-ball screen (pick-and-roll):

A pick-and-roll involves a screen that is set for the ballhandler. The ballhandler has the choice of shooting, driving to the basket, or passing to the screener who has rolled toward the basket or an open area. The player defending the screener must step out and slow down the ballhandler so the defender can fight through the screen and regain good defensive position. The player defending the screener must immediately hustle back to defend his man who has rolled. The two defenders on a pick-and-roll should seldom switch, because it is likely to create a mismatch, since centers or forwards often are the screeners for the shorter players. The player defending the ballhandler must fight over the screen and/or trap the ballhandler when the teammate steps out.

The following suggestions summarize steps that the players defending the screener and the ballhandler in a pick-and-roll situation should take:

If a defender has been scraped off by one or more screens, the defender may take the most direct route to the spot the offensive player is trying to reach.

- The defender guarding the ballhandler:

  - Know his opponent's skills and tendencies. Is the player a good outside shooter? Does he like to drive?
  - If his opponent is a good shooter, he should fight through every screen. His teammate may have to step out to help.

- The defender guarding the screener:

  - It is very important that the defender guarding the screener communicate to his teammates that the screen is being set.
  - He may have to step out to block the path of the dribbler. The purpose of this movement is to force the dribbler to stop and pick up his dribble or to dribble further away from the basket to get around the defender. This action allows the ballhandler's defender time to fight through the screen and re-establish good inside defensive position.
  - The defender who stepped out must now hustle back to defend his man before he can get open and receive a pass.
  - He should never allow a ballhandler coming around the screen to have an open shot or an unobstructed lane to the basket. He must protect the basket.

☐ Defending an off-the-ball screen:

A man-to-man offense will often consist of a series of screens as the players move around the floor.

  - If the off-the-ball screen would result in an opponent receiving a pass in his scoring range, the player defending the screener must step out to disrupt the cut or deny the pass. He must not hesitate in finding his man again and establishing good defensive position.
  - If the screen would result in a player being unable to receive a pass in his scoring range, he may elect to not step-out.

☐ Defending the off-the-ball backscreen. If a defensive player's man goes across the lane to set a backscreen:

  - The defensive player should step in front and block the path of the offensive player coming off the screen. This allows the screened defensive player time to recover to a good defensive position.

➤ The player who steps out to stop the cutter must then hustle back to guard his own man.

❑ Defending the high post screen at the three-point line:

With the popularity of the three-point shot, many offenses currently use single- or double-high post screens at the three-point line to start a half-court offense or in other offensive sets. As a result, in today's game, posts more than ever need to be mobile, have excellent passing skills, and have good facing-the-basket shooting skills.

When the defensive posts sees his man is going to set a high-post screen, he should be prepared to step out past the screen at a 45- to 90-degree angle to the player setting a screen in order to block the path of the dribbler. The player stepping out must be certain to be very close to the screener so that no space is left for the ballhandler to dribble through. The intent of the step-out is to cause the ballhandler to pick up his dribble or slow down and dribble several feet back toward the mid-court line in order to get around the defender. This scenario allows time for the defender being screened to recover to a good defensive position.

If the opponents are effective at the pick-and-roll, the post may step out quickly for an instant to slow down the dribbler before quickly switching back. Occasionally, the defense will use the high-post screen as an opportunity to trap a guard. If so, the other defenders, must shift and play help defense on the closest outlet players, being careful not to leave an offensive player unguarded under the basket.

Defending the Three-Point Shot at the End of the Game

In the last minute of the game, the defense may have to defend against a three-point shot if the opponent is three or more points behind. In these situations, the defenders near the three-point line should switch men if the offensive players come around a screen near the three-point line. The immediate threat that the defender faces is allowing a player an open three-point shot, not a player driving to a basket. However, each defender must be ready to defend an opponent's drive to the basket.

If only a few seconds are left in the game, and the opponent is three or more points behind, the defenders near the three-point line can almost completely disregard a drive to the basket. The defenders should closely defend any ballhandler and deny any pass to a player near the three-point line.

The intent of the step-out is to cause the ballhandler to pick up his dribble or slow down and dribble several feet back toward the midcourt line in order to get around the defender.

Common Mistakes Involving Screens

- Circling wide around the screen leaves room for the defender to squeeze by while maintaining a good defensive position.
- Not setting up the defender for the screen.
- The pass is late getting to the cutter coming around a screen.
- Screens are not defended aggressively.
- The defenders do not communicate and warn each other about screens.
- The player defending the screener does not step out to stop or slow down the person coming around the screen.
- Players seldom reset a screen.

Summary Points

Screens should be an integral part of every offense. Players must become adept in executing and defending screens. This skill is one that coaches sometimes incorrectly assume that all players possess. In reality, an approximate amount of practice time should be devoted to working on executing and defending screens.

Screens should be an integral part of every offense.

CHAPTER 26

A great passer is usually a good penetrator who opens up his teammates and passing lanes. However, a great passer may be any player who consistently delivers a very catchable pass to the open teammate at the right time.

Why Do So Few Great Passers Exist?

A great passer can make everyone else on the team much better. A television announcer recently stated that great passers were born with the natural instincts that allow them to be an excellent passer. Unfortunately, this is a common misconception. While it is true that every person has a different potential for performing a particular physical skill based on his or her genetic makeup, passing is a learned skill. Almost every great passer is an unselfish player, who neither worries about scoring points, his name in the newspapers getting headlines. As such, great passers tend to be the ultimate team players.

Passing is Learned One Small Step at a Time

As his fundamental skills are developed and improved over time, an accomplished passer typically gets the courage to try different passes until he has developed an uncanny ability to deliver the ball in a variety of ways. In the process, this player executes these passes so many times that his passing skills become second nature and appear to be a natural talent. In fact, great passers aren't developed in their junior or senior years in high school or in college. Rather, most great passers start their developmental efforts much earlier. All players require and should be given encouragement and recognition of a job well done during this slow developmental process.

A great passer can make everyone else on the team much better.

Great Passers Are Good at Other Skills

Great-passing point guards are usually terrific ballhandlers who are very good at attacking the basket. Every great passer should have enough scoring skill to cause the defense to commit to him if he beats his man. Once the defense considers the player as an offensive threat, passing lanes will open up more easily. While great passers are usually point guards, the point to remember is that every player can be a great passer.

A great passer exhibits the following characteristics:

- Court awareness. The ballhandler should know where every player is, as well as his open teammate.
- Outstanding peripheral vision. This skill can be developed and improved.
- The ability to anticipate. Anticipation is important if the pass is to be delivered at the precise moment when the teammate is open.
- The ability to deliver the ball on time. If a player has good court awareness and anticipation, he is always ready to deliver the ball on time. The passer must have his head up looking beyond his defender to visualize the play developing. By anticipating that a teammate will become open, a passer has time to prepare his body to be in position to deliver the pass so it will arrive at the second that the teammate first becomes open.
- The ability to deliver the ball quickly. Passes are more effective when they are delivered quickly without tipping off the defense.
- The ability to choose the right pass and make it catchable:
  - The pass must be the correct pass for the situation. For example, a bounce pass may be better than a chest pass in certain situations because it may be more difficult for a defender to deflect or intercept it.
  - The ball must be delivered to the teammate in a position where it is very easy to catch so the player can immediately initiate an offensive move.
  - The ball must delivered as crisply as possible, but not be so hard that the teammate cannot catch it cleanly. This factor is especially true for shorter passes.
- The ability to lead the teammate receiving the ball to a desirable scoring position. If a teammate is looking at the passer, the teammate is not able to see what is happening behind him. A great pass will not only be delivered quickly and on time, it should lead the teammate to an open area where it will be easier for him to get off a shot.

If a player has good court awareness and anticipation, he is always ready to deliver the ball on time.

Timing of the Pass

The pass should be delivered to the teammate the moment he is most open and ready for the ball. If a pass is delivered too soon, the teammate will not be ready or may not be open. If the ball is delivered too late, the defense will be given time to recover.

Inexperienced players tend to wait for teammates to get open before deciding to pass the ball. It takes a second or two to decide to pass and then to actually pass the ball. During this time, the defender can regain his defensive position.

A passer must have good vision of the floor and anticipate when the teammate will become open. The passer must be mentally and physically ready to pass the ball just before the teammate gets open. A good passer sees not only his teammate, but also his defender. He instantly recognizes whether or not the teammate will be open.

Focus on a Small Target Area

Many players are happy just to pass to a teammate without focusing on a small target area. A bad pass can easily result when the target area for a pass is very large, and the pass is slightly off. Passers are much more accurate if they focus on a small target, such as the teammate's hands. Even if the pass is slightly off, the ball can still be caught.

What to Do After Passing the Ball

Whether running an offense or improvising, the passer should do one of the following things after passing the ball:

- Drifts or breaks a few steps to a more open area when his defender sags down to help on defense.
- Breaks to the basket expecting a return pass (i.e., give-and-go).
- Sets a screen for the player he passed to (i.e., screen or pick-and-roll).
- Moves away from where he passed and sets a screen for a teammate (i.e., pass and screen away).

A good passer sees not only his teammate, but also his defender.

Types of Passes

The three basic passes that every player should master are:

❑ The two-handed chest pass:

The ball is held with both hands at chest level. A step is taken toward the receiver as you push your hands away from your chest. The palms of your hands should be facing each other upon release of the ball. This pass should be thrown with force.

❑ The two-handed bounce pass:

The ball is held the same as the chest pass, but your thumbs should face upward when you release the ball. The ball should be bounced hard and should hit the floor about three-fourths of the way toward the receiver. The bounce pass is difficult to intercept because a defender has to reach very low to try and deflect it. The bounce pass is easier to catch since it approaches with less force than a chest pass. The bounce pass is a great pass that many players use too little.

As the player becomes a more-experienced passer, he may be more likely to use the one-handed bounce pass. This type of bounce pass is a great entry pass into the post. The player often fakes one way and reaches around the defender to deliver the one-handed bounce pass to the post. It should be delivered low, away from the post defender, and briskly.

The bounce pass can be a very effective pass in the lane area, either on a fast break or after penetration by the ballhandler. When another defender commits to stop the drive, the ballhandler bounce-passes the ball between players to the open teammate.

❑ The overhead pass:

The overhead pass involves throwing the ball with two hands over the head. This type of pass allows the player to pass the ball crisply, with distance and control.

It should be noted that a player should become proficient with each of these types of passes before trying one-handed passes. Both the chest pass and the bounce pass can be made with one hand, as well as can some of the following other types of passes:

❑ Hook pass:

The hook pass is a quick pass made off the dribble. The pass is made in a similar manner to a jump-hook shot with the player not squaring up in the direction of the pass. This type of pass is often used by the player dribbling the ball as an entry pass to a player who has become open around the basket. The basic objective of this type of pass is to deliver the pass before the defense has time to react.

❑ Shovel pass:

The shovel pass is an underhand pass to a teammate who is a few feet away. The passer sometimes reaches around a defender to deliver this type of pass.

❑ Touch pass:

The touch pass is executed without the passer ever completely catching the ball. The passer receives the pass and softly tips or redirects the ball toward an open teammate. This pass should be made with both hands to ensure accuracy.

❑ Skip pass:

The skip pass is an advanced level pass that is used when players have exceptional strength and passing and catching abilities. When throwing this type of pass, the player must be strong enough to pass the ball crisply over the defense and across the floor to an open teammate who is on the backside of the defense.

❑ Lob pass:

A lob pass should be used only when a player is lobbing the ball up so a teammate can catch and dunk the ball in one motion. A lob pass is a slow pass that allows time for defenders to react. Youth basketball coaches should be aware of the fact that youngsters often try to lob many of their passes.

❑ Pass off the dribble:

A pass off the dribble is made when the passer delivers the pass directly from the dribble without ever picking the ball up with two hands. The ball is picked up and delivered with one hand only. This type of pass involves a more advanced passing technique. It should not be practiced or used until the player has become very proficient with the basic types of passes. Passes off the dribble should be as accurate as any other pass or they shouldn't be made.

The Post as a Passer

Passing is often a lost art in post play. Yet, it is one of the most valuable things a post player can do to help the team and to improve his importance to the team. Although it doesn't take great athletic skills to be a great passer, it does require the player be unselfish and a team player.

The touch pass is executed without the passer ever completely catching the ball.

Although it doesn't take great athletic skills to be a great passer, it does require the player be unselfish and a team player.

With the current emphasis on three-point shooting, a good-passing post player can open his teammates up for easy shots. A player who is fighting to earn a spot on the team or earn a starting role can get an advantage by learning to be a great passer.

Fakes, court awareness, anticipation, and an assortment of passes can assist the post in becoming a proficient passer. Faking can help freeze the defenders and set up the pass. Court awareness and anticipation allow the passer to deliver the pass to the right player at the correct time by using whatever pass is most effective. A post's ability to pass can help make his offensive moves even more effective.

Entry Passes to the Post

When the guard or forward is tightly defended, he may have to fake his defender to one side to be able to deliver the pass to the post. Keep in mind that the person guarding the ballhandler outside has his back to the basket and can't see where the post is. A fake should be easier to sell. A fake move or pass in the opposite direction may cause the defender to move just enough to create a lane for the pass. A fake shot may also trigger the aggressive defender to jump or move enough to create a passing lane.

The passer can see the defense as it develops behind the post. Therefore, the passer may want to lead the post with a pass to an open area. For example, if the defender is playing too far up top on the post, a lane to the basket may be open. As the teammate posts up, the passer may pass to the side away from the defender and toward an open lane to the basket. The post may not be ready for this type of pass unless it has been practiced, since it requires timing and good execution by both the passer and the post.

If the post is double-teamed after catching the entry pass, he should look for an open teammate on the other side or make an outlet pass back to the guard.

If the post is double-teamed after catching the entry pass, he should look for an open teammate on the other side or make an outlet pass back to the guard. An inside-outside game often results in open shots. The guard who made the original pass to the post should have drifted to an open area if his man doubled-down to help defense the post. If the post passes back out to the guard, drifting to a new area will give the guard a split second more before the defender can find him. The guard then shoots, makes a move, reverses the ball to the other side, or makes a re-entry pass to the post.

The re-entry pass to the post will often find the post in a much better position to score the second time the ball comes inside. When a post passes out to the wing area, the defensive post's natural tendency is to straighten up and relax slightly. As a result, the offensive post should immediately reposition in a better scoring position. The other defenders will have moved back trying to prevent a pass to their man. They will not be in as good of a position to double-team quickly.

If the post is being fronted, and the entry pass can't be made from the wing position, the passer should quickly rotate the ball to a teammate near the top of the circle where there is a better entry angle, while the post works to keep the defender pinned in the same relative position. All passes must be crisp and quick.

The post must body-up against the defender and keep him outside, while the ball is being rotated toward the top of the circle. A quick entry pass from the top of the circle or the opposite wing area will often result in an easy basket. If the pass is from the top of the circle to a low post, it is a high-low entry pass. In this situation, many offenses will automatically open up the lane by bringing their off-side post to the top of the circle or slightly off to the other side. This post or forward will then make the high-low entry pass to the post.

The Guard-Post Two-Man Game

The two-man game is one of the oldest and most effective ways of scoring. The options in the two-man game include:

- The guard passes to the post from the wing area (i.e., entry pass).
- If the post can't shoot because he's being double-teamed, one option is to pass back either to the guard (outlet pass) on the same side of the court that he is on, or to another guard on the other side of the court.
- One of the options the guard now has is to pass back to the post, who has re-posted in a better position (i.e., re-entry pass).

Outlet Passes

After a defensive rebound or a turnover, a quick outlet pass to a teammate at the sideline or up the court initiates the transition game. If a team wants to have a good transition game, it must be able to get the ball up the court before the defense can recover.

A great outlet passer immediately looks upcourt toward the outlet position as he is gathering in the rebound. He immediately pivots and delivers the pass. The time that is saved may be the difference in

> **A great outlet passer immediately looks upcourt toward the outlet position as he is gathering in the rebound.**

whether the offense beats the defense down the court to the basket. If the first option is covered, the rebounder should pass to the second outlet option. The outlet pass should be emphasized in drills and in practice.

Inbound Passes

The defender guarding the player inbounding the ball will usually have his back to the other players. The inbounder can make the pass easier by faking his defender slightly to one side. The passer should have visualized the play developing and already determined which player is going to be open. The inbounder's fake has to be timed so the pass is delivered at the precise moment. Small ball fakes are usually effective when inbounding the ball.

Inbound passes can only be effective if the player gets open by using screens and cutting to open areas. Coaches must be alert to instruct players how to get open and how to stay open if the pass isn't delivered at the correct time.

The inbounder is likely to open for a return pass, whether the ball is inbounded from the sidecourt or baseline. If defensive pressure occurs after a stoppage of play, the inbounding player should be selected based on the situation and the attributes he possesses.

Teaching Passing

Most young players are more impressed with dribbling than passing. They do not understand that even the fastest player on the team cannot outrun a pass. In reality, passes are the most effective way to attack a defense.

A coach can emphasize the importance of passing by lining all of his players up on the baseline and promising any player that he can start the entire season if he can run to mid-court before the coach can get the ball there by passing. To further emphasize his point, the coach can give his players two or three steps headstart before passing. Every player will soon realize that no one can run faster than the ball can be passed.

❑ Not passing to an open teammate:

The coach should point out when passes are not made to open players. If a player misses the opportunity to pass to an open teammate during practice, be sure to point it out to the player immediately. Sometimes, it is necessary to move all the players back to where they were when the pass was missed. Let the player see where the open player was. This series of actions emphasizes:

- The importance of passing to open teammates
- Keeping the head up to see the floor
- Widening the field of vision
- Where open areas may be in these situations

❑ Peripheral Vision:

A coach must remind players to use their peripheral vision at all times. While teaching offense, running drills, or scrimmaging, a player may need to be reminded to see the whole floor and use peripheral vision. These reminders emphasize the importance of peripheral vision and help ensure that the players will get in the habit of seeing the entire floor. For example, if a player misses a wide-open teammate in a drill or scrimmage, the coach must remind the player that he did not pass to the correct player. After time, the players will learn to find the open teammate.

Peripheral vision is a person's ability to see what is happening on either side of him, while focusing straight ahead. Great passers seem to have the ability to see where people are without looking in that direction. Although coaches appreciate players with good peripheral vision, they rarely devote any time to teaching anyone how to improve on natural ability to see the entire court.

Most people focus straight ahead, and thus, narrow their focus of vision. When they want to see laterally, they simply turn their heads. As a result, people seldom develop their full range of peripheral vision. Players need to open a focus of awareness laterally. A player can develop a better level of peripheral vision with practice. Improved peripheral vision will enable the offensive player to see the floor better, thereby:

- Allowing him to improve his anticipation skills
- Recognizing open players more easily
- Facilitating the player's ability to see screens, traps, and double teams earlier, thereby allowing time to react
- Allowing a passer to not tip off the pass by looking directly at the teammate

Great passers seem to have the ability to see where people are without looking in that direction.

• *Peripheral vision drill.* This drill is designed to assist the player in developing his peripheral vision, while developing his confidence that he can execute skills accurately and effectively. This drill emphasizes a player's peripheral vision and passing skills. The person receiving the ball is in charge of the drill, so he should clearly understand its techniques and intentions.

• *Identifying the Field of Vision.* In this drill, the receiver starts out eight to 12 feet to the side and slightly behind the passer. The receiver places his right hand slightly in front of his body and comes forward until the passer first sees the hand while he is focused straight ahead. The passer will try to deliver flip passes with his left hand to the target. The goal is for the ball to be passed so the receiver does not have to move his hand. Once the passer can do this, the receiver moves the target higher or lower. Flip passes are then replaced by bounce passes. The types of passes, the speed of the passes, and the targets for the passes are routinely varied once the player is on task. The drill is then reversed to the left side. One of the main purposes of the drill is to develop confidence in passing with either hand. As a result, after a while, the passer will start to be comfortable using his peripheral vision.

Passing While Moving

Basketball is not played standing still. As a consequence, the player must learn to execute the aforementioned passing skills while on the move. The player must first become comfortable repeating these drills while walking slowly forward. The speed of the walk is gradually increased. The next day, the two drills described are repeated. Once the passes are consistently delivered on target, these drills should be repeated, while dribbling forward. The player should deliver flip and bounce passes off the dribble. The speed of the dribble should then be gradually increased until the player is comfortable passing, while dribbling at full speed.

Once the player begins to develop his peripheral vision, he should be willing to continue to work on it both at home and in practice. The player should remember to use his peripheral vision at all times on the court.

The No-Dribble Scrimmage

When you want to sharpen your team's passing and ball movement, or if your team is over-dribbling, the no-dribble scrimmage is a great option. This scrimmage is often used early in the season or periodically during the season if the offense seems sluggish.

In the no-dribble scrimmage, a dribble is considered a turnover. Since the players can't dribble, they will instinctively learn that they must move if they are to get open. Players will also learn that if they work hard to get open, someone will pass them the ball.

This type of scrimmage can be modified to also consider bobbled passes as turnovers. This stipulation will help ensure that the players try to deliver perfect passes and to not let up as they catch passes. As a result, the number of bobbled passes should diminish after these scrimmages are held.

Summary Points

Passing is nearly a lost art in today's world of slams and jams. Yet, a great passer is the one player who makes everyone else better. A coach must help his players to realize the importance of passing within the team concept.

Passing is nearly a lost art in today's world of slams and jams.

CHAPTER 27

Catching the Ball Skills

No matter how perfect a pass is, it is worthless if the receiver doesn't catch the ball. Every game has several turnovers that could have been prevented if a player had caught a pass that should have been caught.

No pass is complete until it is caught cleanly. Some players seldom bobble a ball, while other players often drop easy passes. Why is that?

A few players expect to catch every ball possible, even if it is a poorly thrown pass. They anticipate a bad pass and are ready and focused on the ball. For the players who do not have a positive attitude towards catching passes thrown to them, the coach plays a critical role.

At a minimum, the coach must not tolerate players dropping well-thrown passes. The coach should explain to the player why the ball was dropped and how to catch it more consistently. Even slight bobbles of well-thrown passes in drills should be corrected. One bobble of the ball before gaining control allows the defender to take at least one or two steps. Because defenders are seldom more than one step out of position, the result of not catching the ball cleanly may be a blown scoring opportunity. The coach should encourage hustling to catch a difficult pass or rebound. Whenever possible, the coach should praise these actions in front of the team. Doing so can be a powerful motivating force for all the players to catch the ball better.

At a minimum, the coach must not tolerate players dropping well-thrown passes.

Passing is a Two-Man Game

The passer must deliver a good pass, and the teammate should be ready to catch it cleanly. The receiver must then be ready to do something with the ball. If the player has anticipated the pass, he will have had time to be aware of where everyone is and what he probably will be able to do the instant he catches the ball. An inexperienced player often catches the ball and then tries to decide what to do next. By this time, the defense has swarmed the player. Passes in practice must simulate game situations that:

➤ The passer will be comfortable and confident.
➤ The recipient of the pass will be accustomed to anticipating the pass and will be ready to catch it. In a game, if a passer tries to make passes he hasn't tried before in practice, his teammates often will not be expecting the pass. His teammates may already be moving to block out, rebound, or set a screen.

All factors considered, the pass will be more successful if the receiver does the following:

➤ Has good court awareness before the ball is caught so he can react immediately after the ball is caught.
➤ Gets open and establishes good position.
➤ Is in the ready position. If a player is open, he should be in a ready position so that a quick move or shot may be made. The following examples illustrate this point:
  • If a pass to a guard at the three-point line is from the side, the guard should open up slightly toward the ball. As the ball is cradled into his fingers, the player quickly pivots, squares up, and immediately initiates the shot or move.
  • If the pass is to a guard who anticipates driving to the basket, the player can get a faster start by timing the arrival of the ball to his fingers with a slight step backward, just as the ball is arriving. The player immediately springs off his back foot, thereby exploding with a quick first step.
  • If the pass is being made to the post, the post may make a quicker move by drop-stepping or pinning the defender with his leg just as the ball is arriving in his hands. The defender will be focused on the ball and will be beaten before he realizes what has happened. It is critical that the receiver has his eyes intently focused on the ball and that his shoulders remain squared toward the ball, even though the player has already started the move. Failure to do this will result in a missed pass.
➤ Move to catch the ball if necessary. The ball should be caught, even if a player has to leave his hard-earned position to do it. The receiver may have to step toward the ball if the pass is slow, late in coming, off target, or if the defender has a good deflection or interception angle. If the defender is consistently challenging the passing lane, the player should expect to step toward the ball.
➤ Catches the pass. Focus intently on the ball. Players who have the attitude that they will not bobble a pass seldom do. Adhering to the suggestions in the next section (Developing "Hands") that will assist him in developing this attitude and skill.

In a game, if a passer tries to make passes he hasn't tried before in practice, his teammates often will not be expecting the pass.

Developing "Hands"

A player's ability to catch isn't inherited; it is learned. Many players who have trouble catching the ball simply have never worked on catching passes cleanly. While it is true some players have smaller hands that may make it difficult for them to control the ball with one hand, even those players can learn to catch the ball well if they work on doing the following:

- Be ready and focused
- See the play develop and be mentally ready to catch the pass
- Anticipate and expect the pass to be made to them
- Anticipate a bad pass
- Have their body and hands in a ready position. Their hands should be waist high and ready to catch the ball.
- Go for the ball and focus intently on it. It's their ball!
- Focus intently on the ball while watching the ball into their hands
- Catch the ball with the fingers and finger pads, not the palm of the hands
- Give slightly with their arms as the ball reaches their hands. This step will soften the impact of the pass.
- Squeeze the ball tightly with both hands so it can't be dislodged by contact
- Pivot and be ready to make a move, shot, or pass

Why Players Bobble Passes

Players bobble passes for many reasons, including:

Sometimes a pass is so bad that it is impossible to catch cleanly.

- Trying to make a move before the pass is caught
- Taking their eyes off the ball
- Being anxious. They should relax and let the ball settle into the hands. Soften the catch by letting the hands give slightly toward the body as the ball is caught.
- Not being alert. They should always assume that their teammate will make the pass.
- Not being in the ready position. The player should have his hands waist high in the catching position. He should be slightly on his toes with his knees slightly flexed. From this position, the player is ready to catch a bad pass or ready to spring for a rebound if the ball is shot.

Sometimes a pass is so bad that it is impossible to catch cleanly. In games, many passes are far from perfect. As a result, players should always be alert and ready to catch bad passes. If the ball isn't perfectly passed, and it can't be caught cleanly, the player should be prepared to go after the ball. In these situations, the player's sole purpose should be to gain control of the ball.

Catching and Pivoting

The first action after catching any ball should be to pivot to gain a better position for the next action. Players should practice pivoting as they work on their catching skills. The coach should emphasize the following points:

- The player should be comfortable pivoting with either foot before initiating a move.
- Footwork is critical in establishing an advantage through a properly executed move.
- The player will initiate the next move faster if his knees are slightly flexed as he pivots. From this position, he is ready to execute any move.

❑ Catching and Focusing Drills

Bad pass drills can be helpful in developing the catching abilities of the players. Players can become much better at catching all passes if they practice catching both good and bad passes. Accordingly, the coach should develop a series of bad-pass drills that will enable his players to enhance their ability to catch the ball. The two following drills are designed to emphasize the fundamentals needed to catch any pass, including bad ones:

- ♦ Reaction-and-step drill.

The purpose of this drill is to emphasize the importance of being ready to spring in any direction to get into a proper catching position. If the player is in a good position as the ball approaches, he can adjust if he misjudges the ball or if the pass is off target. The primary objective of the drill is for the players to develop the habit of recognizing a bad pass and moving to establish a catching position. The drill involves the following steps:

If the player is in a good position as the ball approaches, he can adjust if he misjudges the ball or if the pass is off target.

- In this drill, two players are positioned 10 to 15 feet apart. The players take turns catching and passing the ball.
- Each player receiving a pass should be in the ready position.
- The player should spring in any direction or jump to catch the ball.
- The player should hustle to get in front of the ball so that the ball is caught with two hands in front of the receiver.

➤ Each player should gradually stretch the limits of the other player while being very unpredictable in his pattern of passes.

Once the players have become adept at moving to get in good position, the players should focus on the two-man, bad pass drill. This drill teaches players to react, focus intently, and to catch or control the ball, even with only one hand.

◆ The two-man bad pass drill.

This drill is designed to help the players learn to be ready to catch any pass, learn to focus intently on the ball until the ball is in the hands, and to learn soften the impact of the ball as it hits his fingertips. This drill involves the following steps:

➤ Two players line up 10 to 15 feet from each other.
➤ Each player tries to throw bad passes—low and at the feet, high, or to either side.
➤ The passes should be catchable if the receiver can take one long step in any direction. The receiver tries to catch the ball with two hands. If necessary, he stretches and uses one hand to control or cradle the ball.
➤ The receiver should try to keep a pivot foot on the ground if possible. The players may jump or move both feet only if the pass is too far off target to catch any other way.
➤ If the ball is so far off target that it can't be caught cleanly, the player should control the ball with the fingertips of one hand so that the ball will fall straight down, and the player can catch it after only one bounce.
➤ The passes should be varied so the receiver doesn't know what to expect. The passer should mix good passes in this drill to keep the receiver honest. This is a good time for the passer to practice "eye fakes," so the receiver will not know where the ball is going.
➤ As both players get better, at the basic elements of the drill, the speed of the passes can be increased.

Catching the Ball with Contact

Once players have developed good ball-catching skills, whether it be catching passes, intercepting passes, or rebounding, the players should get used to being slapped at, grabbed, bumped, and pushed while attempting to catch the ball. The players should be fully aware that, more often than not, fouls are not called every time contact is made. As such, drill should be designed and performed to get the players used to contact. The players must get used to contact and their focus must be narrowed and intensified.

CHAPTER 28

Rebounding involves having an attitude! Rebounding is more than out-jumping everyone for the ball. A great rebounder is determined to get every rebound. He truly believes that every ball is his, and he works hard to get it. A player must want to rebound.

The Team Controlling the Backboards Wins the Game

Rebounding is a non-shooting skill that requires desire and hard work. The good rebounder is often overlooked, but his contributions are critical. In that regard, the following observations apply:

- An offensive rebound is as important as saving a ball from going out of bounds. An offensive rebound gives your team another chance to score.
- Every defensive rebound is as important as a blocked shot, because it prevents the opponent from getting another shot. If the other team shoots 50 percent, every other defensive rebound prevents two or three points.

A great rebounder is determined to get every rebound.

A good rebounder must block out every time a shot is taken. He must assume every shot will be missed, and must anticipate where the ball will be. The rebounder must believe that every missed shot belongs to him and so go aggressively after every ball.

Essential Traits of a Successful Rebounder

A great rebounder possesses the following characteristics:

- Has proper defensive position
- Immediately blocks out once the ball leaves the shooter's fingertips
- Assumes every shot will be missed
- Anticipates the rebound angle

- Establishes good rebound position
- Is a quick jumper
- Tips the ball to keep it alive, if he can't get it himself
- Follows his shot

❑ Blocking Out

When any shot is taken, you should immediately prevent your man from getting good rebound position. During the time a ball is in the air from a perimeter shot, you should find your opponent and block his path to the basket. Blocking out consists of three separate activities: finding your man, making contact with him, and maintaining contact until it is time to go for the ball.

• *Find your man.* If your team is playing man-to-man defense, find the man you are guarding right away. In a zone defense, you do not have an assigned man since you are guarding an area of the court; find the nearest opponent that is going for the rebound.

• *Make contact.* Defenders may make contact in two ways:

- Pivot (reverse position): You should pivot and position your back to make contact with your opponent. Take a low, wide stance with your rear against your opponent. Your elbows are up and out, and your hands are up and ready to rebound. If you have maintained contact, you can feel when the player you are blocking out tries to move around. You must move to maintain the blocking position. At the correct time, you explode for the ball.

- Step in the path: If you find yourself away from your man when the shot is released (you may be out of position or helping down on defense), you may not be able to use the pivot method. You must anticipate your opponent's path to the basket and beat him to it.

When any shot is taken, you should immediately prevent your man from getting good rebound position.

• *Maintain contact.* Move your feet to maintain contact. This contact will make it easier to know where your opponent is as he moves. Maintain contact until it is time to go for the ball.

The smallest player on the court can prevent the tallest opponent from getting a rebound by blocking him out. Of course, the players would need to be an adequate distance away from the basket so the tall player couldn't reach over the shorter player. When rebounding, remember to find someone, make contact to block them out, and maintain the contact until you explode toward the ball.

❏ Anticipating the Shot

The ability to anticipate the shot allows a player to get a rebounding advantage. This advantage is achieved by gaining desirable position and blocking out opposing players. Know your team's offense and learn your teammates' favorite shots and moves as well as their favorite spots on the floor to shoot from.

A good rebounder may be away from the basket when the shot is taken. If the player knows his teammates, he will know whether a player is likely to shoot the ball in a certain situation. If the teammate is likely to shoot, the rebounder should be ready to break to the basket once the player initiates the shot. The rebounder will often find a crease around the basket as the other players are fighting for position.

❏ Assume Every Shot Will Be Missed

You should always assume the shot will be missed. Doing so will enable you to get many more rebounds. Ask yourself, where will the rebound go?

In this regard, one of the most important factors to consider is the projected angle of the rebound. Once the shot is taken, the rebounder must determine where the ball is going and position himself for the rebound before his opponent can. Unfortunately, players seldom work on learning where the rebound is most likely to go. Yet, the player who can readily determine the rebound angle can get better rebound position.

The simplest way to learn how to judge where the rebound is likely to go is to shoot the ball and try to rebound the ball before it can hit the floor. If it hits the floor, try to get to it in as few bounces as possible. When a player does this exercise by himself, he will learn to follow his shot and pay attention to the rebound angle. Drills involving multiple players can be of great help in this regard.

The ability to anticipate the shot allows a player to get a rebounding advantage.

The following factors affect where the ball goes:

- Is the shot from long range or close in?
- Does the shot have a nice, high arch, or is it a bullet?
- Is the ball going to be long or short?
- Is the ball slightly off target? If so, where is it going to hit on the rim?
- From where on the floor is the shot being taken?

With practice, the player can learn to make instant determinations of where the ball is going accurately. Drills can be designed to help the team learn this skill. The simplest way to learn to judge rebound angles is for the player to practice shooting and rebounding missed shots before they hit the floor, either alone or with another player.

With regard to rebound angles, you should remember the following: Long shots bounce further from the basket. Flat shots with little arch hit hard and bounce farther from the basket. Shots from the corner do not have a backboard to hit.

❑ Follow Your Shot

The first person to know if the shot is off and where the ball is likely to go is the shooter. The shooter should follow his shot. If he gets the rebound, it will be easier to drive past the charging players or pass to an open teammate under the basket.

If a player has the responsibility to get back on defense to stop fast breaks, the coach may not want him following his shot. If in doubt, ask your coach what he wants.

❑ Gaining Offensive Rebound Position

An offensive player must work harder to gain rebound position since the defender usually has inside position. Hustle and use your head. Gain the proper rebound position before or as the shot is taken. Offensive rebounding position is best gained by taking advantage of the defender as he focuses on the ballhandler, and by knowing your teammates' tendencies concerning passing or shooting in any particular situation. The following suggestions are a few ways a player can get good positioning:

> **The first person to know if the shot is off and where the ball is likely to go is the shooter.**

- ➤ If your defender on the weakside drifts a step or two slightly toward the ballside, slide over and pin him there by blocking him out. This should open up the weakside for a rebound.
- ➤ An offensive player near the basket who is blocked out may be able to gain inside position by looping around the defender and coming underneath the basket from the baseline area.
- ➤ You have two choices when a teammate drives to the basket and your defender moves over to help stop the drive: anticipate a pass or go for a rebound. Your defender creates an open lane to the basket when he plays help defense.
- ➤ An open lane to the basket often develops on the weakside, just inside the lane when the ball is being shot from the opposite side between the wing and baseline areas. An offensive player can slash down the lane from the free-throw line or elbow area on the weakside.

❏ **If a Player Can't Get the Rebound, Keep it Alive**

As a player fights for rebounding position, he sometimes doesn't have good position and can't get his hands on the ball to catch it. If the rebounder can stretch enough to reach in with one hand and tip the ball back up in the air, he and his teammates will have another opportunity to rebound. Some great rebounders tip the ball two or three times before gaining control of the ball. In fact, they try to tip it to an open area where they can out-hustle the other rebounders to the ball. Dennis Rodman and Popeye Jones were two NBA players who made a good living at their craft in the 1990s by keeping rebounds alive.

❏ **The Quick Jumper**

The ability to jump, land, and quickly jump again is an essential trait of the great rebounders. Can a player learn to jump quicker? Yes, but he must work hard. In this regard, strength training and jumping rope can be helpful. For example, jumping rope will build muscles needed to jump quickly, and the player will learn to land on his toes and jump without overflexing his knees. When a player lands after pulling down a rebound, his legs should flex slightly, before quickly springing back up.

What Should a Player Do When He Gets a Rebound?

A player should do the following when he gets a rebound:

> *A short offensive rebound.* If a player grabs an offensive rebound, he should immediately put the ball back up (fake and shoot quickly), or pass the ball to an open teammate. Don't hesitate, or the defense will swarm you.

> *A long offensive rebound.* If a player catches a long offensive rebound, he should make a move toward the basket and/or pass to an open teammate under the basket right away. Because the defenders will be moving toward the rebounder, they will often be out of position to stop either a sudden move to the basket or a pass to a teammate who has been left open near the basket.

> *A short defensive rebound.* When the rebound is made near the basket, the player should look to pass to the outlet and get the ball upcourt. The player should instinctively know where the first and second outlet positions are, as well as the safety outlet. Great rebounders often look to see where the outlet pass should

The ability to jump, land, and quickly jump again is an essential trait of the great rebounders.

go before they land. The faster the ball gets to the outlet man, the better the chance of beating the defense down the court.

> *A long defensive rebound.* If a player catches a long defensive rebound, he should pivot and look to initiate the transition game with a dribble and/or pass to a teammate upcourt. Do not hesitate or the defense will have time to get in good defensive position. When bringing the ball down to initiate the dribble, approach diagonally and get low. The first dribble or two will most likely be when players will be reaching in trying to deflect the ball.

What Should an Offensive Player Do When the Opponent Gets a Defensive Rebound?

To prevent an easy transition basket after the defense gets a rebound, offensive players must:

> *Defend the basket.* The players near the top of the key must get back downcourt to protect the lane and the basket.

> *Deny the outlet pass.* If a player is out-rebounded by his man, he should not allow the rebounder to immediately make an outlet pass. Get in his face and keep your arms high, but be sure not to foul in frustration.

Summary Points

Great rebounders often look to see where the outlet pass should go before they land.

The coach must stress the importance of rebounding to his players. Players often think about scoring first. Some may realize the importance of playing great defense or making great passes, but too few set their goal to be a great rebounder.

CHAPTER 29

A great dribbler must not only be able to control the ball well, he must be an excellent passer who keeps his head up and has good vision of the floor, even when he is intensely defended. A great dribbler can get the ball upcourt against pressure defenses, can break down defenses with dribble penetration, and can open up teammates so they then can receive a pass in a scoring position. As such, an excellent ballhandler is a special asset to the team.

Types of Dribbles

❑ Control Dribble (Low Dribble)

The control dribble is used when a player is closely defended or when he is dribbling in a crowded area. The low dribble is used to get out of a congested area, drive around a defender, or to advance the ball upcourt. The ballhandler's body is used as a shield from the defender, and the ball is dribbled low to the floor so the player can react more quickly. The advantage of the control dribble is that it is harder to deflect or steal.

With a control dribble, the ball should seldom come up as high as the knee. In a crowded situation, the ball may need to be dribbled even lower. The general rule of thumb is that the closer the defender, the lower the dribble should be.

On a quick drive around a defender, the ballhandler's inside arm and leg should lead the way, because the ball is dribbled with the opposite hand in such a manner that the body of the dribbler shields the ball from the defender. On a fast break, the ballhandler may suddenly have to switch from a speed dribble to a control dribble, while attacking the basket rapidly. This slightly crouched position will allow the player to react faster if he attacks the defense with dribble penetration.

A great dribbler must not only be able to control the ball well, he must be an excellent passer who keeps his head up and has good vision of the floor, even when he is intensely defended.

❑ Speed (High) Dribble

The speed dribble is used when the ballhandler is in front of the defense, or is in the open and is driving to the basket. If a ballhandler advances the ball up the court using the speed dribble, he should switch to the control dribble as he gets closer to a defender.

The speed dribble is bounced waist high and pushed much farther out in front of the dribbler. The dribbler is not as crouched over as he is with the control dribble. The player is running more upright, and is ready to pass to an open teammate or slow down and switch to a more controlled dribble as he approaches a congested area.

The ball should always be dribbled outside of the ballhandler's feet. Inexperienced players will often try to dribble directly in front of their body as they race down the court.

❑ Cross-Over Dribble

The cross-over dribble is used with either a control or speed dribble. The cross-over dribble allows the player to execute a change of direction or a change of pace to drive by or establish a better position against the defender.

In a cross-over dribble, the ballhandler's dribbling hand flicks the ball to the opposite side by pushing the ball downward and laterally in front of the body. His hand is slightly outside the ball, instead of on top. His opposite hand continues the dribble.

The ball should always be dribbled outside of the ballhandler's feet.

When a player is crossing-over on a fast break, a high bounce is often used. However, a low cross-over is used when initiating a move around a defender.

❑ Step-Back, Cross-Over Dribble

When the dribbler is closely defended, the step-back, cross-over dribble can be used to switch the dribble to the opposite hand. As the player steps back with his forward leg, a cross-over dribble is simultaneously initiated. The ball is brought low across the body and slightly backwards.

❑ Between-the-Leg Dribble

The between-the-leg dribble is used to switch the dribble from side to side without exposing the ball to the defender. Because of the precision required to perform this maneuver while being defended, this type of dribble is not recommended for inexperienced players.

❑ Behind-the-Back Dribble

Although the behind-the-back dribble is seldom used, it can occasionally be helpful. As with the between-the-leg dribble, more time should be spent on practicing the other dribbles first.

Suggestions for Dribbling Properly

Ballhandlers can be better dribblers by adhering to the following guidelines:

- *Do not dribble unless you know where you are going.* Coaches cringe when they see a player dribble the ball one time for no reason. A post who catches the ball and dribbles one time without moving his feet before shooting will find it difficult to be successful. He has given the defense time to swarm him. The guard who uses up his dribble for no reason severely limits his options.

- *Don't watch the ball.* The most common mistake involving dribbling is looking down and watching the ball. If a player's eyes are looking down, he will never be a good dribbler. The dribbler will have poor court awareness and anticipation. Do not make the mistake of looking down to pick up your dribble. Focus on the court, the defenders, and the target of your pass or shot.

- *Maintain the proper height of your dribble.* Dribble lower and faster as you are guarded more closely. The ball will be back in your hand faster, allowing you to react faster and allowing less time for the defender to reach in and steal the ball. Dribble high and more forward when you are in the open and want to go fast.

As appropriate, use the high-low dribble. The sudden change in dribble height can make it difficult for a defender to adjust his reach as he goes for the ball. Use the high-low dribble as you dribble into a crowd, perform a cross-over dribble, or challenge an aggressive defender.

- *Maintain proper dribbling and court awareness.* Keep your head up and your eyes looking forward. A player must be able to see the court if he is to know where or when to dribble, cut, or pass. After the player has learned to dribble without looking at the ball, he should develop enough confidence in his dribbling skills so he doesn't feel he has to watch the defender.

The most common mistake involving dribbling is looking down and watching the ball.

Look beyond the defender. The dribbler should then learn to look past the defender so he can visualize the floor. Being aware of what is happening further down court is the secret of being a good ballhandler who is able to make good decisions. A good ballhandler should control the defender. The defender should not dictate what the dribbler can do.

➤ *Keep in mind that court awareness can be learned.* Being aware of where defenders and teammates are is easier if you understand what the defense is trying to do and what your teammates should do in response.

The following tips can also enhance a player's ability to dribble effectively:

➤ Look first, dribble last. Pass ahead whenever you can.
➤ Too much dribbling hurts team play.
➤ Keep away from sidelines and corners.
➤ Always end a dribble with a good pass or shot.

Hesitation Dribble

The hesitation dribble is a move in which the dribbler hesitates in order to get the defender to relax and straighten up. The hesitation dribble is used when the defender is in good defensive position. The dribbler slows down and slightly stands more erect as he approaches the three-point line area. As the defender also starts to relax and stand more erect, the dribbler quickly accelerates past the defender.

The hesitation dribble can also be used to create enough space for a cross-over dribble and a change of direction when the defender has perfect position to deny a drive to the basket. For example, in this situation, a player driving down the right side of the lane may hesitate, crossover, and drive down the middle of the lane to the opposite side of the basket for a reverse layup or a left-handed layup.

Picking Up the Dribble

One of the worst mistakes a player can make involving dribbling is to dribble up to a defender and to pick up his dribble. This factor is especially true in the backcourt, near midcourt, or at the sideline. An aggressive defensive team will immediately trap the player. The offensive player then has few options left.

If the ballhandler's head is up as he dribbles, he can see both the defenders and the play as it develops. The ballhandler should already

A good ballhandler should control the defender.

know what he is going to do before the dribble is picked up, and it should be done instantaneously. The ball can also be passed off the dribble. The player should keep all his options open by keeping his dribble alive until it is time to shoot, drive, or pass.

Being Trapped at Midcourt

Avoiding a trap at midcourt, while bringing the ball up, is sometimes difficult. Inexperienced players often cross midcourt and pick up their dribble, hoping to pass the ball. As a rule, they are simply happy to get the ball across midcourt before 10 seconds elapses and now they want someone else to take the ball. This is a cardinal sin of basketball, made even worse if the player was not closely defended. When approaching midcourt, the ballhandler should do the following:

- Keep his head up to get a clear vision of the defenders and the overall defense as it develops.
- Do not stay too close to the sideline. Drift slightly toward the middle of the court so that it will be more difficult to be trapped.
- Be ready to pass before reaching midcourt and/or before reaching the defender who wants to trap. When other defenders leave their men to help with the trap, the teammate should drift slightly to open the area even more. The ballhandler should then deliver the pass before the trappers arrive. It is important that players understand the types of traps a team sets so they will know where the defenders are likely to come from and who will usually be open.
- Blow past a single defender awaiting him and immediately attack the basket. Make the defender pay for trying to stop him so far from the basket.

If a ballhandler realizes that he is being trapped in the backcourt, and there is no one to whom he can pass, he can dribble backwards one or two steps before driving around the trapper. A step-back, cross-over dribble should be made toward the middle of the court. If the ballhandler is in the middle of the court, he should not get too near the sideline where he can be trapped easily.

Learn to Dribble with Either Hand

Great ballhandlers often seem to be ambidextrous because they have worked so long on dribbling well with either hand, and their ability to dribble looks natural. As players learn to dribble, they should work on each hand equally. The tendency of most players is to dribble only with their

Great ballhandlers often seem to be ambidextrous because they have worked so long on dribbling well with either hand, and their ability to dribble looks natural.

dominant hand, since it is so much easier. Players have to be forced to learn to be ambidextrous. As a rule, they will not do it on their own (particularly younger players).

The One-Handed Dribbler

Coaches at various levels occasionally have a talented player on the team who has no confidence dribbling with his off-hand. This player is easily defended when matched against a quality defender. It is the junior high coaches' responsibility to see that no one-handed dribbler ever reaches the JV or varsity level. All coaches should require their players to use both hands equally in practice as well as in games.

If a player wants to play basketball in high school or college, he must be comfortable dribbling with either hand. If not, the defense will overplay the dribbler and force the player to pick up the dribble or switch the dribble to the hand with which the player has little confidence.

If a player is one-handed, it is because he hasn't made the necessary commitment to being a better dribbler. Such a player must work hard in drills against aggressive defenders. Furthermore, this player could be required to use only his off-hand for several weeks during the off-season practices. In addition, The coach should consult with the player and develop a program the player can follow at home or during the summer.

The following example can help demonstrate how an excellent player can be handicapped, simply because no one ever insisted that this player learn to dribble with their off hand:

> **If a player is one-handed, it is because he hasn't made the necessary commitment to being a better dribbler.**

"A tall, lightning-quick player with good jumping ability made all-state and received a full scholarship to a top-ranked NCAA Division I school. What was the problem? Being a one-handed dribbler was the problem. With a burst of speed, the player could blow by almost any defensive player at the high school level. At the collegiate level, however, her effectiveness was severely limited by the speed and defensive ability of the collegiate players around her. Since other more-balanced offensive players were on the team, her role was reduced to being a defensive specialist, where she could use her athletic ability to shut down opposing players. While this is an important role for any player, this player had special scoring abilities, especially under pressure and in important games, that were never developed and utilized in college.

This player had been a post in junior high because she was taller and could outjump everyone for the rebound. During her sophomore year, she was promoted to the varsity and switched to a wing position. The player had few guard or wing skills. The player improved dramatically throughout her high school career. Somehow during this time, she never became comfortable dribbling with her left hand. If she had worked during the summer and off-season practices, she could have become more comfortable with her off hand. With several months of intensive work, the player would have been much more skilled and confident. The unaddressed factor is why was this player never forced to learn to dribble with both hands equally?"

The One-Sided Player

A one-sided player has a tendency of always favoring one side of the court when dribbling or setting up the offense. A one-sided player may only drive or shoot from one area. All players have their favorite spots, but a player with an excessive tendency is likely to be shut down by a good defensive team. Similar to the story recited in the previous section, the following story illustrates the quandary that arises when a particular problem is not addressed when it should be:

"A guard was so one-sided that she always dribbled the ball upcourt with the right hand and near the out-of-bounds line. If she got a rebound or a pass on the defensive left side of the basket and if she was defended closely, she would dribble across the court to the opposite corner, keeping the baseline to her right. When the player approached the corner, she would then start upcourt keeping, the sideline to her right. This player was trying to avoid losing the ball if she were forced to dribble with her left hand. Why was this not corrected in practice? Why was it not corrected in junior high?"

Dribble Penetration Breaking Down the Defense

A player who drives by his defender and attacks or penetrates the middle of the defense is causing other defenders to step out and commit. Dribble penetration is often called breaking down the defense because it forces other defenders to leave their man or assigned area to stop the dribbler. This action can open up teammates for a pass and an easy basket. Dribble penetration open up players around the basket, as well as players outside at the three-point line.

Dribble penetration is usually used against a man-to-man defense, but it can also be used against a zone defense. While a zone defense cannot be beaten by a player dribbling the ball, an excellent ballhandler may be able to penetrate the zone when the defenders are caught a step out of position. For example, the point guard cannot penetrate the zone by initiating the offense with a dribble because the defense is in good

Dribble penetration is often called breaking down the defense because it forces other defenders to leave their man or assigned area to stop the dribbler.

position. After the ball has been rotated from side to side, an offensive player may catch the defense slightly out of position, thereby creating a crease in the defense. The dribbler may only be able to penetrate a zone for a few feet, but it opens up other teammates for good shots. A quick move into the crease can create an open area near the free-throw line. As a result, a shot can be taken, or the ball can be passed to an open teammate. As a rule, the open teammates will be either under the basket or at the three-point line.

Dribbling in Special Situations

❑ Practice Dribbling in a Crowd

As players practice their dribbling skills, they should become comfortable dribbling in a crowd. An effort should be made to practice situations requiring special dribbling skills. As players practice dribbling around or between defenders, their body should be used as a shield as much as possible. The height and speed of the dribble should change as the dribbler goes through the tightest areas. For example, when a player uses a cross-over dribble to go by a defender, he should use a high-to-low dribble, a control (normal) dribble, or an even lower dribble.

❑ Practice Initiating a Fast Break in a Crowd

Ballhandlers should practice initiating a fast break after getting a rebound near the free-throw line. Toss a ball up and catch it to simulate a long rebound near the free-throw line. Pivot and start dribbling downcourt with the ball, very low the first several dribbles in case a defender is reaching in to steal the ball. By this time, the dribbler should have determined if a teammate is open ahead of him, or if he has a clear lane to the basket. Practice this move until it becomes natural, and then practice initiating the move with a low, cross-over dribble.

If a good ballhandler gets a rebound close to the basket near the side of the lane, he should initiate the move by pivoting away from the basket toward the sideline and defenders. The initial move should be with the ball in the hand nearest the sideline when he starts to dribble up the court. Initiate the move with a low dribble, even if a high-to-low move—crossing low in front of the body—must be used to initiate the dribble. Look upcourt to the outlet position to see if teammates are open for a pass. If not, continue dribbling downcourt, while looking for an open teammate.

Dribbling on a Fast Break

Players need to learn to attack the basket and not slow down before shooting a layup. Why work hard to get open and then let the defenders catch up by slowing down? The layup must be made in front of the body, with a finger roll to soften the shot.

In a one-on-one fast break situation, if the defender is in good defensive position, an important factor to consider involves who is in control—the ballhandler or the defender? As such, the defender is in control:

- If the ballhandler is one-handed or a one-sided player.
- If the dribbler is not confident scoring when he makes a move to his weakside.

On the other hand, the ballhandler is in control:

- If he goes to his right or left with equal ease.
- If he can dribble fast while making rapid changes of direction with ease.
- If he is effective scoring anywhere near the basket.

Players should work on fast-break situations and the correct moves to employ in such situations if they are to be successful. The following situations may occur in a one-on-one fast-break opportunity. You should practice the following circumstances at home or at a local playground with another defender as part of your workout so you are comfortable when these situations arise in a game. Initially, work on these situations at a controlled speed to enhance your technique. When ready, practice them at full game speed.

♦ The defender is in back of the dribbler, but is closing fast:

- Don't slow down; make the layup.
- Cut off the angle of pursuit by drifting slightly in front of the defender.
- If you do slow down, shoot the ball in front of you so your body shields the ball from the defender.

♦ The defender is beside the dribbler with inside position:

- Don't slow down.
- Dribble in for a short shot, protect the ball, and anticipate powering through a foul.

- Use a hesitation dribble near the three-point line, followed by a continuation to the basket or a cross-over dribble with a drive to the other side of the hoop.
- Jump-stop and make a jump shot from eight to 10 feet away from the basket.

♦ The defender is in perfect defensive position, inside and slightly ahead of the dribbler by one step:

- Use a hesitation dribble and a cross-over move near the three-point line.
- Jump-stop and make a jump shot from eight to 10 feet or at the free-throw line if you are comfortable with that distance.
- Stopping near the free-throw line so the defender is forced to stay near the ballhandler to prevent a shot. This step opens up lanes near the basket for teammates to fill from either side.

Cardinal No-No's of Dribbling

- Don't dribble unless you know where you are going.
- Don't pick up your dribble when you cross midcourt.
- Don't dribble into a corner or near the sideline against a trapping team.
- Don't get in the habit of dribbling one time before shooting.
- Don't look at the ball as you dribble.
- Don't dribble to a double-team you see coming and pick up your dribble.

One of the cardinal no-no's of dribbling is to always dribble one time before shooting.

Summary Points

Dribbling effectively is a learned skill that can be developed through hours of focused practice. Ballhandlers should be able to dribble with either hand and should be able to execute the various types of basic dribbles.

CHAPTER 30

A fake is a movement that simulates another move, shot, or pass in an attempt to get the opponent slightly out of position. The effectiveness of a player can be greatly enhanced by his ability to fake. One of the major differences between skilled and unskilled players is their ability to fake. Most fakes are offensive in nature. A fake is usually immediately followed by a pivot, shot, dribble, move, cut, screen, or pass. To fake more effectively, players should:

❑ Keep Fakes Simple and Sudden

Fakes must be realistic to be effective. This objective can only be accomplished by paying attention to detail and practicing the fakes until they appear realistic.

❑ Be unpredictable; Use a Variety of Fakes, Shots, and Moves

A fake is most effective when the defender is afraid that the offensive player will score or make a move to the basket upon getting the ball. For example, if a guard has just hit two outside shots, the defender will probably be very susceptible to a fake shot, followed by a sudden move to the basket.

One of the major differences between skilled and unskilled players is their ability to fake.

Types of Fakes

❑ Offensive Fakes

➢ *Ball fake.* When making a ball fake, an offensive player moves the ball as he would if he were going to initiate a move, pass, or shot. His hand position should be the same, but his arms are kept flexed. His arms should never be fully extended and should seldom be extended more than halfway. This positioning allows the player to pull the ball back and initiate the next move. A full extension of the offensive player's arms would allow more time for the defender to recover.

➤ *Head-and-shoulder fake.* The head-and-shoulder fake works well with a ball fake. When used together, the defender is more likely to believe the fake is real if the offensive player's body moves in the same manner as it does when he shoots, jumps, or initiates a move to the side. A player should work to perfect his head-and-shoulder fake so it is identical to the way he normally initiates a move. When faking laterally, the head and shoulders should lean a few inches in one direction, before the player makes a move in the opposite direction.

➤ *Foot or step fake.* The purpose of the foot or step fake is to get the defender to react by moving in that direction, thereby creating a space for the offensive player. The step part of the fake should start the same as would a move in that direction, but the first step should be a shorter one. The step should be approximately a half to two-thirds of a full stride so the player can re-pivot more quickly. The offensive player either then makes a move in another direction, shoots or passes the ball (refer to the discussion on a jab step).

➤ *Eye fake.* A player can look away to cause the defender to step in that direction. This one step is usually enough to create a passing lane or a lane for a move to the basket. The player should know what is happening on the court prior to utilizing an eye fake. The player can then use his peripheral vision as he looks away from the area to which the move or pass will be made.

➤ *Change-of-pace fakes.* A change of pace fake can involve having an offensive player change the speed at which he is dribbling or cutting to gain an advantage against a defender. When employing a change-of-pace dribble, the ballhandler changes the speed at which he is moving. As a rule, in this situation, the dribbler is advancing slowly, before suddenly accelerating ahead of the defender. However, if the defender is in perfect position on a fast break, the ballhandler can slow down for a step or two around the three-point line, before cutting behind the defender and accelerating across the lane toward the basket.

The purpose of the foot or step fake is to get the defender to react by moving in that direction, thereby creating a space for the offensive player.

A change-of-pace fake can also involve a dribble fake. The dribble fake is often used in fast-break or two-on-one situations to pull the defender to one side and create a better passing lane for a teammate breaking to the basket. Once the ballhandler realizes the defender has good defensive position, he dribbles to one side of the lane. If the defender doesn't follow, the player continues the drive to the basket. If the defender shifts over to follow the ballhandler, a lane is created for a pass to the cutter.

A "change-of-pace before cutting" can also be employed as a change-of-pace fake. This type of fake is often used to lull the defender into relaxing, before breaking to another area of the court or cutting around a screen. This has also been called the sleep fake, because the offensive player relaxes as if nothing is about to happen. The player appears to be uninvolved. He turns away from the action slowly. He is actually paying close attention through the corner of his eye. He is waiting for the right moment to cut to the basket.

The backdoor cut is a type of change-of-pace fake used against a defender playing tight denial defense. An offensive player breaks out to the three-point line, looking for a pass. If defended tightly, he fakes, while relaxing for a moment. He drops his hands, starts to straighten up slightly, and acts as if he is going to stop and do nothing. As the defender turns to look toward the ball, the offensive player suddenly cuts back door toward the basket.

> *Fakes before cutting.* As a rule, three types of fakes can be employed before cutting—sleep fake, step-away fake, and step-behind fake. The sleep fake was previously discussed in the section on "change-of-pace before cutting."

The step-away fake involves having the offensive player take several steps in a direction away from the way the player plans to cut. The sleep fake and step-away fake can be done together.

The step-behind fake is the third type of fake that can be performed before cutting. This fake works best against a zone defense. The offensive player saunters behind the defense so he can't be seen by the defenders who are focused on the ballhandler. The player wants the defense to forget about him. The player then makes eye contact or signals to the ballhandler as he breaks to an open area for the pass. This move is often used near the basket on the baseline.

> *The high-low dribble and cross-over dribble.* These are both considered types of fakes because the defender is faked into thinking the dribbler is going to continue dribbling in the same manner. When the player gets in the appropriate position, relative to

The backdoor cut is a type of change-of-pace fake used against a defender playing tight denial defense.

the defender, he changes the type of dribble he is using to get by the defender.

❑ Defensive Fakes

When executing a defensive fake, the defender may fake the offense into thinking he is out of position or isn't paying close attention. The defensive player may then steal the pass or the dribble. The defender on the backside of the defense may hide behind other players who are between him and the ballhandler. The defender is hoping the offensive player will pass the ball, without realizing he is in position to intercept the pass.

> **When executing a defensive fake, the defender may fake the offense into thinking he is out of position or isn't paying close attention.**

CHAPTER 31

A move is a specific action the ballhandler makes in order to beat his man. A move consists of a combination of basketball skills and/or a change of direction intended to cause the defender to be out of position. The move may result in an immediate shot or pass without a dribble, or the player may drive by his man toward the basket, resulting in a shot or pass.

Many moves or shots are initiated by a realistic fake, with the intention of causing the opponent to step or lean in the wrong direction. If an offensive player can cause the defensive player to be one-half to one-step out of position, a quick shot or move will have the defender beaten. The following factors apply when making a move:

- Fakes should be simple and sudden.
- Moves should involve very few dribbles, if any.
- Dribbling should only be done to get someplace in a hurry.

Beating Your Man

The purpose of any move is to beat your man. The defender is beaten when he is out of good defensive position or slightly out of control. The result is a one-half to one-step advantage for the offensive player. The defender is beaten when he over-commits, crosses his feet, leans and reaches, charges toward the offensive player, or jumps in the air trying to block a faked shot. Keep in mind that beating your man is worthless if you don't make something happen quickly.

The purpose of any move is to beat your man.

A Quick First Step

A quick first step is one of the most important parts of an effective move. The ballhandler's first step should be explosive in order to allow the dribbler to get a step advantage on the defender. The ballhandler's legs must be slightly flexed, coiled, and ready to spring forward. The player pushes hard off the back foot or the foot opposite the direction the move is made. The push is finished by pushing hard with the toes. Young players are rarely taught how to spring off their toes or how to cut sharply.

When driving by a player, the first dribble should be a low and fast. When executing a crossover dribble, the crossover to the other hand should go from high to low to make it hard for a defender to reach down to the ball.

If the offensive player sees an open lane and wants to make a move as soon as he catches the ball, he can time the catch so that he is springing forward off his back foot. At that moment, his back leg is flexed and coiled, and ready to spring forward as he brings the ball down toward the floor. The player must then initiate the dribble so that a walking violation is not called.

Know Your Man and Test Him Early

A player should know as much as possible about the defender who is guarding him. The offensive player should be scouting and evaluating his opponent from the opening tip-off. The offensive player should learn his opponent's speed, tendencies, or habits—whether it is trying to block every shot, leaning or reaching for the ball, playing very tight defense, or playing off the ball too much. If the offensive player has been aggressive and has challenged the opponent, he will have seen most of the defender's tendencies before the first eight or ten minutes of the game. The offensive player should take advantage of these tendencies the rest of the game.

Time on the Bench is an Opportunity to Scout the Opponent

Take advantage of your time on the bench to evaluate the opposing team's offensive and defensive schemes. What is the opposing team's game plan? Evaluate the players you are likely to be matched against when you go in the game. Few players take advantage of this opportunity to scout their opponent. This knowledge will help you be more effective if and when you return to the game.

Footwork

Proper footwork is mandatory if a move is to be successful. If the player has established the wrong pivot foot, a move may be thwarted, or a shot will be taken off the wrong foot. Proper footwork prevents unnecessary steps or dribbles, helps the player establish position, and enables the player to shoot correctly. The player must work on his footwork as a

Proper footwork is mandatory if a move is to be successful.

move is learned. Even players in the NBA continue to work on this seldom-discussed skill.

Knowledge of the Open Lanes

The player must know when and where lanes are likely to open up in the offense, so he is ready to immediately make his move. No player can drive to the basket if the lane is clogged. He must know where the open shots will most likely exist.

Moves Are Learned

Many young players watch college and professional players make a fantastic move and believe it is natural. They don't realize these players have practiced these or very similar moves countless times in drills, on playgrounds, and in driveways. Some professional players work all summer trying to perfect one or two moves. If you see a move you like, get out and work on it.

As you work on a move, you must first learn the correct footwork. Proper footwork is what allows the move to be executed properly. As the technique is perfected, you must learn how to set up the move, usually with some type of fake. Then, you should increase the quickness of the moves, while maintaining proper balance.

The Simplest Moves

The simplest move for a guard or wing is to catch the pass and immediately shoot or blow past the defender with the dribble. If the defender is out of position or is charging toward the offensive player, the guard should explode toward the basket. If a post has great position and/or a height advantage, the simplest move is a quick pivot and shot before other defenders can sag down to double-team.

Some professional players work all summer trying to perfect one or two moves.

If the defender is in good defensive position and a good athlete, the offensive player will have to make a move that will help put the defender at a slight disadvantage. When an all-around player fakes, the defender will take the fake since he has no idea what the player is likely to do. The more unpredictable a player is, the easier it is to get an open shot.

Initiating a Move to the Basket

Court awareness and situation awareness are the first factors involved in initiating a move. By the time the ball arrives, the player should already have a sense of whether he should shoot, pass, or fake and make a move. A player who catches the ball, looks around, and then decides what to do will usually have difficulty scoring.

A player can gain an advantage before he gets the ball by moving without the ball and/or using screens. Often, the defensive player will relax for a moment or look to help his teammates, for example:

- A guard drifts to an open area if his defensive man sags to help-defend the lane.
- The offensive player pops out to the three-point line looking for a pass. When he doesn't get the ball, his defender relaxes or turns his head toward the ballhandler. The player then cuts backdoor toward the basket.
- A post passes the ball back outside when he is double-teamed. The defenders look for their man, and the defensive post relaxes for a moment. This situation is when the post should gain much better post position by reposting.
- Players should learn to use screens well. Screens are intended to get a player open.

The position of the defender determines the ease of initiating a move. For example, if the defender is out of position, he will be easy to beat. If time exists to shoot or make a move toward the basket, the offensive player should act immediately. On the other hand, if there isn't time to shoot, the defender will be very susceptible to a fake, followed by a cutting move behind the defender in the direction the defender came.

For example, if a wing is on the right side of the court at the three-point line and the defender comes hard from the left, the ballhandler might fake a shot and make a move to the left, thereby cutting behind the defender. With regard to imitating a move, the following circumstances illustrate possible scenarios:

- If the defender is in good position, the ballhandler should be ready to fake hard one way and make a move in another direction. He should remember to be unpredictable.
- If the defender is in good position, a post can initiate a drop-step move toward the basket at the time the ball is being caught. The post pins the defender with his leg and pivots to the basket. This move should not be made if the pass isn't catchable, since the first objective should always be to maintain possession.
- If a post's defender fronts on the high side, while the post is above the low-post area, the wing can fake toward the top of the

circle and drive the baseline. Upon seeing the fake, the post should shift to keep the defender pinned and prevent him from stopping the ballhandler's drive.

❏ When to Initiate a Move

If a ballhandler has vision beyond his defender, he not only knows where his defender is, he can also see the offense develop and the defense react. The ballhandler is ready to react once a lane is created. When the ballhandler knows where the defenders are and who is likely to give help defense after he beats his man, he should be prepared to make the correct decision. Consider for example a wing who has the ball and is positioned at the three-point line in the wing area. If the wing looks past the defender, he may see the following:

- The low post being fronted on the high side creates an opportunity for a pass to the post on the base-line side. The wing may drive the baseline, since the defending post has given position to stop the drive.
- The low post comes out to set a backscreen on the wing's defender. The wing should keep his defender busy until he drives around the screen at the right time.
- The low-post area on the ballside is being vacated as a teammate goes elsewhere. The wing may drive once the teammate's defender turns to go with him. If the wing doesn't drive, he should look for a cutter.

Practicing Moves

Initially, a move should be practiced by paying very close attention to proper footwork and technique. Once the player is comfortable with a move and can routinely execute the move and shot successfully, he should practice the move on the opposite side of the court. Remember, that in this instance, the footwork will be reversed.

Complementary moves should be mastered next. Complementary moves are moves that vary from the initial move, but the direction of the move is reversed after either a fake is made or an entirely different type of shot is taken. These, too, should be practiced on both sides of the court. Remember, it is better to do a few moves well than a lot of moves poorly. (Refer to the section on practice sessions in the chapter on "Shooting.")

If a ballhandler has vision beyond his defender, he not only knows where his defender is, he can also see the offense develop and the defense react.

Moves for a Guard

❑ The Spot-Up Shooter

Some guards are not good ballhandlers. As such, they are not effective in one-on-one situations. Their strongest skills are initiated once they receive the pass in the open. The spot-up shooter depends on other players to penetrate the defense and pass the ball back out to him. The spot-up shooter comes off a screen, catches the pass, and shoots in one fluid motion. If a player has the reputation of being only a spot-up shooter, he will often be easy to shut down—even if the player is a great three-point shooter.

In reality, spot-up shooters seldom get fouled. If a player is a spot-up shooter and a great free-throw shooter, he will rarely get the chance to use his free-throw shooting skills. A spot-up shooter should work to develop his one-on-one skills, so he can become comfortable driving to the basket. Then, he will have a much better chance of getting an open shot or a free-throw opportunity.

A guard must beat the defender off the dribble or use a screen to get open. Furthermore, guards and forwards must become comfortable and confident scoring in most one-on-one situations. Guards get open against a man-to-man defense by moving without the ball and using a screen or a series of screens.

A penetrating guard who can break down the defense is invaluable because he opens up so many of his teammates for easy shots. If a guard penetrates the lane he must first be looking to score, but he should also anticipate other defenders stepping out to stop the drive. If so, the guard should look to pass to the open teammate in the area from where the defender came.

A guard must beat the defender off the dribble or use a screen to get open.

Certain moves are basically designed for guards and wings, but forwards need both guard and post skills as well. While the next two sections discuss moves that guards can make, these moves apply to all players.

❑ The Simplest Moves for a Guard

➢ If the defender is off you when you catch the ball, you can immediately shoot or drive to the basket.
➢ If the defender is charging toward you, you can fake a shot and drive behind the defender and toward an open area.

> When you, as the ballhandler, are closely guarded, you can either fake a move or pass in one direction before driving in the opposite direction or drive by the defender with a quick first step.

The following example illustrates a one-on-one move that can be made by a guard who is positioned near the three-point line. While facing the defender, the ballhandler is bent low and forward, with his arms dangling down. From this position, the ball can be moved from side to side with little effort. The ball is held firmly in both hands. The offensive player suddenly gives a head, shoulder, and ball fake to one side, before driving in the opposite direction. If the defender has been beaten by this move more than once, the ballhandler may have to double-fake before driving to the side of the original move. With a double-fake, the offensive player gives a slight fake to one side followed by a hard fake to the opposite side. The ballhandler then makes his move back to the side of the original fake.

❑ Other Moves for Guards:

The following moves may assist the guard in getting free when he is tightly guarded. When a player is well-guarded, he may need a variety of moves to get open. Once a player has developed several basic moves, he should perfect additional moves in an effort to become unpredictable. However, every player should keep in mind that it is more important to do a few moves well, than a lot of moves poorly.

> *The jab step.* One of the best ways to beat a defender is with a jab step. The jab step is a quick, short step made directly at the outside foot of the defender. The purpose of the jab step is to cause the defender to react. The player then responds with an appropriate move. To be effective, the player must be in the triple-threat position, from which he can dribble, shoot, or pass. As a rule, the following three basic moves can be executed to follow a well-executed jab step:

- If the defender doesn't react, drive in the direction of the jab step. Take a second step with the same foot, and continue with a dribble until you are by the defender. Drive, don't fake, if the defender has been faked in that direction several times before.
- If the defender takes a half-step back after you jab step at him, cross over with the foot you stepped with and drive by him. When you cross over, place your foot beside or beyond the defender's lead foot, thereby hindering his recovery.

Once a player has developed several basic moves, he should perfect additional moves in an effort to become unpredictable.

- Make certain to dribble fast enough to avoid a walking violation. The ball must hit the floor before your pivot foot leaves it the ground.
- Shoot a jump shot if the defender jumps back a full step. Your foot is pulled back as you jump and shoot. To get the shot off faster, keep your pivot leg slightly flexed as the jab step is brought back. Your body should already be flexed and ready to jump.

➤ The crossover dribble. The crossover dribble is an effective way to change directions fast, while dribbling. The player brings the ball in front of his body as he changes hands. This move is often executed with sudden acceleration as the ball is brought from a high-to-low dribble with the opposite hand. Changing the height of the dribble makes it harder for the defenders to get a hand on the ball when they reach for it.

A crossover dribble is used to initiate a move to the basket by a guard. Often on a fast break, the ballhandler may use a crossover dribble near the elbow in order to get around a defender who is in position to deny the drive.

➤ *Spin move.* Ballhandlers who are driving toward the basket occasionally use the spin move when the crossover dribble is unavailable. This move is usually made near the free-throw line to avoid getting caught in traffic under the basket. The player dribbles toward the defender, plants his foot, pivots backwards, and spins away. As the player comes out of the spin, the dribble is continued toward the basket. The primary drawback with a spin move is that the ballhandler loses vision of the floor ahead of him. As he spins he can't see defenders as they converge. Spin moves are more effective if they are used sparingly.

➤ *Hesitation dribble.* If a defender is in ideal defensive position as a player is driving to the basket, a hesitation dribble may be effective in getting the defender slightly out of position for a brief instant. This hesitation creates a space for the ballhandler to either drive to the basket or change the direction of his dribble. The ballhandler slows down and straightens up slightly, before accelerating toward the basket. The offensive player is giving the defender time to react before he accelerates. This move needs to be started far enough from the basket to give the ballhandler adequate time and space for another move.

- *Step-back move.* With the step-back move, the player creates a space to get a clear shot by taking one step away from the basket and the defender. A jump shot is typically taken within 10 to 12 feet of the basket, usually by a forward or a post. The shot may be taken farther away from the basket if the shooter has enough strength and skill. This is an advanced move, since the player is moving away from the basket as the shot is being taken.

- *Step-through move.* The step-through move is made as the dribble is picked up. If two defenders blocking the path of the ballhandler leave enough space, the player may be able to slide through the space and shoot the ball. As the player approaches the defenders, he picks up the dribble and grasps it tightly with both hands. He takes one long step toward the backboard and splits the defenders. The player springs off this foot, while leaning toward the basket to shoot a jumper or a finger-roll. The key is to step past the defenders, spring off the lead foot, and lean forward, while shooting to prevent the defenders from blocking the shot.

A step-through move can be used to split a trap. If the two defender leaves a slight space between them, the ballhandler may step between and through to deliver a pass.

Dribbling/Driving Options

❑ Dribbling Between Two Staggered Defenders

Trying to dribble between defenders is a mistake many players make that usually results in a turnover. However, times occur when a great dribbler has enough space to slide between the defenders and break down the defense. The dribbler uses his body to shield the first defender from the ball by dribbling with his opposite hand. The ballhandler must be ready to switch hands with a low crossover dribble to prevent a steal by the second defender. The dribbler must bend lower as he executes the crossover dribble. The second defender is then shielded from the ball by the ballhandler's body.

Trying to dribble between defenders is a mistake many players make that usually results in a turnover.

❑ Driving from the Wing Position

Wings, or players in the wing position, should look to drive if a lane exists to the basket. Lanes will usually open up by driving toward the free-throw line or driving the baseline. With regard to driving from the wing position, the following suggestions may apply:

- A ballhandler must be able to visualize the screen developing and immediately determine where the screen will be set. If a post or forward comes out to the perimeter to set a screen, it will probably be from behind and slightly to one side of your defender. A fake first in the opposite direction may help set up the screen even better.
- Many offenses set screens to allow a wing to drive over the top of the screen and into the free-throw lane. These screens may be set by other guards, forwards, or a post stepping out near the three-point line. This is the most common situation resulting in a drive from the wing position.
- If a wing sees the post being fronted away from the basket, he should fake and drive around his man. The post must seal his man away from the basket to prevent him from dropping down and stopping the base-line drive.

❏ Driving the Baseline

Finishing a drive along the baseline involves scoring a basket. Make sure to use the backboard; swishing a driving base-line shot without using the backboard is much more difficult. Among your options for finishing the baseline drive are:

- Square up to the backboard and bank the shot, using your body as a shield. Do not bring the ball up over your head where it can be blocked from behind. Keep the ball slightly out in front of you and toward the basket. Jumping up and slightly backward may create a little more room for the shot and might draw a foul.
- Swish the shot. (Note: this is a very hard shot to make.)
- Dunk it. (Obviously, you must first have this particular skill.)
- Dish to an open teammate around the lane.
- Pass out to a teammate at the three-point line. The clearest lane for this pass is often along the baseline to the opposite corner. This outlet is for the baseline drive. Teammates on the opposite side should know to drift to the corner if a baseline drive is made.

A player who is a good shooter from the corners should be able to drive the baseline against 2-1-2 or 1-3-1 zone defenses.

❏ Driving the Baseline Against a Zone

A player who is a good shooter from the corners should be able to drive the baseline against 2-1-2 or 1-3-1 zone defenses. If the offensive player has made baskets from the corner, a defender will undoubtedly charge toward the player, as he receives the pass. A fake shot, followed by a quick move along the baseline, can result in an open area. The offensive player's options are to either pull up and shoot an eight- to ten-foot base-line jump shot or continue his drive to the basket. If the offensive player continues his drive, a defensive post will normally come over to stop the drive or block the shot.

If defenders are waiting for the driving player near the basket, he should anticipate that he will need to plant and cut sharply away from the baseline when he is near the low-post area. This sudden move allows the shooter to find a small area in which he can shoot over the defensive post. For example, the offensive player can shoot a fall-away bank shot from about six to eight feet. Because this move is difficult, it should be practiced until the player is confident of executing it properly. Among the other options this player has are the following:

- Driving in for a layup if the defense is slow to react.
- Passing to an open teammate when defenders step out to stop a drive to the basket. Teammates are likely to be open for a pass in the following areas:
  - Under the basket across the lane
  - On the weakside at the free-throw line
  - On the weakside at the wing area
  - In the weakside corner area

Moves for a Forward

A forward is a cross between a guard and a post, and he should strive to attain the skills and moves of both. The same moves used by posts and guards should be learned by forwards.

Certain plays or parts of the offense are designed to get the forward open. One such play is called "a screen for the screener." One common way to run this play is to have the forward at the foul line, the post at the right low-post position, and the shooting guard at the opposite low-post position. The other guard or forward is at the right-wing position. The point guard dribbles to the left side of the lane, as the power forward moves down the right side of the lane to set a screen for the post, who breaks out to the free-throw line. By this time, the shooting guard has come across the lane to set a screen for the power forward. The point guard has two possible passes—first, to the post at the free-throw line; or second, to the forward under the basket on the left side. The forward should use these screens to get free for the pass.

A forward is a cross between a guard and a post, and he should strive to attain the skills and moves of both.

Moves for a Post

What should the post do when he gets the ball after establishing good low-post position? Among his options are the following:

- If the post has position for a good shot, he should take it immediately.
- If the defensive player is in good defensive position, the post may have to make a move to get a good shot.
- If the post is double- or triple-teamed, he should find the teammate who is left unguarded and pass it to him as soon as possible. In this regard:
  - The offensive post can quickly re-post and gain better scoring position, since the defensive post will often relax once the ball is passed back.
  - The offensive post can go screen for a teammate, thereby creating a lane to the basket.

Posts should seldom dribble the ball. If the post must dribble, it should only involve one or two quick dribbles to get to a more open area. If a tall player dribbles the ball, it is easier for a short player who has good hands to steal it.

Quick, sudden, simple moves are the most effective moves for the post. Since a post is often double- or triple-teamed, it is important that he is decisive upon catching the ball. Any delay or complicated move may allow the defense time to swarm the post.

❑ Basic Post Moves

When a post is well-defended, he cannot get off a shot without making a move. In this regard, a post should become proficient in the following four basic moves:

Quick, sudden, simple moves are the most effective moves for the post.

- Pivot toward the baseline, square up, and shoot a jump shot
- Fake toward the baseline, pivot toward the free-throw lane, and shoot
- Pivot toward the middle of the lane and shoot a jump shot
- Fake toward the middle of the lane, pivot toward the baseline, and shoot

The post should alternate these moves so the defender has no idea what to expect. The post shouldn't fake if he doesn't need to. For example, if the defender is playing off the post several feet, a basic pull-up jumper may be all that is needed.

- *The pull-up jump shot.* If the defender is playing off a step or so and not chesting the post (i.e., leaning against or touching the post with his forearm), the post should pivot, square-up, and shoot a jump shot from the position where the ball was caught. When executing a pull-up jumper:

- The post should catch the ball with both feet planted so that he can pivot in either direction. The post should practice pivoting and shooting both ways.
- The post should use the backboard whenever possible. He should learn to shoot softly and with a high arch.

Practice these shots until you become proficient with them. The post should become adept at making these moves from either side of the lane. Once the post has perfected these basic moves, he is ready to learn the following advanced moves:

➢ *The drop step.* The post should establish low-post position with his back toward the basket. When the pass is received, both feet should be planted so that either foot can be used as the pivot foot. If the defender is over-playing the post to one side, the drop step can be taken on the other side of the defender. The following example illustrates how the post might react when he is on the right low-post area and the defender is over-playing slightly to the high side:

- Anticipate that the pass probably will be a bounce pass; as a result, he should be ready for a low ball.
- After catching the ball, use a head, shoulder, and slight ball fake to the right as his left foot is drop stepped to hook the defender.
- The drop step actually has the post moving his left foot closer to the baseline and the basket while moving his leg more inward toward the lane, so his left leg actually goes around or hooks the defender's left leg.
- Then, pivot to the left toward the baseline. His right foot is swung around so that the post is now facing the basket. The post has then gained inside position toward the basket, and the defender is behind the post. A layup finishes the move.

Once the defender is on the post's back, he can only block the shot if the shooter makes the mistake of bringing the ball up over his head to shoot.

Once the defender is on the post's back, he can only block the shot if the shooter makes the mistake of bringing the ball up over his head to shoot. The post should use his body as a shield and either lay the ball up or shoot a short shot, with the ball more forward than normal.

If the pass is catchable, the post can sometimes drop step as the ball is being caught. As a result, the post makes a direct move to the basket.

In contrast to the previously cited example, a drop step can be done with the post's right foot toward the lane, if the defender is over-playing toward the baseline instead of on the high side. The right foot is used to hook the defender's right leg, and the post then pivots toward his right toward the middle of the lane. The finishing shot is often either a jump shot, a fading jump shot toward the middle of the lane, or a fall-away jump shot.

> *The power move to the basket.* Sometimes a post is forced to catch the ball several feet farther away from the basket than he would like. He can still drop step, however, if his drop step is followed by one power dribble. He should then finish his shot strongly and explode to the basket—dunking the ball or taking it as close to the goal as possible. He should remember to use his body as a shield.

> *The power move across the lane.* The post should be ready to make a move upon catching the ball. The simplest move is to pivot toward the lane and shoot. An effective head-and-shoulder fake toward the baseline, followed by a pivot toward the lane, will often result in an open shot, especially if the post has been using the drop step. The move may be either of the following:

- A jump shot, jumping straight up or drifting slightly across the lane.

- A quick head fake toward the baseline, if the defender is expecting a power move to the basket. The post should follow this fake with a completed pivot and one power dribble toward the middle of the lane. The move is finished with a jump shot or a jump-hook.

The post should be ready to make a move upon catching the ball.

The power-move, with a dribble across the lane, can also be completed with a jump-stop, with the post springing toward the basket rather than across the lane. The jump-stop allows the post to change direction rapidly and more effectively.

> *The up-and-under move.* The up-and-under move is performed when the post catches the pass with his back to the basket, pivots, fakes a shot, and then drives past the post and shoots. This move is performed in one of two ways. First, the post catches the pass, and then:
> - Pivots 180 degrees to square-up facing the defender.
> - Fakes a shot to get the defender to commit.
> - Drives around the defender for a shot after the defender takes the fake.

In the second option, the post catches the pass, and then:

- Pivots 90-degrees off the foot farthest from the baseline.
- Fakes a move into the lane.
- Repivots again with the lead foot toward the basket.
- Then jumps toward the basket and either shoots or lays up the ball.

For example, when the post is on the left side of the basket in the low-post position with his back to the basket, he should:

- Give a slight head-and-shoulder fake toward the baseline.
- Pivot 90-degrees inside, faking a move into the lane with a step into the lane with the right foot.
- Pull the right foot back and step with the right foot toward the basket and past the defender.
- Jump toward the basket and shoot the ball. (A dribble should only be taken when the post is too far from the basket.)

➤ *The spin move.* A spin move by a post is really a sudden drop step, followed by a power move to the basket. When attempting a spin move, the post should be mindful of the following factors:

- The offensive player fakes by giving the appearance that he isn't about to shoot, before he suddenly spins and explodes to the basket.
- The player should also initiate this move with a ball and a head-and-shoulder fake in the opposite direction, followed by a spin toward the basket.
- The move is finished by a shot or a power move to the basket.
- A spin move is more effective if it is used when the defender has his body up against the post. The defender is trying to prevent the post from getting a better low-post position. The closer the defender, the easier it is for the post to spin around him.

A spin move by a post is really a sudden drop step, followed by a power move to the basket.

➤ *Facing-the-basket moves.* In today's game, in which the post is often setting screens near the three-point line, a post with wing skills can be invaluable to his team. The post who can hit the mid-range jump shot, pass, fake, and drive to the basket will open up the court for himself and his teammates.

❑ Posts Should Expect to Be Fouled

The post should learn to power-up through the foul and finish his shot. This step requires good upper-body and hand strength. Once a post is proficient at making a variety of shots, he should work on them in a contact drill. As a result, he can get used to being fouled and finishing his shot.

Powering-through while being fouled will enable the post to have a chance for two free throws or a three-point play, if the field goal is made. If a post wants to be a good scorer, he should work hard to be a good free-throw shooter. The post usually goes to the free-throw line more than any other position on the court.

Summary Points

Moves must be practiced if they are to be perfected. Proper footwork is critical to the post. No move is natural until it has been practiced enough that it feels natural. Moves can be practiced alone or with another player. When practicing moves, pay attention to detail so your fakes and moves are game-realistic. Learn to execute the moves as quickly as possible and under control. Always keep in mind that no move is successful if the shot isn't made!

Moves must be practiced if they are to be perfected.

CHAPTER 32

Two-Man Games

Basketball is a series of two- and three-man games within an offensive scheme. Sound fundamentals and execution of the two- and three-man games are requirements for success on the court. Two-man games can be practiced in drills with or without either defenders or additional players. In this regard, well-designed drills will emphasize two-man games, while stressing entry passes, screens, defense, and other offensive and defensive fundamentals. These drills should address components of the team's offensive scheme.

What is a Two-Man Game?

Two-man games are integral to the most basic offenses in basketball. In these games, two players work together to get one of the players open for a shot. As such, two-man games are typically part of a team's normal offense. A two-man game is more effective if the offensive scheme opens up an area of the court by rotating the ball to the weakside, or by moving a teammate and his defender from the ballside to the opposite side of the court. The following examples illustrate several of the more commonly run types of two-man games:

❏ The Give-and-Go

The give-and-go is perhaps the oldest play in basketball, but still very effective today. It takes advantage of the defender's tendency to relax or turn to look for the ball after the offensive player passes. At that moment, the passer cuts toward the basket or to an open area, looking for a return pass. The give-and-go is used successfully at all levels of play, including the professional level. This basic play should be the first play that a younger player learns. The give-and-go stresses the importance of movement without the ball, teamwork, and unselfishness.

The give-and-go is perhaps the oldest play in basketball, but still very effective today.

❏ The Pick-and-Roll

The pick-and-roll may be the second oldest play in basketball. Like the give-and-go, the pick-and-roll is a basic offensive play that is effective at any competitive level. The pick-and-roll is one viable option that is available when a player sets a screen for the ballhandler. With regard to the pick-and-roll, the following scenario applies:

➢ If the screener's defender steps out to stop the ballhandler, the screener reverse-pivots toward the ballhandler's defender and rolls toward the basket or to an open area, while looking for a pass.
➢ As the screener reverse-pivots, he creates a passing lane by blocking the path of the ballhandler's defensive man. The defender is now behind the screener, and the screener has no defender between him and the basket, unless another defender comes over to help.
➢ When the pass is received, the player with the ball immediately makes a move to the basket or takes a shot.
➢ A mismatch may occur if the defenders have switched against the screen, since posts and guards often screen for one another.

After a player sets a screen for the ballhandler, he has several options, including:

➢ Pick-and-roll toward the basket (as previously described)
➢ Pick-and-screen away—screen for another teammate
➢ Pick-and-flair—roll to an open area away from the basket
➢ Pick-and-step back out—step back out toward or beyond the three-point line

The pick-and-roll is one viable option that is available when a player sets a screen for the ballhandler.

This basic play is seldom used effectively at the junior high or high school level because few coaches have or take the time to teach it. To be effective, the team must have good spacing and be a threat to score outside. At the youth league and junior high levels, however, most of the players are packed in the lane, thus preventing a pick-and-roll move.

❏ The Pass-and-Screen

With the pass-and-screen, the ballhandler passes and then screens for a teammate. If he screens for the person to whom he passed, it is another pick-and-roll situation. If he screens for another player who breaks off

the screen looking for a pass, it is called pass-and-screen-away. After screening, the player should then do one of the following:
- Go for an offensive rebound
- Remain in the area, if left open
- Move to an open area
- Cut around a screen
- Set a screen for a teammate

❑ The Backdoor Cut

The backdoor cut to the basket is made when an offensive player explodes toward the basket, looking for a pass—often a bounce pass. Backdoor cuts are much more effective against an aggressive, man-to-man defense.

Inside-Outside Game

Utilizing the inside-outside game is one of the best ways to get an open shot in basketball. In today's game of tight man-to-man defenses and good three-point shooters, the inside-outside game can be an effective offensive weapon. It requires two unselfish players working together for the good of the team.

The traditional inside-outside game starts when a guard passes the ball inside to a post. If double- or triple-teamed, the post passes the ball back outside to an open guard. The guard should drift slightly to a more open area, as his man sags down to help defend the post. Among the options that the offensive players have with the inside-outside game are the following:

❑ The guard's initial options include:

- Drive or take an outside shot
- Pass inside to the post

❑ The post's options after catching the pass from the guard include:

- Shoot the ball or make a move to the basket
- Pass the ball back outside if well defended, either individually or by a double- or triple-team. This pass often goes to the player who made the initial pass inside. The passer should drift to a more open spot. The pass could go to any player who is open on either side of the basket.

Utilizing the inside-outside game is one of the best ways to get an open shot in basketball.

❑ The guard's options when the ball is passed back outside include:

➢ Shoot or drive
➢ Rotate the ball to a more open player, if the defense has rotated to cover this option
➢ Pass the ball back inside once the post has reposted again

The Inside-Outside-Inside Game

The inside-outside-inside game is simply a continuation of the inside-outside game. After the post passes back outside, he should immediately do one of the three following things:

➢ Post-up again, trying to establish better post position
➢ Establish rebounding position if the guard is going to shoot
➢ Set a screen for a teammate

When the post has posted again, he is likely to be more open. The helping defenders are trying to get back to their men, and because the post's defender tends to relax when his man has passed the ball, he is no longer an immediate threat to score. The post should then look for a return pass from the guard.

The inside-outside-inside game is simply a continuation of the inside-outside game.

CHAPTER 33

Developing and executing an offense involves coordinating the positioning and movements of the players so they have the best opportunities to use their offensive skills and score. An offense is designed to get players open for easy shots, while making it very difficult for the opponent to get help defense. With regard to executing an offense effectively, players sometimes have difficulty realizing the importance of the concepts of spacing and timing.

Creating Lanes

With spacing, timing, and player movement, the offense creates lanes for passes or drives to the basket. The creation of lanes allows offenses to work. Young coaches sometimes do not understand that an offense must create lanes, and they must teach the players where and when those lanes are likely to occur.

Players should not be camped out in or around the low-post area, thereby clogging up the lane. Player movement in the lane is necessary if the posts and forwards are to get open and create lanes by taking their defensive man with them as they clear an area. Perimeter players can drive to the basket when the post (or a player in the post area nearest them) turns and moves across the lane or away from the basket.

The creation of lanes allows offenses to work.

Spacing

Spacing is critical in any offense, whether in a transitional, press-breaker, or half-court offense. If offensive players are too close together, the following limiting factors may exist:

- The players are easier to guard.
- There are no passing lanes.
- The free-throw lane is clogged, thereby preventing moves or cuts to the basket.

As such, an offense should space the offensive players evenly over the court so the defense has to guard the entire floor.

Timing

Timing involves the execution of a move, pass, cut, or screen at the proper time in order to get the easiest pass or shot possible. If the timing of the play is off, the floor spacing will be off, resulting in congested areas. The timing of the initiation of the half-court offense against an aggressive man-to-man defense must be practiced so the players will know when to break.

Adequate spacing and proper timing of an offense ensures the players will have lanes for the two- and three-man games. Once players understand the timing of the offense, they can anticipate where and when an open area will occur for a drive or cut to the basket. As teammates move to other areas of the court, they create openings or lanes. Moves must be made immediately after the lane opens up, since they are usually only there for an instant. For example, a wing has the ball and has been unable to make an entry pass to the low post. As the low post on the ballside rolls across the lane to set a screen, the wing immediately has an opening to drive to the basket. A quick fake and drive result in a score.

❑ Timing of Cuts

Players often rush the offense and make a cut into an area too soon, thereby clogging up the offense. It only takes one player cutting too soon to foul up a scoring opportunity. Players need to learn to let the offense come to them. This means letting the offense develop as it is designed. At the proper time, the players should undertake the appropriate action.

Once players understand the timing of the offense, they can anticipate where and when an open area will occur for a drive or cut to the basket.

Players also rush the offense when they break a split-second before a screen is set. If the player breaks before the screener is set, not only will the screen fail, the screener will be called for a moving-screen violation. Accordingly, the offensive players should be patient and let the offense happen.

❑ Timing of Passes

The passer must be ready to deliver the ball to the cutter on time. If the passer is late getting the ball to the right point at the right time, the advantage the cutter worked so hard to gain may be lost, since his defender will usually have time to catch up.

If a cutter is coming around a screen, the passer should focus on the cutter, his defender, and the screener's defender so the passer can anticipate if the teammate is going to be open. One factor that the passer must consider is whether the screener's defender is stepping out to impede the cutter.

If the passer anticipates that the cutter is going to be open, he should start to complete the pass. The pass should arrive just as the player comes around the screen. The teammate must be ready to catch the pass. He must be looking for the ball and have his hands in the "ready" position. Good timing requires that a passer know the offense, can anticipate whether or not the player will be open, and can deliver a pass at the best time.

❑ The Effect of Bobbled Passes on the Offense's Timing

The simple fact is that bobbled passes and bad passes will occur in games. A bobbled pass will upset the timing of the offense. During practice, the players can gain experience in delaying a cut or break if they see a pass being bobbled. All players should work extra hard learning to catch bad passes. One bobbled pass can be the difference in winning and losing.

Offense is a Series of Two- and Three-Man Games

Keeping the backside defenders busy is often overlooked when an offense is being taught. As the two- or three-man games are being executed, the other players should keep their defenders busy so that they can't help on defense. The other players should be ready to go for a rebound, set a screen for a teammate, cut to an open area, or fake other moves. If the team can't get a good shot, the offense continues and involves the other players in two- or three-man games.

The Tempo of the Game

The type of defense employed establishes the tempo of a game by dictating the type of offense that must be used to counteract it. The offense only controls the tempo when a transition or fast-break offense is utilized.

The offense only controls the tempo when a transition or fast-break offense is utilized.

Types of Offenses

Most successful teams are able to execute a variety of offenses well. As a result, they are relatively well-prepared for any type of defense. Teams should be adept at running both up-tempo and half-court offenses. A fast-break offense after a missed shot or a turnover will discourage the other team from trying to set up a full-court press defense. Teams must also be prepared to handle a variety of special situations, such as endline, sideline, and last-second plays.

The following types of offenses can be run. Remember that the opponent's defense will dictate the offense used, except when a transition offense is utilized.

- Transition offense (after a turnover or defensive rebound)
- Fast-break offense (against a press after a basket with no stoppage of play)
- Press offense (against a press after a basket and stoppage of play)
- Half-court offenses:
  - man-to-man offenses
  - zone offenses

Transition Offense

The primary purpose of the transition offense is to create the open shots that the offense would normally work for in a half-court offense. The transition offense begins the instant the defense gains possession of the ball. The success of the transition offense is determined by how quickly and accurately the players initiate the offense. No time exists to look around and decide what to do after a rebound or turnover. A delay will allow the defense time to recover and get back.

The following examples illustrate how important it is to start the fast break with good rebounding:

- Long shots often result in long rebounds—perfect for initiating the transition offense. Any player who catches a long rebound should make a move toward the opposite basket, as he looks to pass upcourt or continue his advance.

If a player gets a rebound near the free-throw line, he should pivot and start downcourt, keeping the first few dribbles low as defenders will likely be reaching in. He should also look up court to see if a teammate has released early and is open for a pass.

- With short defensive rebounds near the basket, the player must immediately look to pass to the first or secondary outlets.

The success of the transition offense is determined by how quickly and accurately the players initiate the offense.

❑ Releasing Early

A defender who has anticipated that his teammate will gain possession of a free ball should release early in an attempt to get open for a fast-break pass. If a defensive player near the top of the circle or the weak-side wing area determines that his teammate will gain control of the ball, he can break toward the other end of the court. If the player can take a few steps without his opponent seeing him, he will be wide open if his teammate can get the pass to him.

The risk in this situation is that the teammate may not get the ball, and an opponent will be left unguarded. If the player takes the first few steps and sees that he has misjudged, he must hustle back to get in his defensive position before the offense discovers the open man.

❑ The Transition Offense Must Challenge the Defense

If the ballhandler leading the fastbreak is in the middle of the floor, the defense has more options to defend. The player can drive the lane, pass to the right or left, or pull up and shoot at the free-throw line. In this situation, his choices are:

➢ Pass to a teammate on the wing who is cutting to the basket
➢ Continue driving to the basket with the intention of scoring, but ready to dish to an open teammate if his defender comes out to stop the drive
➢ Pass to an open player at the three-point line
➢ Pull up and shoot a short- or mid-range jump shot
➢ Pull back out and look for a trailing cutter
➢ If the cutters are not open, start the regular half-court offense

Since the guards are usually the first defenders back, they are the ones responsible for stopping the offense from driving the lane. If a layup or short shot is not available initially in the transition offense, the three-point shot is usually open on one side of the floor, quite often on the opposite wing, but also in the near corner.

When a teammate receives the pass near the three-point line, the defensive pressure may come from a guard charging from the lane, where he had been positioned to help stop a drive to the basket. If the three-point shot is not taken, a good fake, followed by a move toward the basket, will often result in an open mid-range shot or a lane to the basket. If the player neither shoots nor drives, he should look for a cutter or pass the ball to another teammate.

If the ballhandler leading the fastbreak is in the middle of the floor, the defense has more options to defend.

Once the transition offense has been run to its completion and the defense has re-established its normal defense, the offense should run its half-court offense.

❏ A One-on-Two Break

Coaches often tell their teams that whenever they are out-numbered by defenders on a fast break, they should pull the ball out and look to set up their half-court offense. This advice is usually very sound. However, if a player is a great scorer and ballhandler, he should sometimes challenge the defense, even if he is out-numbered by one or two players. A crease may exist in the defense that allows for an easy field goal or an opportunity to get fouled in the act of shooting.

If the dribbler senses that there are no creases, he should pull the ball out and look to pass to the cutters. Sometimes, the defense relaxes for an instant if the dribbler has turned his back on the goal to get the ball out to the three-point line. If no cutters or other teammates are open, the player should look to set up the half-court offense.

The coach should clearly define to his team in practice that he expects the good scorer to occasionally challenge the defense in this situation. The other players should be informed that if they become highly proficient in their abilities, they will be allowed to do the same. Until then, the other players are expected to pull the ball out in a one-on-two situation, unless the defenders are totally out of position.

❏ Which Teams Should Play Transition Offense?

The transition offense is a way for a less-skilled or less-athletic team to compete against a better team.

Some coaches do not use a transition offense because they consider it an undisciplined style of play. It can be. However, it is the coach's responsibility to see that it isn't. The transition offense is a way for a less-skilled or less-athletic team to compete against a better team. Open shots off the transition offense may come easier than when a team is in a half-court offense against a stronger team.

❏ The Difference Between Transition Offense and Fast-Break Offense

The two are very much alike. However, the two can be differentiated because they have different purposes. The purpose of the transition offense is to get downcourt and get a high-percentage shot before the defense has time to set up. The purpose of the fast-break offense is to get the ball inbounds after a made basket or turnover, before a press-defense position can be established.

The Fast-Break Offense

The best way to break a press after a made basket is to not give the defense time to get set up. The fast break offense is a press-prevention or a press-breaking offense. One of the primary steps involved in a fast-break offense is to inbound the ball before the defenders can get set in their desired positions.

A defensive press works by having everyone in the proper position. The offense should not allow the defense to set-up. The closest offensive player to the basket should catch the ball after a basket. This offensive player should not even let the ball hit the floor. He should catch the ball and step out-of-bounds, as he looks upcourt, and then to the other outlet positions.

The fast-break offense works as follows:

- The fast-break offense utilizes the closest rebounder to get the ball and hustle to step out-of-bounds to make a quick pass.
- The player nearest the outlet area on the ballside breaks toward the sideline. He is the primary outlet.
- The player nearest the top of the circle releases upcourt and diagonally toward the sideline on the ballside, while looking for a pass from the outlet area.
- The teammate closest to the wing area on the weakside immediately releases and cuts toward the opposite lane, anticipating a pass. Ideally, this scenario would result in that player getting an uncontested layup.
- The player in the low-post area on the weakside will be the secondary outlet. He breaks toward the opposite side of the free-throw lane. If he is already there, he can break back toward the weakside, low-post area.

The fast break offense should involve a quick series of reads and options for the inbound pass. The following is one possible scenario in this situation, including options:

- As the inbounder steps out-of-bounds, he glances upcourt, looking for a teammate near midcourt.
- The inbounder passes to a teammate in the primary outlet area, near the sideline on the ballside of the court.
- The secondary option is near the free-throw line on the ballside. The player may also break back either toward the weakside or toward the inbounder.

The best way to break a press after a made basket is to not give the defense time to get set up.

➢ The next option for the inbounder should be to pass to the original strongside outlet who is breaking back toward the inbounder.

When the inbound pass goes to the first, second, or third outlet, the player must decide upon one of several options, including:

❑ If the inbound pass goes to the primary outlet:

➢ He immediately starts upcourt.
➢ He looks to pass to a teammate across midcourt, near the sideline.
➢ He looks to pass to a teammate cutting near midcourt from the weakside.
➢ If neither player is open, the dribbler advances toward the middle of the court and attacks the basket.

❑ If the inbound pass goes to the secondary outlet, the outlet player would:

➢ Immediately start upcourt looking to pass to one of two original players who released early.
➢ Pass to the teammate from the sideline outlet area who will be breaking straight up court or angling slightly to the middle of the court.
➢ Pass back to the inbounder cutting upcourt.

If the pass goes to the third outlet, which is the primary outlet after he breaks back to the inbounder, the outlet passes back to the inbounder cutting upcourt. The team should then concentrate on getting the ball upcourt and starting the offense, since the defense will have had time to establish its positions.

If the fast-break offense does not result in an easy shot, the offense should look to pass to the last two offensive players as they cut into and through the lane. These passes offer additional opportunities to catch defenders out of position or to create mismatches.

The fast-break offense (a press-prevention offense) is different than the offenses that some coaches run, in which the post and forwards get upcourt, and a specific guard or wing inbounds the ball to another guard. Since guards play farther from the basket on defense, it takes time for them to get out-of-bounds under the basket and throw the ball in. Any delay allows enough time for the defense to get into its press positions. The fast-break offense should be stressed throughout the season so it becomes second nature to the players.

> **If the fast-break offense does not result in an easy shot, the offense should look to pass to the last two offensive players as they cut into and through the lane.**

The Press Offense

If a stoppage of play has allowed the press defense to set up, the team will have to implement its press offense. The type of defensive press a team is facing will determine the press offense used. The following factors should be remembered about all press offenses:

- Spread the floor to spread the defense.
- Move the ball quickly. Passing is faster than dribbling.
- Come back to the ball to get open, if needed.
- After the ball has been advanced past the first wave of defenders, somewhere near or beyond midcourt, the ball should be advanced toward the basket. The ballhandler either attacks the basket or passes to the open players who are usually upcourt near the sideline, in the middle of the court, or on the weakside.

❑ Reminders for the press offense:

- When inbounding the ball after a basket, the player can run the baseline and pass to a teammate who has stepped out of bounds behind the baseline. This player can inbound the ball. Only five seconds are allowed to make the inbound pass. The player can't run the baseline after a violation or after the ball is knocked out-of-bounds. The referee will point to the floor to inform the player that this play is a spot-inbounding situation.

- The player receiving the ball should avoid the corners, where it is relatively easy to be trapped by the press. If you are dribbling up the sideline, veer toward the middle of the court.

- If you are dribbling toward a trap, your options include:
    ♦ Be ready to pass to an open teammate upcourt before getting to the trap.
    ♦ If you are too close to get the pass off, pull backwards a step or two and dribble around the trap.
    ♦ Dribble back a step or two to create a lane to pass to a teammate who is coming back to help.
    ♦ Never dribble up to a defender and pick up your dribble unless you have an open teammate to whom you can pass.

- Do not pick up your dribble until you are ready to pass to an open teammate. Never pick up your dribble immediately upon crossing midcourt. Younger players are often so happy to get across midcourt that they pick up the ball and then try to decide

The player receiving the ball should avoid the corners, where it is relatively easy to be trapped by the press.

what to do. The ballhandler should want to blow by any defender who is waiting near midcourt. If the ballhandler has good vision of the floor, he should already know whether he is going to pass before he gets to the defender, or if he is going to dribble past the defenders. If you get past the defender, go straight for the basket, since the offense now has the advantage.

- Attack the basket.

❏ How to prevent being trapped:

Teams will trap in all types of defenses. A player may prevent or beat traps by doing the following:

- Being aware of the position of his teammates and the defenders.
- Keeping his head and eyes up.
- Dribbling equally well with either hand. Not favoring one side of the floor.
- Not being predictable.
- Knowing which teams like to trap. Learning where and when the defense is likely to trap.
- Being ready to pass before the trap can occur and after the trapper has definitely committed. If he sees a double-team coming, then passing to the teammate who is being left unguarded by the defender coming to trap.
- Not trapping himself. Not positioning himself against the sideline or the mid-court line. These lines act as another defender.

Half-Court Offenses

If a fast break or transition offensive opportunity isn't available, the point guard should set up the half-court offense.

If a fast break or transition offensive opportunity isn't available, the point guard should set up the half-court offense. Sometimes, the defense will not press, but they will harass the point guard by applying a full-court, man-to-man defense. If so, a post can help free up the point guard. When the defensive pressure on the point guard is reduced, it will be easier to initiate the half-court offense.

Teams will sometimes use an aggressive full-court, man-to-man defense on the point guard to generate turnovers, upset the timing of the offense, and frustrate the point guard. A post can be used to free up the point guard in the open court. All other players should go to the other end of the court so their defenders will go with them.

The post inbounds the ball to the point guard and goes upcourt past the top of the circle where the post sets a screen. The defense will not switch because it does not want a defensive post trying to guard a point in the open court. These screens can also be used in the backcourt near midcourt. These screens should never be set near the sidelines or immediately across the midcourt where the guard is not free to dribble in any direction without interference.

❑ Ways to vary initiating the half-court offense:

Most half-court offenses start with a pass to the wing near the three-point line. Younger players tend to stand in the designated area and wait for the pass. An active defense can easily deny or intercept the pass to a wing—who isn't active, but unpredictable. Once the offense is understood, the coach should teach the team ways to vary the initiation of the offense. The team should also practice initiating the offense against intense defensive pressure, similar to what they may face in a game. Half-court offenses can be initiated in the following ways:

1. A pass to the wing:

   ➤ If the wings are being guarded loosely, they should wait for the pass near the three-point line.
   ➤ If the wings are being guarded tightly, they should employ the following options:
      ◆ Step in toward the basket one to three steps, and then pop back out to the three-point line, looking for the pass.
      ◆ Pop out from a stack formation, using a screen to get open.
      ◆ Both wings break across court by looping under the basket, looking for screens by the other teammates.
      ◆ Both wings break across court as previously described, except one of the wings stops to set an additional screen for the other wing. The wings then break out either to the other side or near the free-throw line.
      ◆ The wings loop toward the basket as before, but a teammate sets a back screen as the player reverses quickly to pop back out where he started.

2. The post at the top of the circle may set a screen for the ballhandler or a cutter, or he may receive a pass and initiate the offense.

3. Dribble penetration by the point guard. The point guard drives through a crease in the defense and makes the defense commit, thereby opening up a teammate. If no one steps out to stop the

Most half-court offenses start with a pass to the wing near the three-point line.

drive, the player looks to score. A post will often set a screen for the point guard near the top of the circle.

❑ Why do teams run half-court traps?

Defenses run half-court traps for different reasons, including:

- They want to create turnovers.
- They are behind late in the game.
- They want to change the tempo of the game.
- The coach may want to get his team fired-up by playing a more aggressive defense.

Keep in mind that in order to beat the half-court trap, an offense must spread out to spread out the defenders.

❑ Suggestions for beating a half-court trap:

- The ballhandler must have his head up so he can see the entire floor as the play develops. Against a trapping team, the ballhandler must get slightly ahead of his defender so he can dribble away from the sideline as he approaches midcourt. Ten feet before midcourt, the ballhandler should have an idea whether he can beat the trap with a dribble or a pass and to whom. The ballhandler should be prepared to pass off-the-dribble before he gets to the trap, but after the defense has committed a second defender.
- The ballhandler should not get too close to the sideline where a trap is more effective.
- The ballhandler should not pick up his dribble. If he does, his options are limited. He should pick up his dribble only if he is ready to pass and knows to whom. He should pick up his dribble, hold the ball, and then try to decide where to pass.

Some inexperienced players make the mistake of picking up the ball once they pass midcourt, even if they are not defended. In this instance, the player has helped trap himself.

Some inexperienced players make the mistake of picking up the ball once they pass midcourt, even if they are not defended. In this instance, the player has helped trap himself. Instead, the player should try to attack the basket.

If the ballhandler is dribbling into a trap, he should stop, dribble backwards a step or two, and try and go around the trap. He could also back up to create a passing lane and look for an open teammate. If he has crossed midcourt, he should be careful not to step back into the backcourt.

With regard to beating a half-court trap, the following steps can help:

- Ball-fake prior to passing. The defenders are so aggressive that they will usually go for the ball fake. If they are beaten with fakes, they will be less aggressive, thereby creating openings in the defense.
- Use bounce passes when the defender has his arms up. Bounce passes are easier to make and are harder to intercept.
- Move to open areas. Always have someone flashing to the free-throw line.
- Meet the ball. Step or move toward the ball to cut down the chance of having the pass intercepted.

If you are trapped, do not pivot and turn your back on the basket—you can't see your teammates. Pivot side-to-side or pivot backwards to deliver a pass. If a space exists between the trappers, you can step through to get an open angle for a pass.

Man-to-Man Offenses

A man-to-man offense requires players have more individual offensive skills than does a zone offense. As such, the following factors apply:

- A man-to-man offense requires players use multiple skills, such as faking, cutting, setting up and using screens to get open.
- In a man-to-man offense, the ballhandler must have good one-on-one skills. In this regard, he must be able to shoot, drive, and pass.
- Man-to-man offenses also involve a lot of two-man games, such as the give-and-go, pick-and-roll, and pass-and-screen away.

To be successful against a man-to-man defense, a player must not only have great individual offensive skills, he must also have confidence with those skills and a basketball attitude that no one can stop him.

Working extra on fundamentals and practicing intelligently are essential steps if the player is to achieve rapid improvement in his skills. All the skills discussed in this section are important if the player is to be effective against a man-to-man defense.

To be successful against a man-to-man defense, a player must not only have great individual offensive skills, he must also have confidence with those skills and a basketball attitude that no one can stop him.

Zone Offenses

The opponent will play a zone defense if one or more of the following scenarios apply:

- It does not think your team shoots outside well enough to beat them.
- It wants to shut down your inside game, especially if you have good inside players.
- The opponent does not think they can match-up well in a man-to-man defense.

❑ Defeating a zone defense.

The type of zone defense being played determines the zone offense to be utilized. The zone defense negates most screens, pick-and-rolls, and backdoor cuts. Against the zone, the offense must pass the ball, trying to catch the defense slightly out of position and in order to create an opening. Quick passes, ball and player movement, and ball reversal are the keys in beating the zone. Dribbling should be held to a minimum.

In practice, the team must work on being unpredictable when it is executing its quick-passing drills. One of the objectives of the zone offense is to work the defense back and forth until a defender is out of position. The offense penetrates the defense by passing inside or when it is executing dribble penetration. A zone defense can be beaten if the offense can accomplish the following:

- Unpredictable, quick-ball movement from side-to-side, inside-outside, high-to-low, and to the weakside is necessary to upset the coordination and spacing of the defense.
- After the ball penetrates into the heart of the zone, the defense is vulnerable if the offense passes well. Once a player catches the ball inside, defenders will converge on the ballhandler, thereby opening up the ballhandler's teammates for a pass. Dribble penetration can also help break down the defense.
- An outstanding three-point shooting team can create havoc for the zone defense. If one or more players start making three-point shots, the defense will have to come out to defend the shooters. This response will open up the middle of the zone for the posts.

❑ Player movement in the zone offense:

Player movement is not as critical in the zone offense as it is in a man-to-man offense. Player movement is important, however. Some examples of player movement include:

- A wing or forward running the baseline
- Guards or wings drifting to an open area or better scoring area

Quick passes, ball and player movement, and ball reversal are the keys in beating the zone.

- Posts working the lane area, going side-to-side and high-to-low
- A three-point shooter rotates from the top of the circle to the weakside wing area, where he will be more open when the ball is reversed to the weakside

Dribble penetration can used to break down the zone. The ballhandler should not expect to drive to the basket, because once he breaks down the defense, other defenders should come over to stop his drive.

As the ball is brought upcourt, and the half-court offense is initiated, dribble penetration is not usually possible because the defense is set up properly and is focused on the person with the ball. As the ball is passed around from side to side, the defenders may move slightly out of position. At this moment, the ballhandler dribbles into the zone and toward the basket. This dribble penetration can result in an open shot or a good pass to a teammate.

❏ Screening in a zone offense:

Although ball and player movement are the best ways to beat a zone offense, screens can be effective against a zone in some situations. When the ball is reversed against a zone, a screen can be set to prevent an offside defender who has sagged into the lane from getting to his assigned area.

❏ Preparing for a zone defense:

Quick passing drills, with and without defenders, should be practiced. During these drills, the coach should require the team to make quick, accurate passes, while emphasizing inside-outside passing, as well as quick-ball reversal. Bobbled passes are unacceptable. The players should learn to assume the responsibility of mixing up the passing options and sequences.

Last-Second Plays or Shots

A few games are decided in the last few seconds. Accordingly, teams must be prepared and comfortable in these situations. Players must have realistically practiced end-of-quarter and end-of-half plays, so they are calm and relaxed in these situations. These types of plays should be practiced at least once or twice per week. End-of-quarter situations are almost identical to end-of-game plays. Practicing these situations is logical since teams often have the ball and a chance to score at the end of the quarter. Players need to be aware of the clock. This awareness is best learned in practice.

Although ball and player movement are the best ways to beat a zone offense, screens can be effective against a zone in some situations.

The team should have several types of plays for different situations. The plays should have options for different types of shots. Plays should also be planned for situations when very little time is left on the clock.

Teaching an Offense

The following rules apply when teaching offense:

- Keep it simple
- Teach in phases
- Pay attention to details
- Design drills to simulate part of the offense
- Emphasize the importance of every player's actions

While teaching offense, the coach should not hesitate to stop the offense to correct mistakes. Players need to know what they should be doing and where and when they should do it. If players don't learn to run the play correctly in practice, they will never run it correctly in a game.

❑ Offense is taught in three ways:

- Individual skill drills are designed for overall player development and perfecting the offense that will be played.
- Small-group drills are designed for the same reasons. These drills may address parts of the overall offense.
- Team offense. If the small-group drills have been designed to simulate parts of the offenses that are to be used, the coach should put some of the drills together, add other aspects of the offense, and teach keys to the offense, as well as proper timing and spacing. All factors considered, players can learn offenses much faster this way.

If players don't learn to run the play correctly in practice, they will never run it correctly in a game.

❑ Designing an offense:

The first step for a coach in developing an offense is to evaluate the talents of his players. He should understand the strengths and weaknesses of his players, and build his team around them. What are his player's capabilities as passers, shooters, and dribble penetrators? He should then position them accordingly in his offense.

If he has a tall post, a half-court game may be the best offense. If the post can run the floor, the team may do well playing both an up-tempo game as well as a half-court offense. On the other hand, if his best players are guards, and if he does not have a dominant post, the team should develop a more guard-oriented offense.

Ideally, every team should have offensive balance—an inside scorer, good outside shooters, and a good penetrating guard. Few teams have outstanding players that can fill all of these roles. The coach should utilize the talents of his players.

Floor balance is very important to the offense. Floor balance creates spacing and lanes. It also makes the offense more effective, because the scoring threats are spread apart, so the opponent cannot easily defend all of them. For example, if the team has a good post, he may become the fulcrum to the offense against a man-to-man defense. One teammate would be at the wing position and another at the top of the key. These three players have created a triangle. In this situation, the purpose of the offense is to get the ball to the post and see whether the double-down comes from the defender guarding the point or the defender guarding the wing. The post would either pass to the open man, shoot, or pass to a player on the weakside.

When evaluating their talents, the coach should keep an open mind and consider changes in the offense to utilize new skills that a player may develop during the course of the season or during the summer. For example, if an average-sized post in high school develops good facing-the-basket skills during the summer, does the coach continue to position the player at the low post or does the coach develop other ways to use these new skills? An average-height post who can play near and away from the basket will be able to compete more effectively when paired against a taller post. A more up-tempo game, or pulling an opposing tall post away from the basket, may be the key to winning the important game.

When developing an offense, having the players in the correct position for their skills is critical. The goal of the offense is to have the players where they can utilize their strengths to the maximum. For example, most high school teams have only one wing who is good at driving to the basket. Another guard may be a good spot-up, three-point shooter. If the wing drives around a screen, and the defense steps out to prevent his drive, the ballhandler should be able to pass to the three-point shooter. Usually, this player is on the offside at the wing area, in the corner, or at the top of the circle. The player is likely to be open, since his defender will be giving backside help near the lane. However, if the shooter has been asked to set the screen to free up the player for the drive, it will be very difficult for the ballhandler to pass out to the player. The open player on the offside may not be a good shooter.

When developing an offense, having the players in the correct position for their skills is critical.

The aforementioned are only a few examples of factors the coach should consider as he is developing the offense for his team. As the coach studies the offense, he must consider the positioning of the players as the offense develops. In that regard, are the players in the best position to utilize their talents? Are lanes created for both drives and passes? What is the timing of the offense?

Study and Understand the Offense

Most new coaches will agree that they really learn a subject when they are preparing to teach it. Coaches, being former players, have a good understanding of offense and defense. However, until an individual tries to teach these concepts, a coach may not realize how difficult it is to teach.

If a coach is teaching an offense, the very beginning options and the keys for these options must be defined. Players on the offside of the court need to know what to do while the ballhandler and the players on the ballside of the court are playing their two- and three-man games. When to set screens or break to open areas will have to be taught. Timing and spacing are hard concepts for players to understand when they start learning offenses. They want to make something happen right away.

The coach should design the positioning and timing of the offense in such a way that if one option isn't available, other options will be. For example, if the spot-up shooter doesn't shoot, his options are to fake and drive, pass to another wing, or pass to a post who is either breaking high-to-low or coming around a screen on the other side of the lane. If the timing is good, all these options will be open.

Movement of the posts is critical if they are to get open. A post is seldom open if the offense dribbles downcourt and tries to force the ball to the low post. The defense is geared to deny this option. However, when the post is moving within the offense, it will be easier to get open for an entry pass. For example, the post may be at the top of the key in a half-court offense and pass the ball. The post may then break high-to-low, looking for a pass, go set a screen for a wing or forward, or post-up in the low-post area. If the post is a threat to score from 15-to-18 feet, he will open up the lane and create more opportunities for himself and his teammates.

When the post is being guarded by a much taller defender, he can't just post up under the basket. He should use his speed advantage by moving in the lane area.

Drills for Developing an Offense

It is critical not to typecast a player at an early age. The coach should try to develop every player into an all-around player, since it is impossible to know what each player might be capable of later. Players will have to work to develop their skills needed for their positions, but that does not mean they can't continue to develop other skills. In this regard, two types of drills exist:

- Basic drills designed to improve the overall basketball skills of each player
- Drills designed to develop skills specifically for the planned offense or defense

As the players are developing their overall individual skills, the coach may have certain players work extra on certain moves, shots, or techniques that the players will need later in the offense. For example, if a high-post offense is going to be utilized, the coach will still want to teach low-post moves. However, more time during drills will be devoted to the high-post skills that will eventually be essential to the offense, such as screens, moves, fakes, passing, and shooting from further out. The individual drills should be customized for the position players.

Two- and three-man drills, with and without defenders, can address the most basic elements of the offense. As the players work on these drills, the coach should teach the players as if he were teaching the offense. Everything that will be important later should be emphasized. Attention should be paid to detail. The players may feel that they are just doing drills; they may not understand that they are learning the offense and defense. The coach should emphasize the difference to them.

If three-man drills with guards and posts are actually parts of the offense, teaching the offense will be easier, because it is only a matter of putting these drills together in the correct sequence. The time saved by this process can then be spent on improving techniques and execution, rather than on learning an offensive scheme.

Teaching a Half-Court Offense

❑ Conducting a walk-through:

The coach should position the five players in their basic starting spots, and then walk them through the offense, while explaining and demonstrating its most basic elements. The focus should be on understanding the overall concepts, not on executing other skills. These will be added later, once the basic concepts are ingrained in the players.

Utilizing instructional stages in a progressive manner is one viable approach that a coach might use to teach his team an offense. The fol-

As the players are developing their overall individual skills, the coach may have certain players work extra on certain moves, shots, or techniques that the players will need later in the offense.

lowing steps would occur over several practices. Remember, the offense is being taught in stages. The coach should never have his team go to the next stage until everyone is comfortable with the current one.

Attention will be given to the first part of the offense and what all five players' roles are. The importance of spacing, timing, and keeping the defender busy will have to be emphasized, especially to the backside players. When and where to set up screens or cut to open areas must be thoroughly explained.

An offense is designed to put players in positions where they will have the best opportunity to score. Offenses try to create open shots or open lanes for passes or drives to the basket. These openings are only created if the players understand the importance of spacing and timing. Players need to learn when and where lanes will be against a defense. The coach must remind his players when they don't recognize or use lanes as they should.

Sometimes, a player is anxious to make something happen and finds it hard to be patient, especially if he is on the backside. He may see an opening and break for it, only to find he has clogged the lane for the ballhandler who is driving to the basket. Players need to learn to let the offense develop. A set offense allows the players a chance to anticipate their teammates.

Through the entire process of teaching the offense, the coach will need to teach the keys needed to understand what the ballhandler is likely to do at various stages of the offense. The ballhandler always has several options in an offense. If the teammates understand the options available and what they are to do for each option, they can respond with the appropriate action for the option the ballhandler ultimately chooses. For each situation, the other players must learn that, "If he does this, we do that."

❑ Adding the Final Parts of the Offense:

The ball is rotated to the weakside or to cutters breaking from the weakside. Once the players understand the basics of the offense on the ballside, the final parts of the offense are added, including:

➢ A cutter breaking to the ballside and looking for a pass or to set a screen.
➢ Rotating the ball to the weakside.

❑ Employing Quick-Passing Drills:

Quick-passing drills should be employed at different stages of this process to emphasize the importance of:

- Quick-ball movement
- Quick decisions
- Mixing things up and being unpredictable
- The inside-outside game
- Running the offense to completion

A quick-passing drill can be used anytime the coach thinks it's needed. It is critical that the coach make certain that every phase of the offense is practiced thoroughly. The team's play in games will reflect what the coach has emphasized in practice.

❑ Adding a "Passive" Defense:

The coach should work the defense on basic fundamentals of position, playing defense with the feet, and playing help-defense. The primary purpose of the "passive" defense is to let the offense get used to making the correct choices in more realistic situations. The defense should deny drives and steal bad passes without applying additional pressure.

In this stage of the process, all parts of the offense should be reviewed, making certain that all phases are run so every player gets his chance to contribute. Once the coach feels the players are ready, it's time to turn up the heat. As such, these drills can help ensure that the team is used to game-speed conditions.

❑ Intensifying the Defense:

The defense should be required to work as hard as it would in a game. The coach will be working hard to teach offense and defense simultaneously. The quick-passing drills should be repeated with intense defensive pressure.

❑ Adding Variations and Options:

The coach should teach variations and options in the same manner he would the basics of the offense. The players should practice the basic parts of the offense and its variations and options regularly.

The primary purpose of the "passive" defense is to let the offense get used to making the correct choices in more realistic situations.

❑ Mixing It Up:

The importance of mixing up the offensive scheme should be emphasized, so it isn't too predictable. The team, especially the ballhandlers, must learn to be unpredictable.

❑ Establishing "Game Realism":

To be completely prepared, the team should be accustomed to running the offense against an intense defensive effort, as well as a sagging defense, whose goal it is to clog the lane. The team should develop confidence in a variety of defensive situations it is likely to encounter. Games are always faster and more intense than practices.

The team should practice initiating its half-court offense with intensive defensive pressure on the point guard and wings. The mental mindset of the point guard can be much different when he faces pressure defense. First, the point must get the ball across midcourt without a turnover, while intensely defended. He must then make an accurate pass to initiate the offense. The goal is to have the point guard so used to defensive pressure that he feels comfortable and confident and can execute the offense in games, whatever the situation.

It is much easier to initiate the half-court offense without defensive pressure than it is to get the ball up court and initiate the offense against a great full-court defender. Once the players have learned the offense to completion, the point guard should practice dribbling upcourt from behind mid-court. The coach should have the point work the ball upcourt and to a position where he initiates the play against an aggressive man defense. The other players need to learn to judge how and when to get open when the point guard is under this much pressure. If they break too early or too late, the point may not be able to get the ball to them.

Games are always faster and more intense than practices.

The coach should challenge the point guard's ballhandling, confidence, vision of the court, and mental toughness. The point guard must become comfortable initiating the offense with either a drive or an accurate pass to a closely guarded teammate. The other players must learn to wait to initiate their moves until the point is able to deliver the pass. This timing and feel for each others' moves will take time and experience to develop.

❑ Adding variations to initiate the offense:

One of the final stages involved in teaching a half-court offense is to add different variations to initiate the offense. For example, if the wings always go to their spots and wait for a pass, they limit the number of ways to get open. As such, a good defender will be able to anticipate the wings' moves. The coach should teach his players alternate ways to initiate the offense that will make it more unpredictable. Most teams get in the habit of using one side of the court to start the offense. Some defenses will try to hide a weak defender on the left side of the court, since most offenses start on the right side. If the offense can be run from either side, it will be easier to attack the weak link in the defense, and the offense will gain a new element of surprise.

The wings also need other options to get open and initiate the offense. After all, when the point guard brings the ball up, he is going to drive to the basket or pass to right or left. How difficult is it for a defender to guess when to step in the passing lane if a wing only has a few ways to get open?

Only after the offense is fully understood should the coach place the team in a scrimmage situation. No fast breaks, no presses or traps, only full-court man-to-man pressure. At this point, the coach should set up the half-court offense.

The offense should be run to completion in practice so that every player is comfortable with the various options in games. It is the coach's responsibility to make certain that all parts of the offense are given equal attention so that every player on the team knows his job and feels confident doing it.

If the offense starts on one side most of the time, a smart player may be able to score at will in practice. The player should be reminded to spread the ball around and let the other options of the offense have a chance to develop. The first part of the offense may be shut down against a quality opponent, but it is difficult to stop all aspects of a team confident with its offense. Every option of the offense should be run until it becomes second nature to all the players.

It is the coach's responsibility to make certain that all parts of the offense are given equal attention so that every player on the team knows his job and feels confident doing it.

Summary Points

Every player should understand the basic concepts of the offense that his team runs. Knowing how to apply the principles of creating lanes, spacing, and timing is particularly important. Various types of offenses are appropriate for specific defensive situations. Whatever offense is employed, the coach should teach it in a systematic, step-by-step manner.

CHAPTER 34

There are pure shooters, and there are scorers. A pure shooter is an individual who has very good technique and shooting skills when he is open for a shot. A scorer is a player who is capable of scoring points, whether or not he is tightly defended. A scorer makes a move toward the basket, while being defended closely and finds a way to score, even though his shot may not be a pure jump shot. A scorer is often a good free-throw shooter as well.

Shooting is a Learned Skill

Most any player can become a good shooter if he is willing to work hard enough outside of practice. Confidence and a "feel for the shot" are developed through hours of working on technique and game-situation and game-speed shots. Shooting should become a reflex, and the shooter should develop a game-speed rhythm with which he is comfortable and successful.

❑ Learning to shoot:

If a player is going to spend hours practicing, he should learn how to practice efficiently so that he not only develops his ability to make specific shots, but also an all-around "game" that makes him a more effective player.

❑ How does a player with minimal offensive skills learn to shoot?

Youth league and junior high coaches are often faced with this situation. Many of these coaches have lots of kids with minimal skills, few (if any) assistants, and little time. These coaches try to spend as much time with each player as possible, but it never seems to be enough. If the players are to develop, it is very important for them to learn how to practice on their own outside of organized practices. The coach may need to instruct the players and parents what the player can and should do at home.

> **Confidence and a "feel for the shot" are developed through hours of working on technique and game-situation and game-speed shots.**

One of the common mistakes young players who are learning to shoot make is to run out to the three-point line and fire up shot after shot. Since they aren't yet strong enough to reach the hoop with a normal shot, they modify their shots and attempt to "chunk it up." Younger kids are not the only players who do this. It is common to see high school players go straight to the long shots, rather than getting the feel of shorter shots.

❑ Engraining proper shooting techniques:

A player should spend time closer to the basket, working on technique and "getting the feel" of the ball leaving his fingertips correctly. This should be practiced so much that the proper techniques become a good habit.

A player should not be in a hurry to develop his ability to shoot long shots. As a player is developing his shot, his skill level will determine how long he should stay close to the basket. Because his muscles should gradually strengthen over time, the player may be able to shoot farther out every few days or so. Once a shot can be made consistently without straining and with the proper technique, the shooter should move back another foot. The player may need to stay at this distance for some time before going back another foot. In reality, weeks may pass before the shooter is ready to shoot the three-point shot.

Each day the player should start in close and work on shots from all distances and from different areas of the floor, without going over the set distance. As a player continues to use good techniques and makes a high percentage of his shots, he can gradually move farther out. During this time, it is important to add fakes and moves to the basic shooting techniques. The player should try to simulate game-situation shots and shots that he is likely to get from the offense the team chooses to run. This gradual process can accomplish several things, including:

- Engrains the proper shooting technique in the player's minds
- Develops the player's confidence in shooting
- Strengthens the muscles so the player is strong enough to shoot longer shots

The Basic Process of Developing Shots and Moves

The player should learn a shot or move, practice and perfect it, and then build on it. The first shots are best learned from a close distance. Technique and rhythm should be acquired from three to six feet from the basket. Later, the player can learn to shoot farther out from the basket. As new skills are added, the player should always practice and reinforce what was previously learned. Daily shooting drills can help reinforce the player's fundamentals. No player ever gets so good, he can neglect his basic skills.

A coach can employ the following steps to help a player develop his shot:

- Develop the basic shot, and then move the player from his favorite side of court to his weakside.
- Walk through the technique slowly to get the proper footwork, ball movement, and timing. Footwork and balance are an important part of any shot or move, yet are often overlooked.
- Practice the shot without a dribble; catch the ball, pivot, and shoot.
- Add a fake.
- Add a dribble.
- Engrain proper shooting techniques.
- Develop the shot on the opposite side of the floor.
- Footwork will be critical as a player learns to shoot on the weakside because everything is reversed.
- Layups and short shots should be learned with the weakside hand.
- The shot or move must be attempted at a faster pace, once the technique is mastered.

Developing a quicker shot does not mean rushing the shot, but it does mean speeding up the entire pace of the effort without losing balance, timing, and rhythm.

Developing a quicker shot does not mean rushing the shot, but it does mean speeding up the entire pace of the effort without losing balance, timing, and rhythm. Many players get in the habit of practicing a shot deliberately and slowly and never learn to shoot at game-speed. They are intimidated once they're in a game because they have to rush to get their shot off.

- Add a complementary shot or move.

If a player is to be an effective scorer, he must be proficient with more than one move or shot. A scorer must be unpredictable, so his defenders can't overplay in order to deny the favorite shot. Good defenders will know the shooter's favorite shot and where he likes to take it! Complementary shots allow the player to shoot an entirely different shot, or shoot the same shot in a different direction or location. If a player has been successful with a particular move or shot, he should know that the defender will expect that shot and try to deny it. This is when complementary shots are most effective.

> Mix shots and fakes until it is second nature for the player to be unpredictable.

Offensive players are creatures of habit. They tend to fall back on their favorite shot or move. Doing so can make it easier for the defense to shut them down.

Shooting Tips

❑ Square-up to the basket:

A shot is more likely to be on target if the shooter's head and shoulders are squared to the basket when the shot is released. A player's body may be twisted while making a move or getting off a shot, but he should square-up to the basket before releasing the ball. Hook shots and jump-hooks are the exception, since the player's shoulders will be approximately 90-degrees from the backboard.

❑ Stay under control:

If a player is not under control, he will most likely miss the shot. Players should strive to play comfortably at the fastest pace possible. When players try too hard to make something happen, they often are off balance and not squared-up to the basket. As a result, the timing and rhythm of the shot is off.

❑ Shoot with the proper arch:

Why do some players shoot with a flat arch? A flat shot leaves little room for error. When younger players struggle to make a basket, they shoot lower and forward. This results in a low-trajectory shot. As the players get older, they may maintain the same shooting technique unless they're alerted to their deficiencies in this matter. A player should develop a proper shooting arch, even if it means shooting shorter shots until he develops the upper-body strength needed to shoot longer shots with the proper technique.

Young girls, in particular, tend to shoot unorthodox jump shots. As the player jumps and shoots, she tries to get more power by snapping her upper body forward, resulting in a backward thrust. The player bends forward just before the ball is released, and a low-trajectory shot results.

A shot is more likely to be on target if the shooter's head and shoulders are squared to the basket when the shot is released.

The coach should point this out to the player, and help her improve her shooting arch.

❑ Use the backboard:

Many players miss their shots because they have never developed confidence in using the backboard. The backboard can be a scorer's best friend. The backboard should be used when a player is driving from the wing or baseline area.

The player needs to square-up to the goal and bank the ball off the backboard, rather than trying to swish a shot while moving toward or away from the basket. The bank shot should be delivered with a high, soft touch to get a good bounce. Bank shots can be used for many short and intermediate shots from the low-post area and wings.

The backboard shot allows greater room for error, especially if a player shoots harder than he should while under intense defensive pressure. Anyone who plays near the basket should use the backboard anytime he can. If a player is fouled while shooting a shot intended to swish through the net, there is less chance it will go in. Since fouls sometimes go undetected, it is critical that posts and power forwards use the backboard and learn how to shoot with contact.

❑ Follow your shot:

> **The backboard shot allows greater room for error, especially if a player shoots harder than he should while under intense defensive pressure.**

Offensive rebounds often determine which team wins the game. The shooter is usually the first player on the floor to know whether his shot is off and where it is likely to go. A player should finish his shot by following the shot. By doing so, the shooter is often in good position for either an offensive rebound and a follow-up shot, or a dish to an open teammate under the basket. Some occasions exist during which a coach may not want his players to follow their shots. This set of circumstances usually involves a situation when the player has the responsibility of getting back on defense to stop a fast break.

❑ Use the body to shield shot blockers:

Players need to use their bodies to shield the ball from shot-blocking defenders, especially near the basket. The ability of a shooter to shield his shot from the opponent will allow a shorter or less athletic player to score against a taller player. The following suggestions can help accomplish this objective:

- Shoot short shots and layups with the outside hand. Make the defender come across his body to block the shot. This additional space allows the player driving time to get off a high-arching shot over the defender's hand.
- If a defender is close behind near the basket, the shooter should not bring the ball directly above his head. He should use his body as a shield and shoot the layup.
- If a defender is close behind, eight to 15 feet from the basket, the shooter should jump forward and shoot the ball from in front of his body.
- Shoot a jump-hook or hook shot.

❏ Shoot with contact:

A player must learn to power through contact and finish his shot. The shooter should focus on the target. A basket may then result in a three-point play. The player should develop the mental attitude that he will score, even when he is fouled.

If players are used to contact, they will not let the contact affect their shot. Referees often allow some contact, if it doesn't affect the play or allow one player to gain an advantage. Every referee calls games differently, and players should learn to adapt quickly to the referees' tendencies to call—or not call—contact. Referees expect more contact nearer the basket.

Posts and forwards must get used to contact, whether they are shooting or rebounding. Grabbing and pushing occur on almost every play under the basket. The player has to develop the mindset he will power through contact to make the shot. As players develop upper-body strength and the proper mindset, they will gradually start to get more three-point opportunities.

To shield the defenders from the ball and to get a better shooting angle, players should shoot layups and short shots with their left hand when they are on the left side of the basket and with their right hand when they're on the right side. If contact does occur, the shooter has a better chance of shielding the shot.

Practicing shooting while performing contact drills helps prepare the player physically and mentally for contact. In contact-shooting drills, the player is slightly shoved, grabbed, and jostled. These drills should be continued throughout the season.

❑ Draw a foul:

Drawing a foul sometimes is as important as scoring. If an opponent's key player gets in foul trouble, it is wise for the offense to attack that player and try to draw another foul. This foul may change the entire game. Baskets will be much easier as the player backs off and plays passively. Always keep in mind that players who attack the basket shoot free throws.

If you are a good free-throw shooter and want to help your team, you must learn to make moves to the basket. Players who fake well often get fouled by overly aggressive defenders, wanting to block the shot.

Attempts to draw a foul can be even more effective when they involve an aggressive defender who, because he likes to block shots, can be drawn into fouling a ballhandler. A convincing fake, followed by a smart move, will often result in a foul. If an aggressive defender goes for the fake, but is too far away to foul, the offensive player can still draw a foul. The ballhandler subtly initiates the contact with the airborne defender by jumping upwards and sideways, as if trying to go around the defender. This technique must be executed correctly, or the player will be called for charging.

Common Mistakes in Shooting

- The ball is not well balanced if the elbow is out. The shooter's wrist, elbow, and shoulder must be in proper alignment, or the ball is likely to come off to one side. Proper alignment, a good release and follow through, and a soft arch will result in good rotation on the ball.
- A flat trajectory results in a line-drive shot with little room for error. Good shooters have a soft, high arch that results in a "shooter's bounce" when the ball is slightly off target.
- Aiming or guiding the ball is a common cause of missed shots. Shooting should be done in a smooth motion, and not aimed. Aiming or guiding the ball will flatten the trajectory of the shot.

Players who try to guide their shot end up pushing the ball and do not follow through with their wrist. The follow through with the wrist is an important part of a smooth shot. This factor is most obvious with poor free-throw shooters.

How Does a Scorer Find Ways to Score?

A scorer may or may not be a pure shooter, but he always seems to find ways to score, even when he is matched against taller or more athletic players. In this regard, a scorer possesses the following attributes:

- Knows how to get open against a man-to-man or zone defense
- Knows how to use screens
- Finds an open area or a seam in the defense
- Fakes well
- Is a good free-throw shooter and gets to the foul line by "attacking the basket"
- Shoots with either hand while close to the basket
- Uses his body as a shield
- Knows how to draw a foul and still get a shot off
- Has a good feel for finger-rolls and similar ways to manufacture a shot around the basket
- Is proficient with a variety of complementary moves and shots

Shot Selection

Coaches often complain about poor shot selection, but it is the responsibility of the coach to teach each player what good shot selection is. Inexperienced players often think that if they are open, they should shoot. They do not realize that there are times when the player should work the ball to get a better shot for the team.

❏ What is good shot selection?

Good shot selection involves choosing a high-percentage shot that is correct for the current game situation. A player should only take a high-percentage shot. The following examples illustrate game situations in which the coach might prefer better shot selection:

- A shooter is hot. Feed him the ball.
- A key opponent is in foul trouble. Get the ball to the player he is defending. That player should make aggressive moves to the basket in an attempt to draw another foul.
- Take advantage of a mismatch. Get the ball quickly to the teammate and clear out the area in order to make it more difficult for the defense to give help.
- The score is close late in the game. As the game winds down, every possession becomes precious. Any turnover, mistake, or

It is the responsibility of the coach to teach each player what good shot selection is.

poor-percentage shot allows the other team the chance to score and denies your team the opportunity to score.

- If your team is ahead late in the game, it is more important to move the ball around and eat up the clock than it is to score. If a shot is taken, it should be a high-percentage shot. In a stall-offense, coaches usually tell their players to shoot only if they have an uncontested layup—and they better not miss it.
- If the game is tied or very close, the players should try to get the highest percentage shot they can. They should try and get the ball into the hands of the hottest player. Of course, the defense will be trying to prevent that person from getting a shot.

A good player knows when it is better to get a higher-percentage shot.

Getting 'the Feel' for the Shot

The player's shot should be a reflex action. A player is "in a zone" when he has the feel for the ball and can't seem to miss a shot. In this situation, the player is playing the game at a timing and rhythm with which he is comfortable and confident. When a shooter has the feel, he knows the ball is going in the "hole." A good shooter develops a feel for the rhythm and timing of the shot, as well as a feel of the ball coming off his fingertips.

❑ Getting the feel before the game:

- The player should warm up with shots close to the basket. Don't start warming up at the three-point line.
- The player should concentrate on technique the first few shots. He should make certain to shoot with a soft arch and follow through completely with his wrist.
- The player should narrow his focus. He should focus intently on swishing the net, not just making a basket. He should try to feel the ball coming off the fingertips when he shoots.
- The player should swish the net several times in a row before moving farther from the basket. Is the arch high and soft? Is the shot being taken at game speed and with a good rhythm?
- A post should try to swish some of his short shots as well. All factors considered, he should use the backboard for most shots around the basket, if possible.
- Once the player knows he has the feel, he knows he's ready for the game. He should stay active, loose and confident.

❑ Getting the feel at halftime:

Before the start of the second half, it is important that the players come back on the court to loosen up. The players should follow the same routine as before the game. If there is little time, they should relax and concentrate on the shorter shots. It is more important for them to get the feel and rhythm on the short and intermediate shots than three-point shots.

Good Shooters Will Have Off Games

The best shooters in history have had bad games. If a player has a bad game, he should continue to work extra hard on his shooting and don't get down on himself. He should remember that shooting streaks do occur.

❑ Shooting streaks:

A player should never have a slump on defense. Defense involves technique, heart, desire, hustle, and effort. A player should play good defense every minute of every game.

On offense, shooting streaks occur—even for the best shooters. Shooting is technique, rhythm, and confidence. Players will have shooting slumps in games—sometimes for several games. The player is responsible for regaining his confidence and touch by spending extra time on his skills and techniques.

How the coach helps him regain his shooting touch and confidence back sends a message to the player. If a player misses several shots during the game, he will often be down on himself. In those instances, he will need encouragement, not discouragement. The coach should reassure the player that everything is okay. He should remind the player to let the offense develop; he shouldn't force his shots. Going forward, he should continue taking good shots, while working hard on defense and other aspects of the game.

If the slump continues for several games, the player should consult with his coach and work on the following:

- Shooting sessions outside of practice
- Technique and rhythm
- Emphasizing short and medium shots to help re-establish his confidence

- Practicing realistic game-situation shots for half-court offenses and out-of-bounds plays
- Finding ways to get to the free-throw line

Maintaining and Improving Shooting Skills During the Season

Once the season starts, it is sometimes difficult to maintain or improve a player's shooting skills because so much time is allocated to team concepts in practice. Some players need to practice extra if they are to become solid shooters and avoid shooting slumps.

❑ Evaluating a player's shot:

To help a player overcome his poor shooting streak or to change a player's shot so he will be a more consistent scorer, a coach must first be able to evaluate his shot and shooting technique. Game film can be of great help in this regard, since a coach may not know or remember the intricacies of each player's shot.

Shooting Areas

❑ For guards:

The six basic shooting areas of the court for guards are:

- Under the basket (low-post area)
- Baseline (eight to 15 feet)
- Both elbows
- Top of the circle
- Right and left wing area
- Right and left corners

To get open or to help teammates get open, guards must move without the ball from one of these areas to another. As the guards move around the court executing the offense, they should be comfortable shooting or making a move to the basket from the following spot-up areas: top of the circle; right and left wings; and the right and left corners.

Spot-up shooters have to be open to shoot from these areas. If they're not open, scorers can make a move to get open for a shot or a drive to the basket. The scorer not only is able to shoot from the spot-up shooting areas, he can also pull up and hit intermediate-range jump shots.

❑ For posts:

Posts must be comfortable scoring from all areas of the court. In today's game, posts no longer always camp-out under the basket. They work all around the lane and near the three-point line, setting screens and passing. If posts can consistently make three-point shots, they can be a special asset to the team, because they will pull their defenders even further from the basket.

Posts have the following spot-up shooting areas:

- The low post
- Both elbows of the lane
- Free-throw line
- Baseline (10-15 feet from either side of the basket)

❑ For forwards:

Forwards have the following spot-up shooting areas:

- 15 to 17 feet from the basket
- The key
- The wings and baseline

Practice Shooting Sessions

In reality, shooting sessions really work. The following two stories demonstrate that shooting sessions can really be effective:

> "A two-guard was not shooting as well as she knew she could, so she started shooting sessions three to four times a week. Her shooting percentages and confidence immediately soared. She continued to follow this routine for the remainder of the season. That summer found her playing BCI and AAU basketball, where there was plenty of time to work on her shot. When her senior season started, she didn't feel she needed these shooting sessions. After three games of sub-par shooting, she again re-instituted the shooting sessions. The end of her senior year found her making 50 percent of the 160 three-point shots attempted, 64 percent of all her field-goal attempts, and 80 percent of her free throws. She also earned a second district MVP award, all-state honors, and a college scholarship. Her efforts demonstrated that good shooters can be developed through hard work."

> "A man in his thirties was in a gym dribbling up and down the court, as he practiced game-speed shot after shot. A friend would rebound the ball and quickly pass the ball to the man fast-breaking up the court. The player practiced at game speed, paid attention to details, developed his timing and feel, and practiced a variety of shots that complement each other. This was done while running continuously for forty-five minutes.
>
> The college players watched in awe at the realization of how hard this man practiced. They had seen him on television for years, and they thought he did all these moves naturally. It was hard to believe that an NBA All-star, MVP, and future Hall-of-Famer would work this intensely. You see, "Magic" Erwin Johnson had just come out of his premature retirement, and he was practicing on his day off, trying to get the timing and feel back that made him so successful in the past. Years ago, Magic had discovered that sacrifice, hard work, and quality practice are necessary if you are going to be as good as you can be."

Types of Shots

❑ Layups:

Players should learn to make layups with either hand, depending upon from which side of the basket the shot is attempted. By the time a player has finished junior high school, he should be very adept at making layups.

Layups are usually missed because they are shot too hard or the target area was missed. The shot is named a layup because the ball should be shot as if the ball is being laid gently upward. The palm of the shooter's hand is up, and a soft touch is added by an upward flick of the fingers as the ball is being released.

Many young players aren't tall enough or strong enough to shoot a layup properly. These players shoot the ball forward and upward with a flick of the wrist that adds more force to the shot, especially when a player is coming down the court at full speed. A layup shot with too much forward force has little chance of going in.

Some players try to soften the shot by slowing down as they near the free-throw line, so they aren't going too fast when they shoot. Players should execute layups at full speed but with a soft touch.

❑ The jump-stop:

The jump-stop has become an important part of some shots because it allows the player to change directions on the jumper after he has picked up his dribble. The player is under control and able to square up. The player is also able to stop and go straight up for a jump shot off a jump-stop.

A player is allowed to take two steps after picking up the dribble if he jumps into the air for a shot or pass on the second step. A jump-stop involves having the player simultaneously land with both feet and then spring into the air.

❏ The jump shot:

The jump shot is the most common shot in basketball. The player needs to get all the height possible out of his jump. The ball should be released from his fingertips, as his arm reaches full extension of the elbow and at the peak of the jump. A quick jump and a quick release are more important factors than jumping an inch or two higher. The player should remember to square up to the basket when shooting the jump shot.

❏ The baby jumper:

The baby jumper is a shot taken eight to 12 feet from the basket. The player usually has his back to the basket when he catches the pass. He then pivots and jumps while twisting in the air. The player squares his head and shoulders to the basket before releasing the ball. Since he is so close to the basket, he must shoot the ball softly. Forwards and other players who often play around the basket should learn this shot.

❏ The running jump shot:

Some players are too short to out-jump taller defenders. The running jump shot allows the shooter to get the ball off earlier and quicker, before the defenders have a chance to block the shot. The running jumper can be a difficult shot to master, since the player has to shoot a moving shot with a different technique. This shot is good for penetrating point guards and wings who drive into the lane from the three-point line. The player must be careful to slide by the defender and not get called for a charge. This shot can be effective up to 15 feet from the basket.

❏ The step-through shot or leaner:

On the step-through shot, the offensive player steps past the defender and jumps toward the basket, while shooting the ball. The shot is usually taken with the ball slightly forward, so the shooter's body is used as a shield from the defender. This move can be made between two players who have left room between them, but not enough room to dribble through. The up-and-under move, often used by posts, is a type of step-through move.

❏ The jump hook:

The jump hook is often used immediately after catching a pass or gathering in an offensive rebound. The quickness of the release makes this an effective shot around the basket and in a crowd. If this shot is taken with the shooter's shoulder 90-degrees to the basket, the player's body will act as a shield to prevent the defender from blocking the shot.

Playing Above the Rim

❏ The dunk shot:

Dunking has become an important shot in basketball, because it is an extremely accurate shot, and it often has a measurable impact on the fans and teammates. The emotional impact of an impressive dunk can change the momentum of the game.

Players frequently spend too much time trying to master all types of wild dunks. How many times does a player have the opportunity to dunk in a game? The truth of the matter is that the players would be much better off if they did not waste so much practice time on dunks, and worked instead on their technique and fundamentals.

❏ Creating soft shots:

When tall players who can play at or above the rim are close to the basket, they must create ways to get the ball up and over the defender with a soft shot. A jump shot may be too hard a shot for that close a distance. In this instance, the players' shots may be softened with finger rolls, flips of the wrist, or "push" and "puts."

Summary Points

Scoring and shooting are skills that can take a long time to develop and an even longer time to sustain. As such, every player must continually work to maintain the "feel" of his shot.

CHAPTER 35

The free throw may be the most important shot in basketball. It is a learned skill that requires hours of diligent practice.

The Proper Technique for Shooting Free Throws

Free-throw shooting requires balance. The free-throw shooter should always maintain his balance after taking the shot. The shooter's feet should be spread the width of his shoulders. This positioning allows the shooter to have a strong and balanced base. As the shot is finished, the shooter should come up on his toes, but his feet should never leave the ground. The shooter should never fall or jump forward after the shot.

A free-throw shooter should have a sound, repeatable technique that can be executed when the player is tired or under pressure. The shooting technique should eliminate any unnecessary movement, while maintaining proper alignment from the time the ball is picked up, until the second it is released. The following techniques should be adhered to when shooting a free-throw:

- The shooter's shoulders should be squared up to the basket, while his feet should be spread the width of his shoulders.
- His knees should be slightly flexed. His legs will supply much of the power for the shot. The shooter should not make the mistake of making deep-knee flexes and getting too much body movement.
- The shooter should dribble the ball a few times just outside the foot.
- The shooter should catch the ball with his left hand on the side and under the ball and his right hand on top of the ball. His support hand should not be directly under the ball, or the hand will block his line of sight as the shot is taken, thereby affecting his depth perception. The forearm of his right arm should be paral-

lel to the floor, and his elbow should be bent at 90-degrees. The movement involved from going from this basic position to the shooting position is where many free throws are missed.
- ➢ The shooter should take a deep breath, exhale and relax his shoulders.
- ➢ The ball should be brought straight up from the basic catching position to the shooting position. The ball should be above the shooter's shoulder; the tricep area of his arm perpendicular to the floor. The shooter's elbow should be in front of his shoulder and facing the basket. The ball should rest on the fingertips of his hand, and the palm of his hand should not be touching the ball. The fingertips are important in finishing the shot.
- ➢ The ball should be shot with a high, soft arch.
- ➢ The follow through is very important. The shooter's wrist snaps forward and finishes with his fingertips pointing downward. His wrist is relaxed. The shooter should not make the mistake of aiming or pushing the ball.

❑ Proper free-throw alignment at the shooting position:

When the ball is brought up to the shooting position, the shooter's shoulder, elbow, and wrist should be aligned in a straight line, with the elbow facing the basket. The ball should be balanced evenly on all the fingertips. It will be relatively difficult to miss the ball to the right or left with a straight follow through from this position.

• *Free-throws missed to the right or left.* Many free-throws are missed to the right or left, rather than short or long. Some coaches stress finishing the shot as if the player is grabbing the rim to correct this problem. They emphasize the importance of following through with the hand square to the rim. However, the shot is sometimes missed much earlier because of improper alignment, starting the moment the ball is picked up.

Many free-throws are missed to the right or left, rather than short or long.

Many free-throws are missed before the ball ever gets shoulder high. The reason is a flying elbow (i.e., the elbow is pointing out away from the body). For example, if the player catches the ball and brings it straight up in front of his chest, his elbow will be out and aimed right (for a right-handed shooter). When the ball is brought to the shooting position, it is not balanced squarely on the fingertips of his shooting hand. The ball has to be held in position by the left hand. It is very difficult to finish the shot consistently from this unbalanced position, since the ball can easily come off the fingertips in many directions.

❑ Relaxing at the free-throw line:

Standing at the free-throw line waiting for the referee to hand the ball can be a very tense time. In this situation, the shooter needs to be relaxed and confident. The shooter should not be standing at the free-throw line while the referee is trying to get the other players into position. While the shooter is waiting, he should be reviewing a simple checklist and visualizing his free-throw routine, with the ball swishing the net as he holds the perfect follow-through position

When the referee hands the player the ball, he should take a deep breath and exhale completely, while relaxing his shoulders. The player should actually feel his shoulders sag and relax. He should dribble the ball a few times before shooting.

❑ Focus:

The player should learn to focus only on his technique and the checklist prior to taking the shot. Nothing else should be on his mind. A player develops the habit of focusing in practice. The player should step up to the line confidently, concentrating only on this one free-throw.

Who Shoots Free Throws?

Most fouls occur within 12 feet of the basket. Players who make moves to the basket are the players who usually get to shoot free-throws. These players may be guards who drive toward the basket, or posts who shoot and rebound in a crowded area filled with aggressive defenders.

What is a good free-throw percentage? In high school, the varsity should average 70 percent or better. Each player should always have a goal of shooting at least 80 percent or better.

Why are guards expected to be the best free-throw shooters on the team? There is no reason that forwards or posts can't be great free-throw shooters also. In fact, posts and forwards should want to work extra hard on shooting free-throws, since they are the players who are regularly fouled. Free-throw shooting is a learned skill. Great free-throw shooting requires the player to make a commitment to work extra outside of practice to develop good technique and self-confidence.

Making the Important Free Throw

Every free throw in a game counts the same. However, some free throws appear to be more important than others. Free-throws missed early in the game are as important as those at the end of the game. It's just that the earlier free-throws have been forgotten. Every possession seems more important as the clock ticks down.

Every free throw in a game counts the same.

With regard to the critical nature of free-throws, the following factors should apply:

- A player must want the opportunity to make the free-throw. A player can't be tentative or afraid to miss the free-throw or he is likely to miss it. Players need to have good technique, confidence, and a desire to excel.
- A coach must make free-throws important in practice. Good free-throw shooting teams work hard in practice and outside of practice.
- Players need to practice free-throws under pressure. In practices, the coach can simulate pressure by having free-throw competitions. The coach can also create team pressure by engaging in free-throw shooting drills.

A player should not shoot more than two free-throws at a time while practicing. After two free-throws are shot, he should step away from the free-throw line, focus intently as if in a game, step to the line, and make the next two free-throws. In a game, because players rarely shoot more than two free-throws in a row, they should learn the rhythm of shooting two free-throws at a time.

The Net Only

The free-throw shooter should strive to make every free-throw as close to perfect as possible.

Players should not be satisfied just making their free-throws. The free-throw shooter should strive to make every free-throw as close to perfect as possible. The objective should be to have a high arch. The ball should touch only the bottom of the net.

At every appropriate opportunity, every player should set higher goals for himself. In this instance, for example, as the player becomes a better free-throw shooter, he should set higher goals: a higher percentage, more free-throws made in a row, and more swishers.

The Importance of Free-Throws must be Emphasized

The coach may want to take the following steps to demonstrate how important free-throws are to him:

- Set free-throw goals for each player and for the team. Players often shoot worse in games than in practice. The player should set their practice goals a little higher. Subsequently, they can modify their goals, as needed, to set challenging, but reachable, goals.
- Keep a log of each player's free-throw shots and percentages each day. The fact that the coach is evaluating the free-throws tells the players that this skill is important. As a result, they should do it right.
- Work with players on technique before or after practice.
- Establish a free-throw shooting program, for example:
  - Try shooting 1,000 free-throws between the end of the season and the end of school. Shoot 100 free-throws on five days of the week. A written log of free-throws attempted and made should be kept.
  - During the summer, the player should shoot at least another 2,000 recorded free-throws. This target can be achieved in four weeks if the player shoots 500 free-throws per week.
  - During the fall session, before basketball season starts, the player should shoot five hundred free-throws per week.
  - Establish a free-throw club as an outside-of-practice incentive. A series of awards can be given for making 25, 50, 75 or 100 free-throws in a row on the player's own time. For membership in the "club,", the consecutive free-throws must be witnessed by a teammate.

Free-Throw Shooting Drills

Keep practice fun by having the players perform a series of different competitive drills involving free-throws. These drills should be done toward the end or at the end of practice, since most really crucial free-throws are taken at the end of the game when the players are tired. The following drills can be used to emphasize the importance of free-throw shooting:

❑ Eighty percent-or-not-stop drill:

Put an equal number of players at each available basket. Each player shoots 10 free-throws. Shoot two free-throws and then step away from the line before shooting the next two. The other players line up along the lane and rebound. Every player on the team must stay until every player has made 8-of-10 in a set.

❑ First-to-make twenty drill:

Split the team into three or four equally skilled free-throw shooting groups. Players take turns shooting one free-throw at a time until one group has made twenty. The other groups run sprints.

❑ Three-in-a-row drill:

Five to eight players are lined around the lane of each basket. Each player shoots three consecutive free-throws. The object is to make three in a row. For every free-throw missed in a set of three the player immediately runs one lap around the court before rejoining the group. Once a player has made three in a row, he rebounds. No one leaves this end-of-practice drill until every player has made three free-throws in a row. The number of free-throws required to be made can be increased for more advanced players.

❑ One-and-one drill:

At the end of practice, pick a player to shoot a one-and-one. If the player misses the first free-throw, everyone sprints to the other baseline and back. Another player is then selected, and the drill is continued until 10 players in a row have made both ends of a one-and-one. (The numbers of consecutive players required to make both free-throws can be adjusted to the skill level of the players. As the team improves, the number can also be increased.) This drill is a good exercise to start the first day of practice to emphasize the importance of free-throws. It is also a good way to get the players in better condition. Expect the players to run a lot.

❑ Pressure-free-throw drill:

Select the five players who are most likely to be on the court at the end of a close game. Your team has the lead and the ball. Each player will shoot only one free-throw at a time. The two guards who are likely to be doing most of the ballhandling will shoot one extra shot each. These are not to be taken at the same time as the first free-throw. The purpose is to have the five players shoot until they have made seven free-throws in a row.

❑ Swishing-free-throw drill:

Players must set a goal of not just making the free-throws, but swishing as many shots out of 10 taken as they can.

Teaching Youth League and Junior High Players to Shoot Free Throws

Most younger children do not have the strength to shoot at a 10-foot goal from 15 feet. It is more important that children develop proper technique, as opposed to bad habits. Younger players should shoot at an eight-foot goal and from no further than eight to 10 feet away. They should also use a regulation-sized, woman's ball that is slightly smaller and lighter.

Even with a smaller ball, a lower goal, and a shorter distance, the younger players will tend to jump toward the goal. In order to stay behind the free-throw line, youngsters should position themselves a foot or so behind the line and jump toward the basket, often almost throwing the ball. It is important to teach them to position themselves properly and use the correct techniques. If a player does not have the upper-arm strength to get the ball to the rim, he should shoot from a foot closer until he can make the shot. Then, the player should move back to his normal shooting position. It may take a few weeks, but the player will eventually develop more strength from shooting the shots in practice. The coach should not expect younger players to become excellent free-throw shooters in a few weeks. It takes time, as well as lots of practice, patience, and encouragement.

Junior high players will often have the same problems as the younger kids, except they have to shoot at a 10-foot goal from 15 feet. They seldom have good technique and often do not have enough upper-body strength to shoot the ball from that distance. Sometimes, players have the strength and do not realize it. As a consequence, they throw the ball from their hip and jump toward the goal. It is much more important to work on technique the first few weeks of practice, even if it means a player has to shoot from 10 to 12 feet rather than 15. The player's level of strength will develop in a few weeks.

It is more important that children develop proper technique, as opposed to bad habits.

CHAPTER 36

Fouls and Referees

Fouls and referees are part of the game of basketball. A player who is never called for a foul is not playing aggressively. A player never should try to be called for a foul, but if he is playing aggressively, he will be called for something. Players should remember that referees try to do their best. They aren't perfect, and neither are the players. The players should not use referees as an excuse for poor play.

Players Must Adjust to How the Game is Being Called

A player should be aware of and respond accordingly to how the referees are calling the game, for example:

- Referees usually call the game tightly early during the game and immediately after half-time. Their purpose in these situations is to establish control of the game, and not let it get out of hand. Players who tend to get called for fouls may need to adjust their game accordingly the first few minutes of the game. As a rule, referees tend to let things get more physical toward the end of a game. Referees want to let the teams determine a close game so they are usually hesitant to call a slight foul on the last play of the game unless it affects the shot.
- Different referees will emphasize different points in each game. In one game, the refs may call walking. The next game, they may look for the three-second call in the lane. Players must learn to adjust to the way the game is being called.

Players Must Learn How to Play with Fouls

A player must adjust his game when he gets in foul trouble. The coach will usually sit a player on the bench if he gets:

- Two fouls in the first quarter

- Three fouls in the first half or early in the third quarter
- Four fouls early in the fourth quarter

Smart players learn how to play more intelligently when they are in foul trouble. If you are an aggressive defensive player, you will have to be a little more passive. Concentrate more on playing good defensive position and moving your feet. Don't try to stuff shots, slap away a dribble, steal the ball, or take a charge. If you are one of your team's best players, you do not help the team by making a silly foul, and then sitting out the rest of the game.

If a referee has called a foul on a player, he will subconsciously watch the player to see if he fouls again. Play sound basketball, but be careful not to foul again. Allow the ref to forget about you and to focus his attention on other aspects of the game. If you are a key player on your team and in early foul trouble, the other team will probably attack you trying to get you on the bench. Play smart!

The Silly Foul

Sometimes, a player loses the ball or gets a shot blocked, and you can see in his eyes as he is running to the other end of the court that he is going to make a silly foul out of anger. The player is embarrassed, and he wants to get back at his opponent. This action only hurts the player and the team, and it should not be tolerated. When this occurs, this is an appropriate time for the coach to pull the player.

❏ Other examples of silly fouls:

- Fouling while trying to block a three-point shot. This is not a smart foul since this is a low-percentage shot. Defend the shot, but do not slap at the ball or jump into the shooter.
- Fouling a player who is not a threat to score with time running out in the half or on the shot clock is a silly foul. It can result in a four- or five-point swing in the game.

Is a player in foul trouble every game? If so, the coach should talk with the player and instruct him what to do to correct the problem. Many times, the player is making the same types of fouls over and over. If he is still having problems, he may do better if he can see himself in action. The coach should review game films with the player to assess the reasons for his constant fouling.

Smart players learn how to play more intelligently when they are in foul trouble.

Referees Seldom Determine Who Wins

The players and the coach win games, and they are the same ones who lose them. As such, players and the coaches worry about eliminating mistakes, not the referees.

❏ Will referees make mistakes?

Yes, of course they will. After all, they are only human. Younger coaches sometimes make the mistake of yelling at the referees. They complain that they are getting bad calls. Referees are more likely to listen to a coach who seldom talks. A coach should pick his times to talk to the referee. When a difficult, but correct, call goes against your team, the referee will be expecting the coach to be mad. In this situation, the referee will be undoubtedly shocked if the coach says, "Good call". As a result, however, the next time the coach says something to the referee, the referee will be more likely to listen and consider the suggestion. Talk to the referee as you would like to be talked to. Never be belligerent with or berate the referees.

❏ Make the referee aware of violations:

A coach can subtly make a referee aware that an opposing player is continually guilty of a violation. Referees can only focus on a few things at a time. Once aware of a possible violation, the referee will often start looking for it.

> **Referees are more likely to listen to a coach who seldom talks.**

Do not argue every call, or the referee will not listen to you. Make your comments count by contesting only obviously questionable or controversial calls. Arguing any other call makes you look foolish. If a call seems like a bad one, and you are not certain what was called or why, calmly ask for an explanation.

❏ Is it okay to be upset with the referees?

Of course! There will be times when it is understandable to be upset. The coach must not let the way the referee is calling the game overshadow the play of the game. He must stay focused, trying to give his team every advantage he can. However, if the team is at a disadvantage because of bad calls, no calls, or if play is so rough that a player is likely to be hurt, it is the coach's responsibility to bring it to the referees' attention immediately. There are times when the coach must be intense, if he wants his team to be intense.

Technical Fouls

Coaches who have a reputation of getting technical fouls are at a disadvantage before the game starts. The referee will probably not be receptive to suggestions such a coach may offer during the course of the game.

Coaches Must Set Good Examples

- Yelling or screaming at the referees during the game will not help the coaches team.
- If a coach is focused on the referees, he is not concentrating enough on how to help his team. He should keep his mind on the game.
- How would the coach like the coaches to talk to him if he were a referee? Refs will be more responsive when a coach, who seldom complains, questions a call or points out that other violations are occurring. Obnoxious coaches often find that questionable calls always seem to go the other way.
- If a questionable call occurs, or a call is missed, and the coach feels he must say something, he should express himself politely and then forget about it. He should keep his focus on the game.
- An inexperienced coach who continues to complain to other coaches or players about the officiating during the game is setting a bad example for the players. He is diverting the attention of the players on the bench from the game to the coach. In this instance, the focus has been misdirected to the coach and the referees, rather than kept on the players, as it should be.

Coaches who have a reputation of getting technical fouls are at a disadvantage before the game starts.

ABOUT THE AUTHOR

Dr. James Brooks has worked extensively with youth and high school players over the last 28 years. During that time, he helped found the youth basketball league in Abilene, TX, and has coached teams at various age levels. His select high school girls' teams have competed in numerous regional BCI and AAU tournaments, as well as national BCI tournaments. Many of his former players have gone on to play college basketball at the NCAA Division I, II, and III levels.

Brooks was raised in southern Oklahoma and West Texas. In 1969, he received a doctorate degree in dental surgery from the University of Texas Health Science Center in Houston. He then served three years in the U.S. Army. In 1974, he received a masters and a certificate of specialty in periodontics from the University of Texas Health Science Center.

Brooks has seven children, who have experienced the joys and heartaches of athletic competition at the junior high school, high school, and college levels.